MANAGING THE WHITE HOUSE

MANAGING
THE WHITE HOUSE

An Intimate Study of the Presidency

RICHARD TANNER JOHNSON

HARPER & ROW, PUBLISHERS

NEW YORK
EVANSTON
SAN FRANCISCO
LONDON

1817

A MACRO book published in conjunction with MACRO PUBLISHING CORPORATION

Designed by Sidney Feinberg

Library of Congress Cataloging in Publication Data

Johnson, Richard T
    Managing the White House.
    Includes bibliographical references. 1. Presidents—United States—Staff. 2. United States—Executive departments. 3. United States—Politics and government—1933–1945. 4. United States—Politics and government—1945–
I. Title.
JK518.J63 1974   353.03'13   73-5462
ISBN 0-06-012217-X

for Alisa
Ann Carol
and
Jerry

CONTENTS

AUTHOR'S NOTE

A book involves a journey of sorts—for the reader and for the author as well. For me, it has entailed a very long journey indeed. This book had its beginnings in Washington, D.C. in 1968 where I, as a White House Fellow, served initially under Lyndon Johnson and subsequently under Richard Nixon. I remained in Washington through the fall of 1969 and the winter of 1970 as a senior member of the Ash Council staff. I was involved in the reorganization of the Nixon Executive Office that led to the creation of the Office of Management and Budget and the Domestic Council.

The Washington experience taught me many things—some professional, some personal, a few painful. Salient among these learnings was experiencing firsthand the transition of Presidents—watching one depart and another arrive—witnessing (as a result of my Ash Council assignment) Richard Nixon's stated intentions of how he would manage the Executive branch, and subsequently seeing the effects as his intentions were translated into actions. My reaction, in sum, was that much was lost in translation. This President, like his predecessors, was forever destined to struggle with the discrepancy between what he would like to accomplish and what he could, in fact, achieve. From my vantage point, it became increasingly apparent that the President's style, his staffing, his assumptions about people, played a large part in shaping results. From my fascination with this process, the ideas of this book were born.

This book is my responsibility, of course, but many have contributed to its development. I am indebted to Jerry Sternin for recognizing the insights that eventually became this book. While it was in draft form, two friends and colleagues—Alexander George and Eugene Webb—gave me detailed comments. Their criticisms and suggestions have certainly made this a better book and I am enormously in their debt. I am also obligated to others—Richard Lazarus, Aaron Wildavsky, and Colonel John Woodmansee—whose insights and comments made a difference. Finally, I am indebted to Ann Carol Brown who withstood the agonies and ecstasies of this writing—who praised, commented, and criticized, who spirited me away from time to time, and without whose companionship this work might have been completed sooner.

R. T. J.

Five Star Ranch
Pescadero, California

PREFACE

As a result of the Watergate scandal, Americans of varying political persuasion and differing opinions as to the culpability of the President have had the opportunity to watch the unfolding of an extraordinary drama. In the course of these events, the most intimate aspects of staff life in the White House have been unveiled. The inner workings of the Executive office, the hidden aspects of how and why the President organizes his office as he does, how he relates to his advisers and they to each other have taken on far more importance in the public eye as their consequences have become known. As this study of six Presidents reveals, the undercurrents of managerial style have not only affected Richard Nixon but also his predecessors. The way a President manages is important; that is the thesis of this book.

In 1960 Richard Neustadt popularized in his book *Presidential Power* many of the assumptions that have underlain the growth of the Executive branch for the last forty years. In Neustadt's view, the President's capacity to lead the country is in direct proportion to his ability to increase his power stakes—by asserting his freedom to act to his full Constitutional limits, by bringing Congress into line through the imposition of the aura of his office, and finally, by capitalizing on the attention given to his office to forge new priorities among the people. While not all Presidents have exploited these resources, the trend since Roosevelt has been unmistakably toward a stronger Chief Executive. What is more noteworthy is that the trend may be reversing as the circumstances surrounding the Presidency have changed.

Consider first all of the contexts in which the nation came to rely on a strong Chief Executive. The World Wars catapulted the United States into an irrevocable role of world leadership. With the exception of a few lapses into isolationism, the nation found itself drawn into a world of summit conferences, state visits, and limited military interventions, functions which are most readily handled by a strong Executive. Legislatures do not attend summits, speak with a single voice, or act quickly in time of military crisis. Yet the circumstances of World War II and the Cold War years demanded these things. Thus, on the foreign front, the scope of the President's role steadily increased.

Paralleling the President's growing role in foreign affairs were demands on him in connection with the domestic economy. Industrialization had taken the nation a considerable distance from its agrarian beginnings by the 1920s, yet there was still widespread faith in Adam Smith's "hidden hand" to keep the system in balance. Then came the crash of 1929, followed by a depression of such devastating proportions as to convince most citizens that some form of governmental intervention was necessary. Roosevelt's New Deal gave rise not only to programs but also to the continuing expectation that the President should play a major role in ensuring the stability of the domestic economy. By the time Harry Truman inherited the mantle of leadership, the estate of his responsibilities was far more substantial than what Roosevelt had received from Herbert Hoover. Under Truman, foreign policy and domestic policy functions continued to grow in importance. They attained new legitimacy as the National Security Council and the

Council of Economic Advisors were established to help the President in carrying out his role. The trend toward a strong Chief Executive was firmly established.

In subsequent years, new expectations were heaped upon the President as national problems arose. Inevitably, a time would come when the Chief Executive, no matter how fully empowered by legislation, would simply reach the limits of what he could, in fact, accomplish. This watershed occurred in the latter years of Lyndon Johnson's Presidency. On the domestic front, citizens witnessed that many Great Society programs were simply unable to deliver on their promises. On the foreign policy side, the nation's prolonged entanglement in Vietnam likewise demonstrated certain drawbacks to the President's heretofore unchallenged powers to engage forces in "limited" warfare. Thus, by the late sixties, the nation came to realize (with some disillusionment) that giving power to the President might, as with most things, be bound by the law of diminishing returns.

Richard Nixon, as President, seemed to have accepted the changing situation. He did not, as his predecessors, endeavor in his first term to grab hold of the bureaucracy and truly manage the Executive branch. In a curious way he distanced himself from the agencies, drawing a defensive perimeter, as it were, around himself and his Executive office, establishing NSC-like councils within the White House to provide staff support on priority foreign and domestic matters, and otherwise disowning the bureaucracy. When questioned about one of the many fumbles of the Bureau of Indian Affairs, the President readily agreed. "It's a horrible mess," he said. "Someone ought to do something about it." Here was a President talking about a member of his Executive family as if it were wholly outside his sphere of influence *and* responsibility.

All Presidents, to be sure, may not regard the Executive branch with the same aloofness as Richard Nixon. But it is equally clear that the President's traditional spheres of action are not as preeminently his own. Faced on one hand by the limitations of what his domestic agencies can deliver, he turns to foreign policy where he has traditionally had a free hand. Yet here too latitude of action has become more restricted as the line between what is "foreign policy" and what is "domestic policy" have grown less distinct. The 1972–1973 wheat sale to the Soviet Union is a case in point. What may have been viewed by the President as a foreign policy coup turned out to have significant domestic consequences. It is likely that Congress will exercise more influence over such transactions in the future. In a similar vein, the President's freedom of action in the economic sphere faces new constraints as more restrictive economic sanctions, such as wage and price controls, replace the traditional Keynesian measures. As this discussion indicates, many arenas in which the President has traditionally operated with little restriction have grown more contentious and may be subject to increasing Congressional scrutiny.

These trends, which may point toward a diminishing role for the Chief Executive in years to come, are but one piece of the set of problems confronting him. A President who undertakes to manage the agencies is faced with other formidable obstacles. Federal agencies clutter the horizon like bottom-heavy bureaucratic pyramids. What makes these agencies tick?

All bureaucracies tend to be creatures of habit. Their complexity demands reliable forms of coordination. Eventually, standard operating procedures evolve and these routines ensure, if nothing else, that the bureaucracy will have dependable information flows, outlooks, and responses. Well-known episodes, such as the 1962 Cuban missile crisis, document the role that institutionalized procedures can play in shaping events. In that incident the standardized intelligence reporting procedures of the Central Intelligence Agency (CIA) and the Air Force caused a one-week delay in getting the vital information on the missile buildup to the President. Similarly, bureaucratic reflex may best explain the Air Force's insistence on a "surgical

air strike" against the missile sites in Cuba. The problem? The
strike included many nonmissile targets, the destruction of
which virtually guaranteed that the strike would not be "surgical."[1]* As these illustrations reveal, a bureaucracy's programs
for complex actions tend to be drawn from limited repertoires
and are often ill-suited to new situations. Large organizations
tend to have limited flexibility; they endeavor to "do their
part" in terms of what they know best how to do.

These basic characteristics of organizations tend to resist
change as a President strives to assert his will over the Executive branch. At best, they will change incrementally. This presents a fundamental problem for the Chief Executive. The time
frames separating the President and his agencies are markedly
different. Bureaucracies move like glaciers, marking progress,
it would seem, to the pace of geologic time. In contrast, most
Presidents, as creatures of politics, have reflexes attuned to
daily changes in the public pulse. Except for Eisenhower, all
of our last five Presidents came from the Senate. There, as in
the House, accomplishment is measured in terms of votes made
or bills passed. In this setting, time frames correspond to Congressional sessions or election cycles. In contrast, professional
bureaucratic managers, in industry or in government, adopt
time frames of five years or more when planning major organizational changes.[2] This pace is more in harmony with the bureaucratic character. It ignores, however, the Constitutional
reality of quadrennial Presidential elections.

The cyclical demands of electoral politics impose an un-
avoidable constraint upon Presidential management: how does
the President reconcile the short-term demands of election politics with the long-term requirements for bureaucratic change?
One frequently used tactic is to circumvent the bureaucracy
altogether, creating new agencies whenever new programs depart radically from traditional forms. The Peace Corps and the

---

* Notes to the chapters begin on p. 241.

National Aeronautics and Space Administration (NASA) are illustrative and are cited as successful examples.[3] One might ruefully inquire about the long-term consequences of proliferating a new agency for every new program. The risk, of course, is one of increasing the already awesome complexity of the Executive branch.

The Federal bureaucracy is not only large but highly differentiated. Extensive separation between organizational units exists not only among agencies but also among bureaus within agencies. To a degree, such separation is necessary to effectively relate an organization's different parts to its respective missions. But in the Federal sphere, "separatism" becomes a threat to organizational unity as agencies and bureaus move outside the Executive orbit and become the captive of the special interests they serve. The President's prime managerial concern becomes one of integrating—or drawing together—these divergent organizational units and imbuing them with the administration's goals and priorities.

The dynamics of a Federal bureau are by no means explainable in wholly organizational terms. Bureaus do not hang motionless in a political vacuum waiting for Presidential direction; they tend to seek out their own independent bases of support in order to get the power to operate.[4] Every governmental bureau has important stakes in survival. Accordingly, it must cultivate sympathy and support in those who can do it harm—which most often means Congress. In the interest of control, Congress may itself strive to reinforce an agency's responsibility to it. Such interest can and does undermine the authority of the President.

Another feature of the Federal bureaucracy is the appointive process through which political officers are selected and placed in strategic positions within an agency. While such appointments are important, both the President and his Cabinet secretaries frequently operate under considerable restriction—statutory and otherwise. Harold Ickes once complained that "without the power to appoint subordinates, there is no power of control at all."[5]

The President's appointments of undersecretaries and assistant secretaries are subject to many influences. During party turnovers these positions are eminently suited to the repayment of political favors. Congressmen press personal favorites upon the President and his department heads, and the President frequently relents. This may be unfortunate from the standpoint of internal administration. The conflict, again, is between the President's political and managerial roles. If the President comes from Congress, he is probably used to the practice of making selections that balance off party and region; this "compromise orientation" is frequently carried into the White House. While such practices may be consistent with the President's symbolic role of "bringing the nation together," they frequently dilute one of his few means of exerting control over the agencies.

Along with other problems, many agencies tend to have organizational inflexibilities embedded in the legislation which created them. All this seems obscure and unimportant to most incoming Presidents; only later does a President realize that these clauses sharply curtail his capacities to change the system. When the "organizational chart" is written into the legislation, it gives rise to organizational independence by inhibiting changes that might increase responsiveness to the President. Frequently, neither the President nor the secretary can transfer activities from one bureau to another, or even alter their budgets to enforce new priorities.[6] Here, as in the two preceding issues, we confront an inseparable part of the Presidential challenge in managing the bureaucracy: *Congress is part of the problem!* Study commissions frequently tend to forget this—tidying up the boxes that report to the President but ignoring the hidden linkages that also bind these agencies to the past and to the legislative branch.

Woven into this pattern of complex bureau relationships is a fourth distinguishing feature of the bureaucracy—the civil servant. Civil Service regulations protect him from outright dismissal, but he is always vulnerable to informal censure and the "ultimate weapon" of being "promoted" or "transferred" to an irrelevant position. In these latter respects, civil servants are subject to the same kinds of sanctions as executives in all walks of life—public or private.

Stereotypes of phlegmatic or conspiring civil servants are generally overdrawn. Civil servants are, after all, members of society like everyone else. Newcomers to the Executive branch frequently overlook the obvious fact that civil servants belong to organizations and have loyalties to them. The challenge for the President and Cabinet members alike is to look beyond the stereotype: how much of the perceived foot-dragging is "bureaucratic sabotage" and how much is properly attributable to the norms and values of the bureaucratic system in which the civil servant must survive?

Against the backdrop of these constraints—organizational and political—the President installs a Cabinet member and expects him to run his department. The President demands loyalty. But certain forces—of interest, of authority, and of partisanship—impinge on the Cabinet member. These forces have been built into his department by history, by the appointive process, which emanates from Congress, and by the publics that the department serves. The result can be a secretary's growing preoccupation with the internal affairs of his department. The vital problems of his success and survival may cause him to adopt positions which are department-oriented and which diverge from Presidential priorities. Secretaries of Agriculture and Labor frequently find themselves in a crossfire between their constituencies and the President. The dilemma is one of competing responsibilities, loyalties, and demands. The President expects the Cabinet member to represent his interests. On the other hand, the secretary inherits an immense bureaucratic structure; he finds it difficult not to become a part of it—supporting its vested interests and concerning himself with its *esprit de corps*.

As a result of these factors, conflicts between Cabinet members and the White House staff are inevitable. From the White House vantage point, Cabinet members appear disloyal and distracted. An unnamed White House aide states:

It is amazing how soon the Cabinet people get captured by the permanent staffs. Secretary [David] Kennedy [of the Treasury] under Nixon, for example, was captured within days . . . and Nixon's staff didn't even try to improve things. . . . I think you can't expect too much from the [agencies]. It is just too much to expect that they will see things the President's way.[7]

A former aide to both Kennedy and Johnson presents a similar view:

It was an absolutely terrible problem. . . . there are major [conflicts] with Cabinet members and civil servants alike. Even the great Cabinet members like McNamara and Freeman were terrible in evading their share of many of our efforts.[8]

This examination of the Federal agencies and advisory groups reveals a complex network of conflicting loyalties and dependencies. The Presidential assistant is the linchpin that holds the system together, and he is often involved with conflicts that arise between the White House and the agencies. When they occur, there is an almost inevitable tendency for the White House aide to dive in and correct them. The result over recent years has been the increasing involvement of the White House staff in agency affairs. Their statements speak for themselves:

A Kennedy staff hallmark was to seize power from around town. In retrospect, I think [we] were insensitive to the channels of existing government. For example, I think the White House staffers often called people low in the departments and deliberately undercut Cabinet people too much in the early years. In retrospect, I don't think you can coordinate much from the White House. You just don't have the people and the numbers.[9]

Another observer states:

The always delicate distinction between staff or advisory roles of
the White House and operational administrative line responsibilities
in the Cabinet departments became overly blurred during the Kennedy and Johnson years. Too many staff tried to do more than they
were supposed to be doing and gradually came "to give orders"
rather than transmit requests. . . . One danger of this approach,
in the words of one top Johnson aide, was that "after awhile he
[Johnson] never even bothered to sit down with most of the Cabinet members even to discuss their major problems and program
possibilities. Johnson wound up using some of his staff as both line
managers as well as staff and, I think in retrospect, it frequently
didn't work out!"[10]

Interestingly, well over half of the Kennedy, Johnson, and
Nixon domestic policy staff members were lawyers. Perhaps it
is not surprising that these aides tended to establish adversary
relationships with the departments!

Any liaison position, by definition, bridges organizational
boundaries. The bridge becomes a tightrope when White House
aides seek to correct perceived problems by extensive involvement in agency affairs. As the statements above indicate, it
may be counterproductive. The managerial problem for the
President is to draw a line between allowing his staff's interference to proceed unchecked and restricting his aides too tightly.

The White House aide's relationships not only radiate outward to the agencies but upward to the President. Each adviser, to succeed, must establish and maintain that vital link
to the President. Relationships such as those between Roosevelt
and Hopkins, Eisenhower and Adams, Kennedy and Sorensen,
Nixon and Haldeman provide important insight into the character of each President and his approach to managing men.
The ties between the President and his top aides reveal his
needs and fears, his assumptions about people, and why he
manages them as he does. Why does one President employ rivalry, forever generating tension among his staff by promoting

competition among them? Why does another President strive to avoid conflict and promote teamwork? Shortly, we shall delve into these questions.

The President's public role establishes a subtle but important distinction between the President of the United States and the chief executives of lesser enterprises. He has, in effect, the means at his disposal to reach beyond the immediate boundaries of his organization to create new resources. All executives have this prerogative to some extent: entrepreneurs appeal to banks; foundations appeal to donors. But the President of the United States is more than a supplicant asking for help. He has unparalleled legitimacy. In a sense he commands not only the Executive branch but its environment! He can go to the people. If an Executive department is unresponsive, he can expose it to the press. If Congress is recalcitrant, he can assert his will by forging new priorities among the American public. Strong Presidents have done just this. Political scientist Richard E. Neustadt tells us that the President's power is the power to persuade.[11] Neustadt calls our attention to the fact that the President's ultimate power is in the people. In the face of many constraints, the President can work on the system from without and from within.

In summary, the President is confronted with a formidable array of difficulties. However shrewd his judgments, however astute his appointments to the various positions under his command, his advisers and secretaries must cope with the inheritance of the offices they fill. Embedded in these offices are roles and customs, alliances and antagonisms which subtly influence behavior. To some extent, these forces can be overcome. As we shall see, some Presidents have had more success in this regard than others. Part of that success depends upon the President's ability to exploit Congressional receptivity in getting a new bill through, or nudge an agency toward a change that has already been gathering momentum. Part of his success also depends upon his ability to establish clear priorities, to assess his strengths and devise a strategy that exploits them. But above all, if the President is to do these things, he must manage a team of men to provide him with information, staff out his alternatives, and otherwise extend his reach. How this is done matters a great deal. That is what this book is all about.

MANAGING THE WHITE HOUSE

CHAPTER ONE

PRESIDENTIAL STYLE

THE orbits of advisers and agencies that revolve around the President do not, like the heavenly bodies, follow a strict and invariant course. To some extent their paths are determined by Constitution and custom; but, to an important degree, the President himself, as central occupant of the Executive galaxy, shapes the pattern of government.

This book examines the way in which successive Presidents, whether by intent or default, have left their imprint on government. Some, like Dwight D. Eisenhower, may have tried to rationalize the workload by establishing an elaborate staff system, but at the risk of becoming a prisoner of the staff machinery over which they preside. Others, like Franklin D. Roosevelt, may have striven to remain informed by playing aides off against one another, but at the price of exacerbated conflict and at the risk that aides might establish outside alliances to further their interests.

Since the time of George Washington political analysts have speculated about how well the President is managing. This reflects a general belief that the way a President organizes and relates to his close circle of advisers—and through them to the Executive branch—influences policy significantly.

This book will focus on the *process* of management and its *output*, that is, how six Presidents—Franklin D. Roosevelt,

Harry S. Truman, Dwight D. Eisenhower, John F. Kennedy, Lyndon B. Johnson, and Richard M. Nixon—have organized their office and how their approaches have affected results.[1]

In weighing the consequences of Presidential style, it is convenient to label the different patterns of management that Presidents have used—*formalistic, competitive,* and *collegial.* Each of these patterns of management endeavors, in different ways, to resolve the four fundamental dilemmas of decision making. The first has to do with the trade-off between optimality and "doability"—how far can one go in the direction of doing "best" without being "impractical"? The second stems from the mechanisms that screen out or embrace conflicting viewpoints and personalities—how much conflict can a workable decision process tolerate? The third concerns the distortion of information—how much desirable screening can occur in the staffing process without incurring undesirable distortion? The fourth involves the constraint of time—how elaborate can the decision process be without sacrificing responsiveness? The choice of one managerial pattern over another depends upon how the manager resolves these trade-offs.

The point of this undertaking is not just to label a particular approach but to explain why it worked in some instances and failed in others. To the extent that it worked, what were the subtle factors in a President's style that kept his system in balance? How did his staff system reflect and complement his personal preferences and values? Truman's staff funneled in the facts; he made the decision—an aspect of the job he relished. Johnson, on the other hand, sought consensus and struggled mightily to establish agreement among his advisers. Both Presidents sought to make good policy decisions, yet each shaped his decisional machinery differently, rewarded his aides differently—and got different results. In evaluating these results we shall discover that associated with each pattern of management are costs and benefits that predictably surface when a given approach is used. In other words, given a particular style of management, we can anticipate the likely consequences of that style on the quality of decision making and implementation.

It should be stated at the outset that while each President may adopt a dominant pattern of management, his approach may vary from situation to situation. In addition, he must relate to subordinates of widely differing character, and this also may cause him to vary his managerial approach. He must deal with his own staff and personal advisers, and he must devise a way of working with important advisory groups that work closely with his office, like the Cabinet, the National Security Council, and the Council of Economic Advisors. Finally, he must strive to find some way to manage the giant Executive agencies like the Department of Defense (DOD) and Health, Education and Welfare (HEW). From these sources he must gather information and weigh it, make decisions, and pass his choices out again for implementation.

Each President distributes his energies differently, and like most people, he tries to use his experience and draws on what has worked for him before. While each President's approach is to some extent unique, there are striking similarities too.

THE FORMALISTIC APPROACH

Consider the similarities between the Eisenhower and Nixon Administrations. Common to both was an emphasis on order. Both Presidents installed a procedural system of decision making; both tended to underplay their political role—the stress was on finding the best solution to national problems rather than on working out "compromise settlements" among conflicting views. This emphasis on order and analysis was reflected in their choice of advisers: figures like Sherman Adams and Henry A. Kissinger emerged as predominant—the stereotype was analytical and dispassionate. Eisenhower and Nixon tended to discourage staff conflict; open expressions of interpersonal conflict such as competition, bargaining, and hostility were taboo. They sought to preserve substantive conflict by having both sides of an issue presented on paper. Because they had these preferences, each devised a structured decision process that centered upon the reasoned discussion of prepared briefs rather than upon the heat of debate. A formalized staff system collected information and funneled it to the top; complex problems were analyzed into their pros and cons.[2] Ultimately, the President weighed his decision on the merits.

It is noteworthy that the formalized approach, at least in its idealized form, aspires to make "the best" decision. Decisions are expected to stand on their merits; implementation is not stressed in the decision-making process. In this respect, the assumptions underlying this approach bear some resemblance to "decision making" in the economic context: the decision maker is seen as a single agent striving to optimize his goals in the face of given costs.[3] This approach assumes that an optimal solution exists and that it can be identified and implemented; decisions are made and action is taken with complete information on all the alternatives and their consequences.

Clearly, decision making in this rarefied atmosphere bears little resemblance to the Presidency. But the differences, in terms of the basic assumptions of the formalistic approach, are more in degree than in kind. Agreed, Presidential decisions are rarely, if ever, made on the criterion of technical rationality alone. But an interesting feature of this approach is the tendency for technical considerations to be emphasized and political considerations deemphasized. Eisenhower steadfastly urged his Cabinet members to "not compromise on principle."[4] The Nixon invasion of Cambodia may or may not have been justified in terms of technical military criteria, but there is general agreement that he underestimated the political reaction that followed. A later section on the Nixon White House will provide fuller opportunity to examine the assumptions and consequences of the formalistic approach.

THE COMPETITIVE APPROACH

Against any standard of ordered decision making, the managerial approach of Franklin Roosevelt stands as the polar extreme. In passion, as well as administrative persuasion, Roosevelt sought involvement and controversy. He not only tolerated a great deal of conflict, he thrived on it. He sought aggressive advisers of divergent opinions—such as Harry L. Hopkins, Henry Morgenthau, Jr., and Harold L. Ickes—and pitted them against one another.[5] He delegated responsibility and authority in overlapping segments. The resulting clash generated heat, but also information. Roosevelt, pragmatic and opportunistic, sought above all to stay informed and to exploit prevailing political currents. His decision process, forged in the heat of debate, was preconditioned to withstand debate in Congress and the test of public exposure. Roosevelt may have overly sacrificed what was "best" for what was "doable"; but if the acceptance of his proposals was his criterion for success, acceptance is what he got to a greater extent than any President before or since.

Roosevelt exemplifies what will be termed the *competitive* pattern of management. His method of delegation left jurisdictional boundaries to be mapped out by conquest among his subordinates. It promoted conflict which often landed in his lap. He fully recognized the inherent conflicts of interest that surround the Presidency and assumed that, in most instances, the quarrels among his subordinates could not be resolved to the satisfaction of all disputants. Roosevelt thus sought to position himself as the arbitrator, as the "swing vote" in the decision-making process. In many respects his approach was well suited to the White House. The President must live with conflict; it is woven into the fabric of the Presidency. Roosevelt sought to sharpen this conflict as a means of staying informed, promoting creativity, and providing a healthy, renewing jolt to the system. But competition also exacted its price. Intense conflict among his subordinates at times drove them toward extreme and intransigent positions; aides were driven underground—withholding information or leaking tidbits to Congress or to the press in order to weaken adversaries or to limit the President's options.[6] The overlapping assignments which promoted conflict also fostered duplication of effort. A lesser President than Roosevelt might have become more the victim rather than the patron of power politics.

THE COLLEGIAL APPROACH

The two patterns of management, formalistic and competitive, describe the extremes of a range of possibilities. The principal strength of the formalized approach is its emphasis on thorough staff work and its stress on finding the best possible solution to a problem. The risk of this approach is that it may insulate the decision maker. Staff members working in specialized assignments become parochial, "the funneling of information" is ofttimes accompanied by the distortion of information. The more staff layers information has to filter through, the greater the risks of such distortion. There is also a tendency for the formalistic pattern of management to react too slowly or to generate solutions that seem utopian and hard to implement. In contrast, as often employed, the competitive pattern of management focuses attention on the power dimensions of a problem—at times sacrificing its substantive merits. Result: more attention is given to the bargaining than to the analysis. Under such circumstances, there is a tendency toward short-run solutions that are strongly influenced by the immediate political climate.

The collegial pattern of management strives to avoid these pitfalls. The managerial thrust is toward building a team of colleagues who work together to staff out problems and generate solutions which, ideally, fuse the strongest elements of divergent points of view. By virtue of encouraging subordinates to work together, this approach recognizes the existence, and in fact the merit, of conflict. The emphasis, however, is not on the win-lose interplay among competing individuals or ideas but rather on treating conflicting viewpoints as a resource. The collegial approach has as its principal strength the potential of forging solutions that are both substantively sound and politically doable, having taken the strongest arguments of all sides into account. Its greatest limitation stems from its dependence on people working together. Considerable managerial skill and attention is required to build an effective team. Collective endeavor requires patience and takes time.

Of all recent Presidents, perhaps John Kennedy went the furthest on some occasions toward adopting the collegial pattern of management. In the Cuban missile crisis, Kennedy incorporated conflict into his Executive Committee: he included representatives from the Department of Defense known for their commitment to "military solutions," as well as members who favored a diplomatic settlement. Unlike his mismanagement of the policy-making discussions leading to the Bay of Pigs, this time Kennedy did not attempt to stifle the expression of disagreement and debate among his advisers—in fact, he absented himself on several occasions so that it would be fully voiced.[7] He stressed solving the problem and emphasized the group's collective responsibility for coming up with sound recommendations. The resulting solution did not ignore conflict, but neither was it imprisoned by it. From the divergent views of Ex Comm's members, a composite plan was formulated which built upon the strengths of conflicting proposals and which in sum was better than any of the original plans.

These three managerial patterns—formalistic, competitive,

and collegial—describe a range of approaches a President might employ. Clearly the patterns are highly simplified; but each provides a net of a different mesh, so to speak, which we might cast into the murky waters of Presidential performance. These nets will permit us to consider different managerial approaches that have been used in the White House, and their consequences.

CHAPTER TWO

ROOSEVELT'S FEUDING FRATERNITY

On NOVEMBER 2, 1932, Franklin Delano Roosevelt was swept into office on a tide of national frustration. Seething beneath the sea of ballots was an angry, frightened America. At least thirteen million Americans (nearly one-fourth of the labor force) were walking the cold streets in search of work. Everywhere the system was breaking down. The economy, succumbing to grinding deflation, was depressing prices and wages. The burden of debt, incurred in better times, was becoming every day more intolerable: it was bankrupting the railroads, bankrupting local government, straining the banking and credit structure to the breaking point.

It was a strange, numbing crisis, worse than an invading army, for it was everywhere and nowhere; it was in the minds of men. For many Americans it was eroding their faith in a system—a faith that dwindled day by day along with their jobs and savings.

Inaugural Day dawned cold and cheerless. Almost all the nation's banks were closed. Chin outthrust, Roosevelt repeated the oath of office. Then, turning to the acres of grim faces on the Capitol lawn and the unseen millions before their radios at home, he delivered his stirring Inaugural. They had nothing to fear but fear itself. The vast crowd listened in almost dead silence. "It was very, very solemn, and a little terrifying," Eleanor Roosevelt said afterward. "The crowds were so tremendous, and you felt that they would do anything—if only someone would tell them what to do."[1] Roosevelt did.

The legend of the New Deal was born. In those threadbare days of the Depression, the nation seemed caught in the grip of an economic plague. As with the Black Plague of medieval times, the cause of the pestilence was unknown—and incomprehension made it more ominous. In hindsight, the best plan of attack would be an experimental one. Roosevelt's methods seemed tailored to this requirement. He was not, like Herbert Hoover, wedded to a single ideology or bound to a fixed set of principles. In fact, so fluid were his beliefs that at times he seemed adrift in a whirlpool of contradictory philosophies. But Roosevelt was a captain disposed to sail in troubled waters. He had promised action. From a range of sources, ideas were translated into bills and rammed through Congress. Roosevelt played a personal role in authoring the Civilian Conservation Corps and Tennessee Valley Authority. From other sources came proposals for the Reconstruction Finance Corporation (designed to make loans to small businesses that would put people to work), the Home Owners' Loan Corporation (to save small property owners), several public works programs, an Agricultural Adjustment Program (to save farmers from destructive competition), and the National Recovery Act (aimed at reviving industry and reducing unemployment). It was a time of experimentation and, for most Americans, of renewed faith.

"The final greatness of the Presidency," Clinton Rossiter once said, "lies in the truth that it is not just an office of incredible power but a breeding ground of indestructible myth."[2] The myth of Franklin Roosevelt portrays a President of charm and vision. In his first term, legislation was passed altering the fabric of American society; by the time of his death, he had led the nation through two of the greatest crises of its history. His admirers found him a wise, benevolent father—an ardent social reformer and sometimes master planner. Critics added to the legend, ascribing forethought and guile to many aspects of his conduct.

Where does the myth leave off and the man begin? Much can be learned in answer to such a question by examining Roosevelt's style. Several themes underlay FDR's *competitive* methods. The first was his appetite for diverse ideas. The second was his choice of advisers of clashing temperaments and values to supply the diversity of outlooks he sought. Roosevelt sharpened these clashes by virtue of a third attribute of his management style: he granted overlapping delegations of authority. This aggravated the strife within his staff—but guaranteed that he would never be dependent upon the advice of one aide alone. Fourth, and perhaps serving as a mechanism to hold the warring factions together, Roosevelt demanded absolute centrality. By enforcing his primacy he sought to ensure that his subordinates' loyalty to him would never be eroded by their hostility toward one another. In total, these aspects of his style served rather effectively during the innovative New Deal phase of his Presidency. However, as we shall see, his system encountered more difficulty in coping with the requirements for clear priorities and orderly administration that were called for during the war.

First, consider Roosevelt's accessibility. FDR was a public instrument of the most keen receptivity. He was remarkably accessible during his early years in office. Almost a hundred persons could get through to him by telephone without stating their business to a secretary, and government officials with anything serious on their minds had little difficulty in getting appointments. Roosevelt sought opinions from every quarter; he collected ideas, unconcerned with how well they fit together. Sometimes his advisers were flabbergasted by his glib romances with complicated subjects. Once, when his position on tariffs was being prepared and two utterly incompatible proposals were placed before him, he left his experts speechless by airily suggesting they should "weave the two together."[3]

Yet in some respects, receptivity was the secret of Roosevelt's political genius. If a large number of people wanted something very badly, he believed it was important that they be given some measure of satisfaction. Neither contradiction nor incompatibility deterred him from this course. An illustration of this can be seen in his handling of several key pieces of legislation that he initially opposed. When Senator Robert F. Wagner, Sr. introduced the National Labor Relations bill in 1934, Roosevelt was cool toward the measure. The bill, which seemed a radical initiative in its day, provided machinery for employees to establish union representation and gave unions the right to collect dues. In time, the bill would alter fundamentally the nation's politics by vesting massive economic and political power in organized labor. But perhaps in 1934 Roosevelt did not foresee labor's potential as a political force. In May of that year he told reporters with some irritation that the workers "could choose as representatives whomever they wished— including the Ahkoond of Swat or the Royal Geographic Society."[4] Wagner received no help from the White House; in fact, the Senator narrowly prevented the President from lining up with the opposition. Still, Roosevelt endorsed the measure when its popularity became evident.

Political expediency? Perhaps. But Roosevelt's receptivity unquestionably contributed to the miraculous record of the first hundred days. The test of his flexibility came not just from the initiatives forged within the White House but, as in the case of the National Labor Relations Act, from Congress. Still other hallmarks of the New Deal, such as the Emergency Banking Act, the Economy Act, and the Agricultural Adjustment Act, owed a good deal to the initiative of career men who were holdovers from the Hoover Administration. The remarkable fact was that Roosevelt could incorporate ideas from anywhere—whatever the source—and adopt them into his program.

When reporters told Roosevelt his speeches were flat, he dared them to do better. One reporter rose to the challenge and drafted a speech advocating the more equitable distribution of wealth. Roosevelt used it. When his conservative opponent Senator Arthur H. Vandenberg led the initiative for what became the Federal Deposit Insurance Corporation, FDR's principal advisers counseled against it. Convinced, Roosevelt warned Vandenberg he would veto the bill. But as Congress moved toward adjournment, Vandenberg's parliamentary maneuverings threatened to block other needed legislation. When the Senator agreed to modify his bill, delaying its becoming law for six months, Roosevelt deftly accepted the face-saving compromise. Claiming the bill to have "more lives than a cat,"[5] Roosevelt happily signed it into law—and established its place in history as a landmark of the first hundred days.

A curious display of Roosevelt's ability to embrace disparate views occurred in the drafting of the National Recovery Act. When Congress moved to enact a rigid thirty-hour work week, Roosevelt's advisers were divided on the issue. Harold L. Ickes, his waspish Secretary of the Interior, favored a large public works program and opposed any regulation of labor and industry. Others argued that the government should take a regulatory role and, in effect, act as a broker to ensure that the best interests of business, workers, and the economy were served. After extensive discussion, Roosevelt asked, "Why not do both?"[6] Thus an unlikely marriage was consummated, and after a rocky ride through Congress, the NRA was born.

Roosevelt employed the same pattern in implementing the NRA as he did in formulating it. A major proponent of regulation in drafting the bill had been crusty General Hugh S. Johnson. Roosevelt asked him to head the NRA. Later FDR apparently had second thoughts. But not until the announcement to the press did he let Johnson know that he was giving him only half the job; the $4.8 billion public works segment of the NRA would go to Ickes. Johnson threatened to quit and only the timely intervention of an old friend, Secretary of Labor Frances Perkins, kept the General on board. With this shaky takeoff, the NRA eagle soared into existence; administrative anomalies would plague its life. Johnson, bent on vindication, drafted codes overnight and implemented them immediately. He summoned businessmen to Washington and delegated huge policy-making powers in an effort to outpace Ickes. By 1935 the NRA was fluttering through heavy weather. Criticized by business and labor, Roosevelt was forced to clip its wings. In fact, by the time the Supreme Court found it unconstitutional, the NRA was near administrative collapse.

The NRA provides a mold whose image was to be cast again and again in the unfolding drama of the New Deal. Listening amiably to all sides, watching opponents test their views, digesting evidence, Roosevelt gradually felt his way toward conclusions. Yet even then his decisions were rarely clear-cut. "He hated to make sharp decisions between conflicting claims . . . ," noted Francis Biddle. The decision thus emerged, as Biddle describes it, "in the spirit of arbitration; each side getting part of the morsel."[7]

We see here the first theme of Roosevelt's management style blending into the second. Roosevelt's receptivity unquestionably broadened his reach; but his means of implementation relentlessly secured his grasp. Roosevelt's shotgun weddings of ideas joined ideological opponents—like Johnson and Ickes—and these marriages predictably fueled conflict. The outcome reinforced Roosevelt's propensity to play the "final arbitrator." Roosevelt remained in the center; his system molded his aides into the role of adversaries rather than analysts.[8]

Roosevelt's appetite for conflicting advice evolved gradually. As a State Senator he had been viewed by his colleagues as brash and aloof—a man caught up in his own opinions. As Assistant Secretary of the Navy under Woodrow Wilson, Roosevelt's impatience with a single chain of command became visible. His boss, Secretary of the Navy Josephus Daniels, was to be Roosevelt's only administrative superior. Roosevelt chafed under the older man's ways, called him a hillbilly, mimicked the Secretary before society friends, and wrote amazingly tactless memoranda.[9] Roosevelt was a "Big Navy" man and established immediate rapport with the admirals. His zeal led him on to dubious ground; he maintained contacts with conservatives such as Theodore Roosevelt, Henry Cabot Lodge, and other critics of the Wilson Administration. He even passed naval intelligence on to Republicans who used it in attacking Daniels for his naval unpreparedness. But the roots of Roosevelt's style of management were in the making: the unorthodox networks of information, the capacity to maintain a foot in warring camps without being captured by either.

On a sunny day in mid-August 1921, Roosevelt slipped and fell overboard while cruising off Campobello. He felt chill afterward but the next day resumed his vigorous vacation routine. That day, spying a small forest fire, he and his family spent several hours beating out the flames. Later he went for a swim in a nearby lake, jogged a mile and a half, plunged into the piercingly cold water of the Bay of Fundy to cool off, and sat in his dripping trunks for half an hour reading his mail.[10]

Suddenly feeling chill, he went to bed. The next day he had severe pain in his back and legs and a high fever. His wife sent for a doctor, but it was not until two weeks later that a specialist made the correct diagnosis—poliomyelitis. During much of this time Roosevelt was in agony. His legs were lifeless; at one point his arms and back were paralyzed too. Eleanor Roosevelt was later to recall the depths of his despondency: "one night he was out of his head."[11] She watched the contest between determination and defeat. She remembered him crawling like a helpless infant on the sands of some lonely beach in Florida. Ever so slowly, determination prevailed.

His partial recovery was heralded at the Democratic National Convention of 1924 in Madison Square Garden. Roosevelt was asked to make the nominating speech for Alfred E.

Smith. He was thin and pale. He struggled to the platform on crutches and moved with painful slowness toward the security of the speaker's rostrum. Then he smiled with a warmth that embraced the audience. His speech is remembered for the term "happy warrior."[12] Roosevelt applied the term to Smith—but in the poetry is the poet. Roosevelt, the determined warrior, had returned to politics. There was a change in him. Some saw greatness in the man. Since the days at Campobello, a transformation had taken place involving a struggle over mind as well as muscle. Perhaps he now belonged to a different order of things. Perhaps mortality—and other mortals—mattered less.

Was this the source of Roosevelt's ability, as President, to disregard the anguish he often imposed upon his staff? Whatever the case, he remained committed to his philosophy of pitting his advisers against one another. However raucous the conflict, however wearing on his aides his methods were, it must be acknowledged that Roosevelt's system of management served him well during the Depression years. Perhaps the secret behind the meshing of this jagged machinery lay in several characteristics of Roosevelt's style which, in aggregate, seemed to keep his system in balance. The first of these was his tolerance of conflict. "There is something to be said for having a little conflict," he once observed. "A little rivalry is stimulating, you know. It keeps everybody going to prove he is a better fellow than the next man. It keeps them honest too."[13]

Roosevelt's choice of personalities seemed at times calculated to produce strife. Placing under the same roof men of different temperament and viewpoint guaranteed conflict. His juxtaposition of General Johnson with Harold Ickes under the banner of the NRA has been discussed. His assignment of the intellectual Raymond Moley (and later Sumner Welles) to important State Department jobs, which undercut pragmatic Secretary Cordell Hull, had similar effects. In 1933 he persuaded the reluctant Moley to go to London to attend the International Monetary and Economic Conference at which

Hull was the official U.S. representative. Later, Roosevelt reversed signals, placing Moley in an untenable position with Hull. Outraged, Hull placed his ultimatum before the President, saying, in effect, "Either Moley or me!"[14] Moley was recalled from London and soon removed from the State Department. Later, when the chagrined Moley met the President, Roosevelt acted as if nothing had happened.

Painful conflicts such as these were numerous. Roosevelt gave his Secretary of War, Harry H. Woodring, an assistant who was often at odds with his chief. A variation on the theme was Roosevelt's assigning Ickes and Secretary of Agriculture Henry A. Wallace control over conservation and power, and giving rival chieftains in the party overlapping control over patronage. Roosevelt, acting as wrecker and salvage operator combined, was always on hand to pry the colliding personalities apart. He seemed to savor the crash—and ultimately forged workable compromises from the debris.

Cabinet meetings also bore this internecine stamp. The men —and one woman—sitting around the table in 1935 shared little common ground. All forceful personalities, they feigned an outward show of camaraderie that often just barely concealed their suspicions of each other. The peppery Ickes, for example, was a ceaseless source of friction; he fought not only with Hopkins but with NRA chief Hugh Johnson, Frances Perkins, and Henry Morgenthau. Ickes' final battle with Henry Wallace culminated in a blazing face-to-face quarrel in which the principals exchanged charges of lying and disloyalty to the President. In fact, Frances Perkins recounts one occasion when the President was summoned out of a Cabinet meeting by a telephone call. Instants after his exit, the pent-up conflicts of his advisers burst forth and fierce backbiting began. It was the first time the Cabinet members had been alone together as a group—and it was clear by the time he returned that they would not seek out each other's company on their own initiative.[15] In any case, the President reduced the need for his Cabinet members to get along by permitting them to see him after the meeting about those questions that really troubled them. This further discouraged their sharing information or working out problems collectively.

Roosevelt liked to think of his Cabinet and staff as a family. He often referred to himself as "Papa." Braintruster Rexford G. Tugwell complained once "that he treats [us] like children."[16] Writer John Gunther has perceptively noted Roosevelt's repeated reference to the Papa theme. After a speech or press conference, he would say, "How did Papa do?," or to an administrator, "If you do get into trouble come back to Papa."[17] Roosevelt said once that he "needed to have a happy ship."[18] He may have accurately pictured his role as the paternal captain, but a happy ship he never got.

Roosevelt discovered early a near-foolproof device for maintaining the competitive edge: he granted overlapping delegations of authority. The memoirs of his aides provide colorful testimony to the effectiveness of this device. The diaries of Harold Ickes, for example, are interwoven with the overhanging presence of White House aide Harry Hopkins, Secretary of the Treasury Morgenthau, and others.

An example of this is the feud between Harry Hopkins and Secretary Ickes. Roosevelt received an overwhelming endorsement in the Congressional elections of 1934. With this vote of confidence he embarked upon a new and expanded works program. The Works Relief Bill was pushed through Congress along with an appropriation of $5 billion. Once passed, the likely administrators to head the program were Hopkins and Ickes. This dilemma of choice was resolved in characteristic Roosevelt fashion: he chose *both* and placed a third figure—moderate, amiable Frank Walker—in charge of the explosive pair!

Such was the chaotic command structure of the relief program: Ickes, based in the Department of Interior, became head of a cumbersome committee (the Public Works Administration); Hopkins was responsible for the millions of individuals on relief (through the Works Progress Administration); and Frank Walker was placed squarely in the middle. The result was toughest on Roosevelt who inherited staggering obligations in his inevitable role as the final "court of appeals." "In the first three years of the program," recounts Roosevelt aide Robert Sherwood, "something like a quarter of a million individual projects—ranging from suspension bridges to sewing circles—passed through Walker's office to Ickes' committee and thence across the President's overcrowded desk from which the vast majority of projects approved were passed to Hopkins who converted them into actual man-hours of work."[19] Ickes' diary gives us a glimpse of the hours spent in intrigue and in invective—by-products of the cutthroat competition with Hopkins. When, for example, a proposal for the modernization of Atlanta's sewage system appeared, there would be internecine warfare between the PWA and the WPA over jurisdiction. Hopkins and Ickes would each lobby among the Georgia delegation in Congress and ultimately disputes would be referred to the harassed umpire, Frank Walker. "Since his decision usually satisfied no one," continues Sherwood, "both Ickes and Hopkins would execute sweeps around Walker's flanks to the President. FDR would be forced to decide which of them would enjoy the prestige to be derived from laying sewer pipes."[20] Such demands upon the President's time were the price of his system. Nonetheless, his competitive pattern of management served two functions. First it elicited ideas and stimulated debate among competing advisers, each eager to win the President's confidence. Secondly, it kept Roosevelt in the center—for only he could resolve their conflicts.

What tied the system together, as noted earlier, was Roosevelt's absolute demand for centrality. A lesser leader might have been consumed by the strife or have been unable to prevent the warring factions from tearing the system apart. Such was not the case with Roosevelt. First and foremost, he demanded total allegiance. When Donald Richberg was made the secretary to the National Emergency Council (the council was one of FDR's first attempts at "total coordination" of the New Deal programs), newspapers featured Richberg as "the new Assistant President." Roosevelt's reaction was prompt and explosive: "Get hold of [the reporters]," he said to Press Secretary Stephen Early, "and tell them that this kind of thing is not only a lie but that it is a deception and a fraud on the public. It is merely a continuation of previous lies such as the headlines that Moley was running the government; next that Baruch was Acting President; next that Johnson was the man in power; next that Frankfurter had been put over the Cabinet."[21] Later, Roosevelt announced to the Cabinet that Richberg was no more than "an exalted messenger boy."[22]

Roosevelt enforced his primacy ruthlessly. Cabinet members were "teased" when given undue notice in the press. Schlesinger has observed that Roosevelt's "unfeeling needling of his associates expressed a thin streak of sadism of which he was intermittently aware."[23] Soon after Moley's collision with Hull at the London Economic Conference, Moley was invited to a small staff dinner at the White House. Roosevelt began to chide him, and Moley replied with heat. The exchange that ensued terminated the relationship. Moley would dine with the President but once again—at a constrained Hyde Park luncheon.[24]

"However genial his teasing," said Francis Biddle, "it was often . . . pointed with a prick of torment, and went to the essence of a man, pierced him between the ribs into the heart of his weakness."[25] Roosevelt once confessed to Morgenthau: "I [am] so tired, I would enjoy seeing you cry or sticking pins into people and hurting them."[26]

Among the most interesting aspects of Roosevelt's system was his management of rewards. Though effective, the reward system made staff life precarious. His jealousy of the limelight and the sting of his teasing deterred aides from seeking outside rewards in the form of public recognition. He was also strict in policing his aides against their securing outside allies. These deterrents focused his subordinates' attention on the one reward left—access to Roosevelt himself.

The power to influence the President, the power to get things done through him, became the brass ring in Roosevelt's circus. For Cabinet members and advisers alike, Roosevelt managed his White House so that this was the sole reward. Their singular dependence upon him gave him power. He exercised it in subtle ways: by offering or refusing access, by granting or withholding authority, by the distribution of assignments and responsibilities from day to day, by giving or withholding private or public credit for work done, by "extracurricular" favors such as invitations to state dinners or the chance to go on a fishing trip with him. In short, Roosevelt used his power to manipulate these rewards and deprivations.

There are two basic rewards—remuneration and recognition. Financial reward is clearly proscribed in the White House. Of the various kinds of recognition possible, Roosevelt narrowed the reward system to favors over which he had personal control. He was quick to take credit for his Administration's successes but frequently let subordinates stand on their own in the face of criticism. Frances Perkins observed, "He reserved the right not to go out and rescue you if you got into trouble."[27] "It was your battle," said Tugwell, "and you were expected to fight it. If you ran to the President with your troubles, he was affable and even, sometimes, vaguely encouraging, but he never said a public word in support."[28]

The four ingredients of Roosevelt's system—his accessibility, his appetite for conflicting counsel, his overlapping delegations, and his demands for centrality—imposed binds on his subordinates that are best understood by example. Consider the career of Roosevelt's Special Assistant, Thomas G. Corcoran, who ranged from pinnacle to precipice across the New Deal terrain. "Tommy the Cork," as he was called, came to Roosevelt's attention through his skillful preparation of a landmark court case in the early days of the New Deal. Corcoran was a brilliant lawyer—and in this and other appeals, he never lost the Government's case before the court. Some have observed that Corcoran, operating with his small collection of young lawyers out of a cubbyhole in the Reconstruction Finance Corporation's office building, ran the best law firm in the country. Corcoran was warm, vibrant, and charming. He could marshal his charm to get things done through the system. Corcoran sought the top, but he realized that one frequently must trade recognition in exchange for the power to influence. He steadfastly avoided the press. Within the White House he was no flashy eminence but an engineer toiling below decks, keeping the New Deal running.

Corcoran worked on a number of odd jobs for Roosevelt. He participated in speech writing and contributed such phrases as "instinct for the jugular" and "rendezvous with destiny." Although he worshiped ardently at the shrine of FDR, he was also toughly realistic in appreciating Roosevelt's strengths and foibles. He maintained collateral allegiances to important Congressmen, to Justice Brandeis' group, and to several high-level administrators. These plural loyalties were indispensable in carrying out his catalytic role for the President. But while they strengthened his position to forge compromises that paid dividends to the White House, they circumscribed his standing with the President. FDR had a characteristic of demanding nothing less than complete and exclusive devotion. First Louis Howe and later Harry Hopkins passed this exacting test. FDR could sense instinctively when, in even the smallest particulars, the devotion he sought was lacking.[29]

Corcoran preferred to work on the basis of speedy informality. He abhorred committees. This he shared in common with his chief. But unlike FDR, Corcoran tended to harness conflict toward convergent rather than divergent ends. His genius was in eliciting cooperation and teamwork that surmounted administrative fratricide. Corcoran excelled at finding out what the other fellow really wanted, and from that, building durable compromises.

As Corcoran's star rose, so did the antagonism of fellow White House aides. His independence, his teamwork approach, his outside allegiances flawed his armor, and others, covetous of the President's favor, exploited this vulnerability. Perhaps, in addition, Corcoran transgressed upon one of the cardinal tenets of Roosevelt's White House by not assuring his boss of the loyalty and centrality he demanded. It may have been merely by mischance that Corcoran was placed in command of Roosevelt's ill-fated Supreme Court reform and later FDR's unsuccessful purge of the Democratic party. In the course of these protracted engagements, Corcoran was forced to spend great sums of his political capital in the President's interests. The purge of the party ended in defeat and embarrassment for the President. It was even more costly to Corcoran and his future. His active role had made him the focus of public attention. Perhaps Corcoran, in his shrewd understanding of politics, also began to draw back. By the time Roosevelt declared himself for his third term, the split between Corcoran and the President had gone too far to mend. As Corcoran's star waned, Hopkins' ascended. Tugwell recounts that Hopkins acted aggressively to execute the final coup against Corcoran by coaching a cavalcade of visitors who plied the President with hostile reports about Tommy the Cork.[30] Such were the hazards of Roosevelt's competitive approach.

There was a sorry contrast between the attractive, robust Corcoran and the sickly, driven Hopkins. Corcoran clearly seemed the more versatile, but his aspiration to play the catalyst and his skills at brokerage—however valuable to the Administration—were potentially threatening to the master. Hopkins, in contrast, was decidedly more dependent upon Roosevelt. Rude, abrasive, limited in horizon, but fanatically devoted, Hopkins could be counted on to further Roosevelt's interest and no other. Of Roosevelt's many advisers in the White House, Hopkins would last the longest.

A President's top assistants are extensions of the man they serve. To a large extent, Presidents get what they deserve. Yet the personal characteristics of a Presidential aide may have unforeseen consequences on the way in which a President's will is imposed. Aides may amplify or mute a President's strengths or weaknesses. For example, while Corcoran may have smoothed Roosevelt's edges through his ability to build teamwork and weld agreements, Hopkins did not. In fact, in translating Roosevelt's orders, Hopkins may have conveyed more heavy-handedness than was intended.

Hopkins' understanding of Roosevelt's mind and moods made him a formidable competitor for Presidential attention. He was willing to make a total commitment to Roosevelt's cause. Whereas others, like Moley and Corcoran, who because of pride, ideology or personal ambition, held back, Hopkins was completely Roosevelt's. Yet the extraordinary fact was that this very important man in the U.S. Government during a most crucial period of the nation's history had no legitimate official position. His desk was a card table in his bedroom. That bedroom, however, was in the White House. For all this, Hopkins never enjoyed the security with Roosevelt that Howe felt. Once when Hopkins made a derogatory comment about Wendell Willkie, Roosevelt slapped him with as sharp a reproof as his staff had ever heard him utter. Eleanor Roosevelt observed that "Hopkins did not like opposing the President." "He frequently agreed with him regardless of his own views and tried to persuade him in indirect ways."[31]

The phenomenon of Harry Hopkins could be explained entirely in terms of the idiosyncratic properties of this very unusual man. Hopkins' personality and competitive orientation certainly played some part in his controversial career. However, one intent of this analysis is to look beyond the obvious. What factors, aside from Hopkins' personality, might have enhanced the conflict of which he was too intimately a part?

Relationships reveal the assumptions and characteristics of the individuals involved. While there is endless variety in the chemistry that binds people together, there is a tendency for stable relationships to develop mutually compensating and compatible roles. Roosevelt's relationship with Hopkins provides an intriguing illustration of this point. Hopkins was blunt and abrasive. He had a great capacity for work and carried out assignments with Machiavellian efficiency. Roosevelt was ambiguous in commitment, reluctant to offend people, and at times, indecisive. Hopkins could do what FDR would not do. In addition, Hopkins offered loyalty which withstood Roosevelt's periodic tests of ignoring Hopkins, withdrawing support, or appearing indifferent.

Roosevelt's personal demands were endured by Hopkins, but there is some indication that, over time, they may have driven away other talented subordinates—one price of the competitive approach. With the departure of first Moley, then Corcoran, FDR lost lieutenants of exceptional intelligence, and in the latter case, skill. In Hopkins, he got instead a loyal operative whose zeal to please his master at times bordered on sycophancy.

In describing Roosevelt's managerial system, several of its attendant strengths are evident. It kept him informed. It generated heat but also ideas and politically viable compromises that could withstand the test of Congress. In addition, there were several inherent weaknesses. Of particular interest is the sequence of decisions that led to FDR's plan to "pack" the Supreme Court. Ironically, this was less a failure of his system and more the result of his departure from his usual managerial practices.

The Supreme Court struck down the NRA in 1935. Until then, the New Deal's momentum had rolled his programs along unimpeded. Events had imparted to Roosevelt an aura of invincibility and perhaps this was decidedly showing. Roosevelt had been outraged by the court's action. Following his reelection, he plotted a counterattack. But this time (1937), contrary to his usual practice of soliciting diverse views, he worked in secrecy. Even Hopkins was not told of his plans until the last minute.

Timing his message for impact, he called a surprise meeting of key Congressmen a day before his judicial reform proposal was made public. The plan, presented under the flimsiest pretense of providing for Supreme Court Justices' retirement, proposed, in part, that for every Justice over seventy who did not resign, an additional Justice would be appointed. With six Justices in this category, most of whom had voted repeatedly to strike down New Deal measures, it was a bold-faced court-packing effort. He did not, as he described the plan to the Congressional leadership, engage in his usual practice of inviting comments. Instead, he presented it as a given. There was silence; no discussion.

The Court plan encountered immediate and vituperative opposition. But Roosevelt remained wedded to the idea to the end. Perhaps his first fateful misstep was in abandoning a managerial pattern that had always protected him from making such mistakes. In his 1937 Supreme Court initiative, FDR was no longer an arbitrator; he became a party to the dispute.

Quite apart from the managerial issues involved, FDR's tangle with the Big Bench proved costly in many ways. He gambled away his image of invincibility. Congressmen who once feared him now realized that there were votes enough to turn his flank. Gradually, the coalition that had granted him such legislative success began to fall apart.

Roosevelt's strategic error was in not recognizing the basis of his support. Perhaps this revealed a more basic weakness of his managerial style. Attuned to the politics of the moment, it did not enable him to weigh events in the larger context. Roosevelt saw himself simply as a securely entrenched leader of the people. He had been swept into office by bipartisan support. He did not consider that his strength might lie primarily in the immediacy and magnitude of the crisis. He did not see that once the crisis passed, age-old cleavages would reappear.

Another weakness of the Roosevelt system stemmed from its inability to develop real teamwork. Roosevelt's competitive approach worked brilliantly when innovation was the currency of success. His system generated ideas and spotlighted opposing views. But sometimes teamwork is necessary to build a complete analysis of an issue—for example, the 1938 recession.

In late 1937 the economy slumped badly. Unemployment soared. Roosevelt assumed his habitual stance. Playing off conservative budget balancers like Morgenthau and his Budget Director Lewis W. Douglas against free spenders like Corcoran and Hopkins and Ickes, he bided his time. The conflict among his advisers was intense. Corcoran and Ickes gave speeches attacking the nation's business. Roosevelt gave tacit approval. Yet simultaneously, he encouraged Morgenthau to prepare a balanced budget. Roosevelt waited until April of 1938 when, spurred by a precipitous drop in the stock market, he finally adopted a deficit plan.

Roosevelt preferred to move with the grain of events. He had held out—waiting for a sign, a clear mandate from the Congress or the public. But in his concern for the immediate, he had passed by the better course.

Several years before, Roosevelt had met a British economist named John Maynard Keynes. They had conversed over tea, but the meeting was not a great success. Keynes was arrogant and this may have offended Roosevelt.[32] More importantly, Keynes stood for a *system* that prescribed deficit spending of fixed sums for specified lengths of time. Yet in 1938, nothing could have been more of an anathema to Roosevelt than Keynes' formulations and the commitments they entailed.

Roosevelt's system was long on advocates and short on thorough analysis. But an accompanying weakness lay in the very nature of the adversary process which had either driven out his intellectually more powerful advisers (such as Moley) or polarized those that remained. Roosevelt, neither as a thinker nor as a manager, was able to seize the opportunity that Keynesian economics gave him. This failure illuminated a fundamental trade-off of the competitive approach: in structuring his system to provide divergent opinions, he had blunted his aides' capacity to work collectively on good ideas and staff them out. His advisers had been trained to compete with rather than complement one another. In the 1938 recession, as well as in the war effort that would follow, Roosevelt's methods remained much the same as they were in 1932. The situation, however, was changing.

World War II confronted Roosevelt with his second great crisis. As we shall see, his managerial methods, well suited to the experimentation needed during the Depression, were less appropriate to the requirements of war.

Lend Lease marked the nation's first major step into the war. With that step, Roosevelt's problems moved from inventing New Deal programs to mobilizing the nation's productive machinery.[33] This confronted the Administration with a wholly new phenomenon: mere ideas and experimental programs would no longer suffice, as had been the case in 1933. Required instead were clear priorities and the direction necessary to bring the nation to readiness. For this task Roosevelt's pattern of management was somewhat inadequate.

The nature of the relationships between Roosevelt and his advisers did not change with the war. Hopkins, forever jealous of his relationship with FDR, sought to be involved with the vital activities that would ensure his continued presence. Bernard Baruch, one of Roosevelt's perennial sources of outside advice, complained throughout the war that Hopkins was like a jealous woman and was keeping others away from Roosevelt. Later, when FDR sought to enlist Baruch on an important assignment, Hopkins was instrumental in having the request withdrawn.[34] When Lend Lease was launched, Hopkins engineered the appointment of his tractable friend, Edward R. Stettinius, as its director. Stettinius was content to fill the top post while Hopkins ran the show.[35]

More serious to the war effort was Hopkins' success in having the innocuous, affable Donald Nelson made chairman of the War Production Board. To engineer this coup, Hopkins had to head off the nomination of Supreme Court Justice William O. Douglas to whom Roosevelt had already tentatively offered the job. In photo-finish maneuvering, Hopkins exploited Roosevelt's fear of appointing an "assistant President" and slid Nelson into the coveted slot.[36] Hopkins' motives were, as always, unclear—but certainly among them was the fear that the brilliant, aggressive Douglas as head of the WPB might have turned Hopkins into a surplus war commodity.

Hopkins might be faulted. Yet this was the price of a managerial system that kept aides so insecure that they were forever fighting to retain their primacy. Roosevelt's system so riveted his subordinates' attention on maintaining access to him that wider values were ignored. Such was to be the case with the WPB. A tragicomic drama ensued: Nelson, as WPB chairman, bumbled through ten months of contretemps. Decisions lagged, agencies quaked with struggles; there were leaks and counterleaks to the press, embarrassments that Roosevelt could never tolerate. Reluctantly, he removed Nelson by dispatching him to China to untangle one of the many snarls of Chiang Kai-shek's Administration. Apparently Nelson became entwined in the process and was never heard from again during the war.[37]

Hopkins, in fact, suffered a significant loss in favor as a result of this affair. Churchill remarked some months later that in a meeting with Roosevelt and Hopkins, the President had been noticeably cool to his aide; Hopkins explained later that the Nelson fiasco was the cause. Mismanagement in the WPB had sent shock waves through the system. Stimson became so irate at the inefficiencies that he threatened to resign. An entry in his memoirs castigates the President: "Having tinkered for nearly two years with boards and commissions, [the President] finally gave real power to the wrong man. Then, when that man got into trouble, the President coasted along; he neither fully backed Mr. Nelson nor fired him."[38]

Thus Roosevelt's managerial methods suffered from a serious weakness. His need for centrality, his fear of delegation, and his tendency toward fickleness drove aides to establish their indispensability. Hopkins, though not alone, was clearly a champion of the sport. Weaseling himself a trip to London in 1941, Hopkins became Roosevelt's emissary to Churchill. And indeed, Hopkins could be relied upon to convey faithfully the intent of the messages from the President and reliably repeat Churchill's response. Hopkins' gifts were not of a strategic kind. An emissary of greater talent would have had instincts for the longer view as well as the immediate. But Hopkins was a trouble-shooter—not a long-range planner. He pursued but one objective: supplying war matériel, fast. At this, Hopkins excelled.

As a result of his position as liaison between Roosevelt and Churchill, Hopkins parlayed himself into a central role in the war. His on-the-spot knowledge of the fighting fronts, gleaned from Churchill, gave him a corner on the market in directing the war effort. Hopkins discovered that the best way to be influential at home was to always be just leaving or returning from Europe.

Hopkins' often-praised role in the war as the President's expediter has been widely advertised. His genius for action was considerable: he got armaments to the right place at the right time. He lived to win the war, and despite Roosevelt's reach of mind, the Chief did little more. Hopkins could be rude and incredibly abusive. Admiral Emory Land, head of the Maritime Commission, gave him the title, "Generalissimo of the Needle Brigade."[39] He moved constantly, used the telephone with surgical efficiency to knife through red tape, and kept the War Department in a constant state of anxiety with his inquiries and interventions.

Hopkins made much of his capacity to blow open log jams. Indeed, his talents were considerable. But one wonders, in hindsight, if Hopkins might have been in some measure a self-fulfilling prophet. He aided and abetted Roosevelt's chaotic system, placed mediocre or inept men in key positions—then hurried to the system's rescue. Indeed, Hopkins may have been as much the symptom as the remedy of Roosevelt's larger administrative problems. Given Roosevelt's system, Hopkins was essential. But alternatives existed, had FDR been willing to use them.

Beyond the ken of Harry Hopkins sprawled an amoebalike network of emergency organizations established to coordinate the war effort. Consistent with his competitive principles and his determination to retain full command, Roosevelt's wartime organizations followed a consistent pattern: (a) they were typically boards of multiple membership, (b) the members represented divergent interests, (c) the groups either had multiple "directors" or none at all, and (d) their charters were invariably fuzzy.

In January 1942 the President in his State of the Union message announced to Congress his breathtaking set of production goals: 60,000 airplanes, 25,000 tanks, 20,000 antiaircraft guns; these yearly production quotas were to be reached by 1943.[40] While it was one thing for the President to issue clarion calls for production, discipline, and sacrifice, it was something else to set up the necessary administrative machinery to do the job. One observer commented a year later on the nation's uneven response: The bleak fact was that industrial mobilization was faltering to the point of crisis. The priority system—the heart of effective mobilization—was breaking down. The failure had a multitude of causes but not least the President's reluctance to make strategic commitments, his determination not to plan ahead too far, his fear of vesting too much authority in one man or office.

Yet Roosevelt's understructuring of his war organizations persisted. In his first effort to coordinate production, he had established the Office of Emergency Management. It was a predictable Rooseveltian instrument. The Emergency Council had no director but instead an "acting secretary." This post was filled by a veteran government official with thirty-four years of service—a thoroughly tractable lightweight. Roosevelt staffed the council with a large number of representatives from industry and labor.

When this expedient proved unwieldy, Roosevelt resurrected a 1916 act and established an Advisory Commission to the Council on National Defense. To this commission he appointed seven members. Once again, no clear system of leadership was designated. Harold Ickes, who attended the first meeting, recorded impressions in his diary which were a prophecy of things to come:

I became depressed as I sat at this meeting and listened to the President. He must have talked for about an hour straight, and I was reminded of other occasions when he was developing a new idea. He was conciliatory and persuasive and plausible, and yet, it seemed to me, ineffective. He didn't give such an impression of strength as I think this situation calls for, and the plans that he outlined for the members of the commission were nebulous and inchoate. Probably it took him a long time to explain his scheme because it was somewhat intangible even in his own mind.[41]

Roosevelt's desires in 1942 remained the same as they had been a decade earlier: to run the show himself. He was unwilling to delegate broad powers or to establish an all-out superdefense agency. And so the Advisory Commission stumbled along. Donald Nelson, in an illuminating statement both to the Commission and Roosevelt, singled out the failure to appoint a chairman as the Advisory Commission's greatest weakness: "I believe that the President overestimated his own capacity. He undertook to direct the Commission, and frequent meetings were held with him in the chair, meetings at which basic policies and plans were investigated and talked over."[42] Problems arose because the President could not always attend these meetings.

Once again, seeking to correct the deficiencies of the Advisory Commission, Roosevelt requested his Budget Director and the president of General Motors, William Knudsen, to present him with alternatives. Knudsen proposed an industrial mobilization agency, to be headed by a director who would run the entire defense production program. Again, Roosevelt reneged. Instead, he transferred the most critical functions from the Advisory Commission to a new agency, the Office of Production Management. As before, no head was named. Its members included four people—Knudsen representing management, Hillman representing labor, and the Secretaries of War and the Navy. Hillman and Knudsen were designated to "exercise joint authority in directing the defense program." An interesting exchange with the press followed this announcement:

Reporter: "Are [Knudsen and Hillman] equals?"
The President: "That's not the point; they're a firm. Is a firm equals? I don't know. See what I mean? Roosevelt and O'Connor was a law firm in New York; there were just two partners. I don't know whether we were equal or not . . ."
Reporter: "Why is it you don't want a single, responsible head?"
The President: "I have a single, responsible head; his name is Knudsen and Hillman."
Reporter: "Two heads."
The President: "No, that's one head. In other words, aren't you looking for trouble? Would you rather come to one law firm, or two?"[43]

The OPM limped along. On the first anniversary of Pearl Harbor, the Administration still faced a crisis of production.

Production of military airplanes had more than doubled, but it was still far short of the President's target; the output of other armaments fell even further behind his goals. Problems were compounded as the Roosevelt style, "administration by arbitration," began to spill over into the ranks. The two-headed OPM—serving two constituencies with different objectives—behaved predictably. At one point, the Truman Committee investigating wartime inefficiency revealed that corporations whose representatives sat on the OPM had received $3 billion worth of government contracts within a year, while hundreds of smaller competitors starved or subsisted on crumbs. Balancing the industry representatives on the OPM were scores of union officials and labor lawyers whose principal mission seemed to be to see that any grant of favor or relief to an industry group was matched by a corresponding grant to its workers. Hillman was accused on occasion of countermanding contract awards to nonunion employees; Knudsen was sometimes charged with favoring nonunion areas for the location of defense plants.[44] OPM was a house divided and in perpetual conflict with itself.

To some extent, circumstances and the sheer weight of administrative responsibility forced Roosevelt to yield some authority. In late May 1943, FDR created a true supercoordinating agency under the direction of former Supreme Court Justice James F. Byrnes. For Roosevelt, this final move—precipitating vocal Congressional criticism—was an artful compromise. Byrnes was a trusted official whose record in the Senate and on the bench had been conspicuous for its correctness. Roosevelt made his charter to Byrnes clear: "In jurisdictional disputes, I want you to act as a judge."[45] Byrnes, steeped in the tradition of the court, found the juridical posture a natural one. He was skilled in the ways of compromise. He decided disputes on the merits. He did not seek to legislate or expand upon his charter. Byrnes did not aspire for larger powers. He did not exceed his office.

Even the presence of Byrnes, however, could not remedy all

the conflicts emerging from the tangle of wartime agencies. The long-standing dispute between Jesse H. Jones, Secretary of Commerce, and Vice President Wallace burst upon Washington like a Fourth of July display. Roosevelt had joined the two in unholy wedlock: one was empowered to purchase strategic materials; the other held the funds. Ultimately, Roosevelt was forced to fire Jesse Jones. His sternness impressed the country, but his aides were more skeptical. They doubted that the President would change his old administrative habits for long. They were not wrong. Elsewhere in the system, similar conflicts were boiling to the surface with the regularity of geysers at Yellowstone. Because of the development of new weapons, Dr. Vannevar Bush, head of the Office of Scientific Research and Development, whose efforts culminated in the development of the atom bomb, urged the President to create a joint committee on new weapons and equipment to establish a desperately needed bridge between military and civilian research. Roosevelt, wary of important decisions being made without him, insisted that whatever coordination was necessary occur under the Joint Chiefs of Staff. This resulted in a decision point at a level not high enough for top secret developments (like the atom bomb) and yet too high for most conventional weapons.

Secretary of War Stimson stated the situation bluntly: "President [Roosevelt] is the poorest administrator I have ever worked under in respect to the orderly procedure and routine of his performance. He is not a good chooser of men and he does not know how to use them in coordination."[46] But Roosevelt was carrying on his old Rooseveltian tradition of administrative juggling and disorganization; he was no more able in 1944 than he was in 1934 to work through one chief of staff. On his sixty-second birthday, January 29, 1944, FDR complained to Senator Kilgore: "The details of this job are killing me."[47] A total of forty-seven war agencies were reporting directly to him.

It should be noted, however, that while Roosevelt's methods

prevailed in civilian matters, in military affairs he was willing to let the generals decide. Secretary of War Stimson and Chief of Staff General George C. Marshall had recognized the nation's need for a long-term strategy of war during the Atlantic Conference. Gradually, the Joint Chiefs of Staff filled in behind Marshall to provide a solid base of staff work. Remarkably, Roosevelt exhibited none of his usual jealousy toward the military. It was as if they were a different species and not subject to his careful audits of Presidential prerogatives.

The Joint Chiefs of Staff retained their primacy in military planning throughout the war. They proposed and fought for the cross-channel invasion that became "Overlord." A revealing incident occurred when Stimson and Marshall took their plans for "Overlord" to the White House. They were worried about the President's reactions. One observer recalls that in previous meetings, "he had shown, they felt, a tendency to respond too readily to the scattered needs of his allies and his area commanders."[48] Stimson feared he might go in for another "dispersion debauch"; Marshall had tabbed the President's habit of tossing out new operations as his "cigarette-holder gesture."[49] In fact, this time they found their chief more willing to focus on the issue. Whatever the difficulties, he recognized the importance of bolstering the Russians and keeping them in the war. Not only did he endorse a cross-channel attack but dispatched them to London to sell Churchill. Regrettably, the Joint Chiefs who were to perform so admirably in winning the war did not have concomitant responsibility for winning the peace.

Roosevelt employed traditional methods at the great wartime conferences. At the Atlantic Conference, conducted on board a battleship off Newfoundland, Churchill was well prepared. Hopkins was astounded at the size and sophistication of Churchill's staff. Whereas Roosevelt was completely on his own, subject only to the advice of his immediate self-selected entourage whose counsel he could accept or reject, Churchill was constantly reporting to and consulting with the war cabinet in London, addressing communiqués to the Lord Privy Seal, and so forth. During three days of the conference, more than thirty communications passed between the battleship and Whitehall. This was astonishing to the Americans.

From the Atlantic Conference to Yalta, Roosevelt continued to play it loose. He kept no record of his conversations and engaged problems in the same manner as he had during the Depression of 1933.[50] At these conferences Roosevelt tended to take a mediating role between Churchill and Stalin. FDR had learned that by poking fun at Churchill he could make Stalin laugh and use this to his advantage. At Teheran the three met again, each performing in his accustomed manner. Roosevelt sat in the middle, by common consent the moderator and arbitrator.[51]

Perhaps Roosevelt felt out of his element with these masters of grand strategy. Commenting upon Roosevelt's conduct at Teheran, Churchill quoted Hopkins as saying, "The President was inept. He was asked a lot of questions and gave the wrong answers."[52] At the Casablanca Conference, in fact, Roosevelt had inadvertently used the term "unconditional surrender" while spinning a yarn about Ulysses Grant in an off-the-cuff statement to the press.[53] Churchill was chagrined. But the term stuck—leaving historians to ponder whether it contributed to the duration of the war. At his last wartime conference at Yalta, Roosevelt stood true to form. "The President," said James Byrnes, a member of the American delegation, "had made little preparation."[54] Although the State Department had prepared a package of briefing materials on the postwar politics of Europe, neither Roosevelt nor Hopkins opened it on their week-long voyage to the Mediterranean. At the conference, Roosevelt, counting upon longevity, assumed he could establish an informal understanding with Stalin and play it by ear once the Nazis were defeated. He approached Yalta with the same mode of statesmanship that had piloted him through the New Deal—improvisation.

Who, after all, was FDR? A man of exceptional gifts and unusual character, the captain of a ship caught in a stream of events. Roosevelt knew how to drift with a flourish. This served him well as he negotiated the uncertain waters of his first term, but as experienced river captains know, to maintain steerageway, one must move faster than the current. In time, the stream changed; its eddies and banks took on a more certain character. Yet the captain maintained his commitment to an uncertain helm—even when "Full speed ahead" might have been the better order. Such was the dilemma of Roosevelt in the White House and his pattern of management which could not encompass the twelve years it spanned. Between the myth and the man falls the shadow.

CHAPTER THREE

TRUMAN'S MANAGEMENT
BY TRANSGRESSION

"Being President is like riding a tiger," Harry Truman observed after a few months in office. "You either stay on or get swallowed."[1] On more than a few occasions, his metaphor seemed close to prophecy.

In many respects Harry Truman faced one of the most difficult Presidencies since the Civil War. Not since Lincoln had an incoming President faced a Congress as divided as the 79th. But whereas Lincoln's problem was the clear-cut issue of national unity, Truman's problems were multifarious and complex. In the campaigns in Europe and Asia he inherited the mantle of leader-among-equals in the largest-scale war in recorded history. In Europe the end of the war was in sight. Yet in the wake of the conquering Allied armies loomed problems larger than the fighting itself. Europe lay prostrate; victor and vanquished alike were gutted by the war. There was the portent of mass starvation. The old order had been shaken. The tradition, the aristocracy, and the public attitudes that had sustained it were being challenged. In this mosaic of disarray, old patterns clashed with new realities. Britain lingered in hopes of reestablishing the Empire, de Gaulle hastened to reestablish French suzerainty in the Near East. On the Eastern front, Stalin brazenly installed Communist governments before the dust of his advancing regiments could settle. It was for Harry Truman to decide what to do.

At home there was great restlessness. Americans looked forward to a time of resurgence and recovery after all the sacrifice of war. Parents who had survived the Great Depression, sons who had fought, wives who had worked and waited, reflected on a decade of trial and asked—for what? Citizens with aspirations as large as their wartime savings were itching to cash in on victory. Wives wanted their husbands home. Soldiers wanted jobs. Labor wanted wage controls lifted but price ceilings held. Business wanted the opposite. Consumers wanted Depression prices but an end to rationing. And economists warned of serious dislocations if returning veterans were suddenly dumped upon an economy winding down from war.

This was the United States in 1945: frustrated with power by virtue of having it; seeking to fulfill multiple ends but in conflict over means. This was the terrible tiger that Truman would ride. Truman's task was made no easier by having to follow one of the most popular Presidents in history. Truman knew that FDR's prestige would be one of his biggest handicaps. It was inevitable that he would be compared unfavorably. When the nation was stunned by Roosevelt's death on April 12, 1945, part of the shock was attributed to apprehension over his successor. Truman also realized that Roosevelt had done him a disservice by not taking him into his confidence. Now he was on his own, alone and unprepared.

In hindsight, it is clear that Truman faced and made policy decisions of far-reaching importance. Should he airlift supplies to Berlin? Send aid to Greece? Sponsor the Marshall Plan? Support the United Nations? Develop the H-Bomb? Establish NATO? Invade Korea? Truman was left to decide. But unlike a wartime President, he had no clear-cut enemy against whom to rally support. He could not appeal to patriotism and valor. And because there were no clear-cut battles, there were no shining victories. His cruelest test was the insidiousness of the contest.

Following Roosevelt's death Americans had rallied around Truman as they do in times of national crisis. The Gallup poll indicated 87 percent approval—3 percent higher than FDR's top rating. Eighteen months later, as the Congressional elections approached, Truman's standing had plummeted to 32 percent.[2] Problems cropped up everywhere: skyrocketing inflation, black markets, incessant strikes, meat shortages, quarrels among the armed services, firings of Cabinet officers, and housing shortages. Truman became a liability as Election Day neared; Democratic Congressional candidates left his name unspoken. Walter Lippmann sternly warned that the Truman Administration was a grave problem to the nation. "How are the affairs of the country to be conducted," Lippmann questioned rhetorically, "by a President who not only has lost the support of his party but is not in control of his own administration? . . . At the very center of the Truman administration . . . is a vacuum of responsibility and authority."[3] The electorate apparently agreed in a stunning vote of no-confidence; Americans swept Democrats from Congress, giving the Republicans control of both houses for the first time in eighteen years. Senator J. William Fulbright, a Democrat, suggested that Truman appoint Senator Arthur Vandenberg as Secretary of State and then resign to make him President.[4]

"Nevertheless," as political scientist James D. Barber has put it, "this repudiated President, the year after the election debacle of 1946, engineered the most massive peacetime aid program in history, and in 1948 he got it accepted by Congress."[5] Still wholly lacking his own electoral mandate, Truman built outward from piecemeal response to Soviet moves toward a new concept of U.S. foreign policy. The manner in which this occurred sheds light on Truman's management style.

Early in 1947 the British reached their limits on a problem

that had been foreseen as early as 1945: they could no longer afford to pay for bolstering the security of the Greek and Turkish governments. The United States was asked to take over to prevent the Soviet Union from extending its sphere of influence to these countries. A year before, Truman had recognized that he could never find time to make a complete study of problem areas such as Soviet intentions in the Balkans, bombarded as he was day and night by people with information, problems, and schemes. In anticipation of further difficulties in Greece, he requested a comprehensive report on this topic. So, in the summer of 1946 he asked Clark Clifford, his former naval aide, whom he had made his Special Counsel, to staff out a paper on the subject. Advisers within the State Department whose judgments would leave their imprint on U.S. foreign policy for decades—Dean Acheson, George C. Marshall, George Kennan, Charles E. Bohlen, and W. Averell Harriman—grappled with the problem and its significance. A one-hundred-page report was submitted to Truman. It detailed the findings of the investigating teams and gave summaries of consultations with the foreign governments involved. Truman studied the report closely, completing his homework late the same day the report was submitted. In this process, he did not play a policy-formulating role. But *he* was the preeminent decision maker, often startling his advisers with his readiness to act. When Truman convened the climactic meeting on the situation in Greece, his advisers unanimously agreed that the sternest diplomatic and military measures would be justified in thwarting the Soviet scheme. According to one observer, "Truman agreed so readily with this drastic interpretation that General Eisenhower, sitting as Army Chief of Staff, hesitantly raised the question of whether the President understood all the implications of this decision."[6] Truman said he understood. Subsequently Clark Clifford authored a strongly worded statement committing U.S. aid to Greece and Turkey, converting a moderate-toned State Department memorandum into a vigorous historic paper. In

March 1947 Truman set forth in three sentences the essence of the "Truman Doctrine":

I believe that it must be the policy of the United States to support free peoples who are resisting attempted subjugation by armed minorities or by outside pressures.

I believe that we must assist free peoples to work out their destinies in their own ways.

I believe that our help should be primarily through economic and financial aid which is essential to economic stability and orderly political processes.[7]

In May, Congress passed a $400 million aid bill for Greece and Turkey.

Here was the essence of the Truman style and his *formalistic* approach. First, the use of staff machinery to sift difficult questions; second, reliance upon trusted advisers to bring forth from that process sound, workable solutions; third, Presidential willingness to stand behind his counselors; and finally, Truman's deep belief in "doing what was right." He believed that honest decisions, based on facts, would speak for themselves. In his own words, "Since a child at my mother's knee, I have believed in honor, ethics and right living as its own reward. I find a very small minority who agree with me on that premise. . . . I don't care if I get honor, if [the job's done right]."[8]

As this reference to his childhood suggests, Truman's style had its roots planted firmly in Missouri soil. Young Harry was the son of a dirt farmer who dabbled unsuccessfully in politics and speculative ventures. A short, pugnacious man, self-conscious of his height, John Truman was frequently involved in arguments and brawls. Young Harry did not escape unscathed from his father's frustrations. He was scolded unmercifully for the slightest wrongdoing and frequently served as peacemaker in family quarrels.[9]

Harry Truman seemed an old man as a child. As a result of poor eyesight, he had to wear thick glasses from earliest boyhood. He was accident prone and sickly; at nine, diphtheria brought on a partial paralysis of his limbs, so that his mother had to push him around in a baby carriage. These misfortunes cemented the bond between mother and son.[10] Martha Truman was a strong-willed woman with a high sense of moral rectitude. Young Harry learned not only to *know* right from wrong but to *act* accordingly—and face the consequences no matter what. This theme would carry into his Presidency.

Between his mother's rectitude and his father's discipline, Harry learned to walk a narrow line. He learned that the best way to avoid trouble was to keep his nose to the grindstone. In school he was far from a brilliant student, but the home-tested formula of hard work and attention to detail ensured a solid performance. Here was another harbinger of the evolving Truman style.

He liked school and hoped for a college education. But his father's failures forced him to take a job immediately after high school in order to support the family. Although he tried on several occasions to get a college degree, this goal eluded him.

Thus Harry Truman came to manhood. There was little in his early life to provide him with assurance or a sense of command. His father's scoldings, his reputation as a mama's boy, and his lack of education had done little to build inner security and self-confidence. Yet hardship is the mother of character. He had learned that hard work could surmount many obstacles. This made a great deal possible.

World War I provided Truman with a long-awaited opportunity. Since his father's death in 1914, life had been closing in. As the eldest son, he became responsible for the Truman farm and the livelihood of the family. When his National Guard unit was activated, he found a way to manage the farm with hired help. At last, the way was cleared to make a significant break with the past.

The army thrust Truman into entirely new circumstances. One of his first assignments was the operation of the regimental canteen. With an attention to detail that would characterize his performance later in life, Truman ran a canteen that was the only one at camp to turn a profit—a handy $15,000, which represented more than a 650 percent return on the original investment.[11] Then, abruptly, his regiment was moved to Europe. For the first time, Captain Harry was placed in charge of men— and his first assignment was a rowdy artillery battery that had gone through its first three commanding officers. On the first day, his men faked a stampede with their horses and wrecked their barracks in a brawl after taps. Truman lowered the boom. He threatened to bust any sergeant who didn't keep his men in line. Later, on the battlefield, when his men ran under fire, he gave his troups a dressing-down that onlookers found remarkable. "I got up and called them everything I knew," said Truman.[12] A Catholic chaplain who was on the scene recalled, "It took the skin off those boys' ears . . . but it turned them right around."[13]

Truman's army career also gave evidence of his drive to "do right." Once he disobeyed orders by directing fire outside his sector, thereby saving a vulnerable division from annihilation. He was threatened with court-martial for his disobedience but stood by his principles, insisting that he would do the same thing again. He was not court-martialed.

Truman was learning that facing problems head-on, calling the shots as he saw them, was a workable way to manage. It also won him respect—and with that respect he could rely on his men to do the job. He, in turn, provided them with support. This formula of reciprocal loyalty was to become a Truman trademark.

Truman's success as a captain paralleled his growing popularity. He was a sensitive man who could listen, give advice, yet participate in a prank and laugh at a bawdy story. His men liked him and when he returned from the war, he sought to continue what had been a positive and rewarding experience. He did not want to go back to the farm. Instead, he turned to business. Truman was to be badly burned by several unsuccessful ventures. The most famous of these was his haberdashery. In this and subsequent investments, Truman demonstrated a willingness to take risks. Borrowing heavily, he invested $15,-000 in the haberdashery—a tidy sum in those days—all of which was lost. Later he would invest in, and lose on, still more speculative ventures involving banking and oil drilling. Truman, like his father, was willing to gamble for big stakes. But unlike his father, he learned from these early experiences. His subsequent gambles were in politics.

In 1922, deeply in debt, thirty-eight years old, and his haberdashery in financial collapse, Truman inveighed upon the Tom Pendergast machine of Kansas City to let him run for county judge. Ultimately he secured assent and won the election handily. A Missouri county judge is an administrative position (like county executive). In this post, Truman had major responsibility for the maintenance of county roads. Historically, this had been a source of payoffs and corruption. But Truman, dedicated to honest management, handled his job with great propriety. Despite his salutary conduct, he was defeated for re-election in 1924, but was elected again in 1928. His big break came in 1934 when he was selected to run for the U.S. Senate. His candidacy had been almost an accident—he was chosen by Jim Pendergast (Tom Pendergast's nephew) only after three earlier choices had turned down the opportunity! In a precipitously uphill fight, Truman won the election.

Even though Truman attained the high office of U.S. Senator, the ups and downs of his career had left an indelible impression of humility upon him. Election to the Senate altered his fortunes more than it did his self-confidence. The shadow of the Pendergasts followed him to Washington: he was the product of machine politics—not a victor in his own right. Truman's insecurity was compounded by the fact that he was snubbed by FDR and treated with scorn by many colleagues because of his political associations.[14] Throughout his early years in the Senate, Truman was a faithful follower of the New

Deal line. Off the floor he was a convivial fellow and made a number of friends, but he remained pretty much of a cipher in the Senate hierarchy. To many, he was an amiable but undistinguished backbencher who rarely made a speech and who was likely to make a botch of it when he did. His biggest splash, in fact, was a negative one. When Boss Tom Pendergast was imprisoned for income tax evasion, Truman, out of loyalty, stood alone against the reappointment of the Federal attorney who had prosecuted him. "Tom Pendergast has been my friend," he said, "and I don't desert a sinking ship."[15]

Throughout these years, Truman was a lonely man. He spent most of his evenings on Senate work. He developed an appetite for biographies of political and historical figures. Perhaps his fascination with the lives of great men betrayed his aspiration to be part of events of more heroic proportions.

His successes in the Senate came slowly. His careful drafting of the Civil Aeronautics Act was praised by Arthur Krock in *The New York Times* as "the product of unremitting and intelligent toil by legislators of ability and . . . intent upon working out difficult national problems."[16] In 1936 he embarked on a painstaking study of the financial practices of the nation's railroads. With many of the railroads teetering on bankruptcy, President Roosevelt had called the railroads "the most serious problem of the administration."[17] Truman suspected spurious financial reporting. One of the first lines he looked at was the bankrupt Missouri-Pacific. Immediately, he was deluged with threats from lobbyists and Missouri constituents to call off his investigation. Characteristic of his developing style, Truman stuck to his facts, hired the best investigators available, and refused to be intimidated. Soon he was accusing the Missouri-Pacific of false bookkeeping and fraudulent stock transactions—proving his points with the railroad's own financial records.[18]

Truman frequently displayed an unusual measure of determination once committed to a course of action. His legislative assistant commented once that "if anyone put pressure on him, he immediately turned stubborn."[19] Perhaps for Harry Truman, the ledger of self-respect was kept in balance by his exercise of independence. It had been his mainstay in redirecting the artillery barrage in the army, in patronage squabbles with the Pendergasts, and now with colleagues in the Senate. They might scoff at his mannerisms and speech, they might scorn his machine connections, but in the last analysis, he was his own man. Truman's independence would accompany him to the Presidency.

When Truman ran for reelection to the Senate, the political environment in Missouri had taken a serious turn for the worse. Tom Pendergast was in prison and his machine in disarray. To many, Truman stood as the last vestige of corruption and disgrace. He became the target of Republicans and Democrats alike. Franklin Roosevelt sought to replace him with Governor Lloyd Stark and even offered to buy Truman off with a lucrative post in the Executive branch.[20] In a mudslinging campaign that spattered the state, Truman accomplished the miracle: he returned to the Senate a victor in his own right.

In the face of such experience, Truman frequently felt anger and resentment. Margaret Truman writes of his "slow burn" as he watched FDR attempt to install Governor Stark in his Senatorial seat, his "resentment against endless pressure and browbeating."[21] Once he exploded to Steve Early, Roosevelt's Press Secretary. "Listen," he said, "I've got a message for the President. Tell him to stop treating me like an office boy."[22] But Truman's anger was rarely expressed face to face. Even at home, according to his daughter, "he rarely raised his voice . . . and made a point of avoiding arguments."[23] "I think the secret of his success with my mother," Margaret continues, "was his absolute refusal to argue with her. From his very early years, my father was known as a peacemaker in the Truman-Young families. . . . He is still remembered as an expert in resolving arguments. Right straight through his presidential years, he continued to play this role. . . . Occasionally he complained mightily to me . . . about the prevalence of 'prima donnas,' . . . but he continued to exercise this gift for peacemaking in private—and in public."[24] Occasionally he would display his temper in a letter, fired off with sizzling hand to an adversary. Letters permitted him to express anger that he could rarely muster face to face. As President, one such scathing epistle was sent to Secretary of Commerce Henry Wallace because of the latter's pro-Communist public statements. The episode was particularly embarrassing because Truman had signed off on the speech—and even publicly endorsed its comments without reading it. From Truman's point of view, Wallace should have alerted him—and in his pique, sent Wallace an angrily written demand for resignation. Wallace considered the letter so intemperate that he asked that it be withdrawn so that he could retire gracefully.[25]

A distaste for conflict was an important part of Truman's style. This theme was evident in one of Truman's most notable experiences before becoming President—in his handling of the Truman Committee's investigation of wartime inefficiency. As chairman, he insisted on unanimous reports from his committee members—a demand which sometimes required five drafts. Once he was asked to explain his curious stress on unanimity: "Reasonable men don't differ much when they have the facts," he replied.[26] His response was part of the answer; but he also preferred agreement to controversy. There were other signs of his preference for interpersonal peace. Once during the committee's investigations, Jesse Jones, FDR's head of the Reconstruction Finance Corporation and also Secretary of Commerce, was questioned about a monopolistic contract with Alcoa (Aluminum Corporation of America) that was deemed responsible for an alarming aluminum shortage. The powerful Jones exploded in anger and used every iota of influence he had in Washington to make Senator Truman back down. This infuriated Truman. But when Jones reappeared before the committee and weakly admitted that the original contract was prejudicial to government interests, Truman treated him courteously. "No matter how mad he might be at a man personally," said a close friend, "he made it a point never to browbeat him."[27]

The Truman Committee, as one of Truman's last managerial experiences before becoming President, provided a reliable preview of the style he would employ in the White House. In setting up his committee, he selected old friends and men he could trust. Among them were Thomas Connally of Texas and Carl Hatch of New Mexico. He was equally careful in selecting the investigators he borrowed from the government agencies. (This was necessitated by the committee's meager budget.) Among these key men were a future Supreme Court Justice, Tom Clark; a future Democratic National Committee Chairman, William M. Boyle, Jr. of Kansas City; and a future White House Appointments Secretary, Matthew Connelly.

Truman's pursuit of his investigations characterized other aspects of his style—his drive for facts, his determination to do right, and lastly, his emphasis on careful staff work. Having engineered the railroad investigations in his first term in the Senate, he had learned something of the art. When the House voted in 1941 to raise the ceiling on the national debt to $65 billion, Truman was convinced that the spending spree needed a watchdog. Rumors of waste and profiteering from the war effort were rampant. He entered a resolution before the Senate to investigate these allegations. Perhaps because senior Democrats thought him too small for the job, his resolution was approved. But to ensure an extra measure of restraint, he was limited to a budget of $10,000.

After assembling his staff, he set off after the facts. After three months of work, he documented $100 million of waste in the army's $1 billion camp building program.[28] By the close of 1941, his committee held seventy hearings and gathered three thousand pages of testimony. In addition to the formal meetings, Truman called his committee together several times a week for private sessions. Truman moderated—as he would later before the National Security Council and the Cabinet.

When the committee's year-end report was presented, it contained a devastating indictment of that year's defense efforts—and especially of Roosevelt's two-headed Office of Production Management. As a consequence of the Truman report, the War Production Board was established in its place. Throughout the war years, the Truman Committee uncovered staggering evidence of graft, corruption, and inefficiency. By the end of the war, there were estimates that the committee had saved the government $15 billion.[29] These efforts brought Truman wide exposure and by 1944 he was mentioned as a possible member of the Democratic ticket.

Truman's pattern of management had been well developed before he became President. When he took the oath of office April 12, 1945, upon Roosevelt's death, one could have predicted with considerable accuracy how he would manage in the White House. From previous experience he had evolved an approach was that essentially formalistic. He established a staff and assigned them tasks. In Margaret Truman's words:

His approach to the presidency was quite different from Mr. Roosevelt's. He believed in delegating much more authority than Mr. Roosevelt. Mr. Roosevelt really ran his administration as a one-man show, confident of his own enormous popularity and his ability to keep track of all the strings. Dad was convinced that the government was simply too large for such an approach and was determined to get men with more administrative ability—as well as more loyalty to him in the Cabinet.[30]

These two themes, reliance upon staff machinery and delegation based on loyalty, emerge as the central tenets of the Truman system. To quote one close observer, "The chief reason for [Truman's] optimism in the first eighteen months of his second term was the smooth operation of the White House and the various agencies he had created to assist [him] in policy forming and decision making."[31]

Consistent with the formalistic approach, Truman adopted—and made full use of—his institutional machinery: the Joint Chiefs of Staff, the National Security Council, the Central Intelligence Agency, the Council of Economic Advisors are his surviving contributions to the Presidency. These organizations did not exist before he came into office.

President Truman conducted his staff meetings in the same orderly fashion as Senator Truman had run his wartime investigations. He strove for punctuality and liked to spring the door open at precisely 9:30 and wave his aides into the Oval Office. His staff meeting occupied a reliable forty-five minutes each day and was attended by ten to twelve aides. On his desk he had file slots marked with the name of each man. He would look through the files and hand the various men their assignments. But while Truman valued order, his style was never tense or formal. In handing out work he invariably asked each man, "What do you have to do today?" Current problems were discussed, appointments were arranged, and according to one observer, "He tried to hew to the staff approach in making assignments."[32] Over the course of his years in the White House, his schedule acquired further vestiges of regularity. He was briefed each day by the secretary of the National Security Council. His personal appointments were scheduled into fifteen-minute interviews; only rarely did visitors overstay their allotted time. On Mondays Truman met with his Congressional leadership. Unlike FDR, he did not manage legislative matters informally. Other fixed appointments in Truman's schedule were distributed throughout the week. Party politics were discussed with the National Democratic Party Chairman every Wednesday. Meetings with the Secretary of State and the Secretary of Defense, the NSC, and the Cabinet were likewise part of a fixed weekly pattern.

The outward manifestations of Truman's formalistic approach

are easy enough to identify: there is an emphasis on facts, staff machinery funneling information to the top, and the President sitting like a magistrate making the final decisions. But it is of considerable interest to press beyond the outer skin of Truman's managerial system and examine its inner logic. Having traced Truman's life from boyhood to the Presidency, we have identified forces shaping his Presidential style: a deep sense of doing the right thing, an avoidance of interpersonal conflict (perhaps a reaction against his father's argumentative nature and harsh discipline). We have noted too his humility and lack of confidence, his determination to face adversity, and his willingness to count on subordinates and support them in return for their loyalty. These were the underpinnings, and over the course of his career, they coalesced into a style of management that generally served him well.

First of all, Truman's style served to guard him against himself. There is evidence to suggest that Truman felt this necessary. Truman was impetuous—with a tendency to shoot from the hip. As a second-term Senator, he strained whatever relationship existed between himself and FDR by unwittingly approving an article that blasted the Roosevelt Administration for inefficiency. The incident occurred when a publication sent a girl down to Washington with a copy of the manuscript. She exerted pressure on Truman by telling him the presses were ready to roll and begging him to stop everything and read the article. Then she implied that he really didn't have to read it since everything in it was exactly what he had earlier told the writer. Truman compliantly initialed each page without reading it. When *American Magazine* hit the newsstands two days later with the lead article, "We Can Lose the War in Washington," Truman found himself author of a wide-ranging, sensational critique of the whole war effort. Not until months later did FDR forgive and agree to *try* to forget.[33]

A string of early mishaps in the White House struck a similar chord. During his first week in office he carelessly signed an order, without having read it, which drastically reduced Lend Lease. His action raised an outcry in England, indignance in France, and animosity in Russia. The order was withdrawn, but only after embarrassment to all concerned.[34] As noted earlier, he publicly endorsed a pro-Communist speech of Wallace's without having read it—and sent shock waves around the world. His ultimate firing of Wallace was also marred by rash conduct.

Nowhere was his impulsiveness more a liability than before the press. White House aide David Niles said:

FDR treated his press conferences like a poker game, while Truman kept exposing his hand. On purpose, FDR avoided calling on certain reporters who were there only to cause trouble if they could. Truman recognized everyone. FDR was always in control, tossing out trial balloons for public opinion, chiding reporters for asking silly questions and deftly turning aside subjects that he felt shouldn't be brought up. Truman was always direct—a question deserved an answer; he let reporters take advantage of his low boiling point and his general willingness to please.[35]

Repeatedly at press conferences Truman would be trapped by quotations that were attributed to him but that were in fact invented by a reporter who got the President to agree to them. His calling the Korean War a "police action" and the anti-Communist investigations a "red herring" came about in this fashion.[36] But all too frequently, Truman succeeded in hoisting himself on his own petard—his offhand remark at Potsdam, "I like Joe Stalin" or his careless allusions to "using the A-Bomb in Korea."[37] Truman was never to master the media. But fortunately for the nation, his determination to do the right thing, despite his public fumbles, prevented the media from mastering him. A lesser man might have abandoned his objectives for his image.

Perhaps as a matter of self-protection, Truman's managerial system sought men to run interference. Among those men, to be sure, were unsophisticated cronies from Missouri—like Harry

Vaughan—who would cause Truman embarrassment later. Yet a glance at the major decisions of his Administration as described in the diaries of such men as James V. Forrestal, his Secretary of Defense, Averell Harriman and Dean Acheson, captures a process in which talented aides thought through recommended courses of action.

Truman was perhaps aware that incisive analysis was the domain of others. In this arena he must depend upon men with greater mental acuity than he possessed. His role in the process was as ultimate decision maker. In essence, a tacit understanding of complementary roles was the invisible hand in Truman's decision system. Outwardly, it was structured and logical. But from within, it was driven by a delicate reciprocity: the President readily sought advice; but he evened the score by being the one who would decide and bear the consequences. A small plaque with the slogan "The buck stops here" was one of the few objects on Truman's immaculate desk. For the uninitiated it might be mistaken as a register of Presidential complaint against the burdens of his office. More likely, it served as a reminder to Truman's subordinates that the ultimate debt of the team was owed to him alone. Presidents, too, must fight for security and a sense of place. Truman found his place in his ability to make tough decisions and stand by them. This was his stock in trade.

Another important factor in maintaining the system's inner balance was Truman's method of giving rewards. For Truman to delegate with confidence, he required loyalty. Margaret Truman writes of "the modesty that characterized [Truman's] day-to-day operations of the White House. . . . He hated to use the buzzers on his desk to summon a man peremptorily. Nine times out of ten he preferred to go to the aide's office. When he did summon a man, he would usually greet him at the door of the Oval Room office. . . . This constant consideration for others . . . was the real source of the enormous loyalty he generated in those around him."[38]

Truman, while less accessible than Roosevelt, was readily available to the score of aides and top government officials who shaped Administration policy. In addition, access mattered less because his system permitted other forms of recognition. Truman was willing to delegate chunks of responsibility and let subordinates sink or swim accordingly. He was also far more permissive than FDR in allowing his aides their press clippings and invariably stood behind them when the going got tough. Truman stated his views on these matters with characteristic simplicity: "I am willing and want to pass credit around. The objective is the thing, not personal aggrandizement."[39] (In an interesting afterthought, he said, "All Roosevelts want personal aggrandizement. Too bad.") He was indeed generous in bestowing credit, allowing, for example, Secretary of State George Marshall to unveil the Marshall Plan at a Harvard commencement. Equally blessed by publicity was his Special Counsel Clark Clifford, who attained a prominence under Truman that has assured his fortunes since. Absent in the Truman Administration were men like Tommy Corcoran or Raymond Moley, who had faded into a Presidentially-imposed oblivion under FDR. Truman shared the credit.

Truman backed up his aides when they needed him. When Chief Justice Fred M. Vinson's pending visit with Stalin to discuss the European peace was leaked before Truman could inform his Secretary of State, there were rumors that the President had lost confidence in Marshall, who was then in Paris. Marshall was upset. Truman summoned him home for a personal conference, and then, with deep regret, announced to the nation that the Vinson mission was canceled.[40]

In return for his rewards, Truman received quality advice, which kept his Administration ticking. His awareness of this exchange seems apparent in this private memorandum dated June 17, 1945:

Went down the [Potomac] River today on the [Presidential yacht] to discuss plans, issues, and *decisions*. Took Charlie Ross, straight thinker, honest man, who tells me the truth so I understand what he means; Matt Connelly, shrewd Irishman, who raises up the chips and shows me the bugs, honest, fair, "diplomatic" with me; Judge Fred Vinson, straight shooter, knows Congress and how they think, a man to trust; Judge Rosenman, one of the ablest in Washington, keen mind, a lucid pen, a loyal Roosevelt man and an equally loyal Truman man; Steve Early, a keen observer, political and otherwise, has acted as my hatchet man, absolutely loyal and trustworthy, same can be said about Rosenman.[41]

Truman's system worked best when the advice was consistent. The most difficult decisions were those in which there was no agreement among his advisers. Such was the case with the Berlin Airlift. The Air Force, in particular, feared that a commitment to Berlin would weaken its coverage elsewhere. Truman decided to go in and ordered the Air Force into line. An even greater controversy arose over the decision to develop the hydrogen bomb. With counsel divided, Truman's instincts prevailed. Development of the H-Bomb was approved.

The inner logic of Truman's system served, as we have seen, to keep the machinery working and more or less in balance. There is no mystery here. As a manager's style matures, both the man and the method make adjustments. In a sense, they grow up together.

Along with its strengths and internal consistency, Truman's system had important limitations. The formalistic system of management, with its emphasis upon analysis and the orderly flow of information, depends inevitably upon the delegation of authority. Truman's needs and limitations made such delegation essential. But to do so with safety, he needed people around him whom he could trust. Thus he turned to old friends from Missouri and to men who had served on his Senate staff. Harry Vaughan, Truman's friend since World War I, became the President's military aide. Matt Connelly, Truman's Appointments Secretary and chief trouble-shooter, was an old friend from the Senate who had worked on the wartime investigating committee. Donald Dawson, another old friend and Missourian, became Truman's top personnel man. The President's personal physician, Brigadier General Wallace H. Graham, was likewise an old friend and Missourian.

Before the end of the Truman Administration, each of these men would appear as a star witness before a Senate subcommittee investigating fraud and corruption. Vaughan was deeply implicated in a half-dozen charges ranging from having received payoffs for influencing government decisions to smuggling. Connelly was indicted and imprisoned for perjury, bribery, and conspiracy to defraud the government in fixing an income tax case. Dawson was charged with accepting favors in return for engineering several very dubious million-dollar loans from the government to private corporations. Even physician Graham was subpoenaed by the Senate for speculating in the commodity exchange—using confidential information provided by the Department of Agriculture. Graham admitted to these wrongdoings.[42]

An equally important consequence of the formalistic approach, which delegates responsibility and relies upon aides to pass information up, is the warpage that occurs in the chain of command. While this problem never became acute in the Truman Administration, it did occur to some degree. Consider, for example, the situation which developed within the Truman staff during the rash of postwar strikes. By the end of January 1946, one million workers were on the picket line; before the end of the year, the public would suffer no less than five thousand strikes. Here was the making of a domestic crisis and it was clear that Truman needed help. Truman recruited John R. Steelman as Assistant to the President to assist him on domestic matters. Steelman had worked his way up in the Labor Department to become head of the Federal Mediation and Conciliation Service.

It became rapidly apparent that Steelman and Presidential Special Counsel Clifford did not see eye to eye on many matters of policy. For example, on March 30, 1946, when John L. Lewis took 400,000 miners out on strike, Steelman counseled for compromise. Clifford took the opposing view, arguing that the settlement would set a precedent, that others would follow, and that Lewis was challenging the government and should be met head on. Truman heeded Clifford's advice, fought Lewis and won. But the lines were now drawn between the homespun labor expert, Steelman, and the urbane, articulate Clifford.

It was not long before Clifford sensed he was caught up in nothing less than a full-scale battle for the President's mind. Steelman, as a conservative, had an ally in John Snyder, Truman's Secretary of the Treasury; he also maintained contact with influential Congressmen on the Hill. These forces favored a nonexpansionary economic policy; Clifford, in contrast, feared that such a course might invite recession. Gathering allies on the Council of Economic Advisors and elsewhere in the Administration, Clifford began to meet weekly with his group to discuss how they might most effectively influence the President's course of action. Recounts Clifford,

The idea was that our group would try to come to an understanding among ourselves on what directions we would like the President to take. And then, quietly and unobtrusively, each in his own way, we would try to steer the President in that direction.

Naturally we were up against tough competition. Most of the Cabinet and the congressional leaders were urging Mr. Truman to go slow . . . toward the conservative line. We were pushing the other way.

Well, it was two forces fighting for the mind of the President, that's really what it was. It was completely unpublicized, and I don't think Mr. Truman ever realized it was going on. But it was an increasing struggle during those two years, and it got to the point where no quarter was asked and none was given.[43]

The White House is a magnet for conflict. The differing interests of Cabinet departments and constituencies have a unique point of intersection in the Presidency. While Truman's system worked remarkably well, his blind faith in the open flow of information caused him to ignore, or at least underestimate, the degree to which White House aides could become "a constituency" themselves. Roosevelt clearly recognized this problem. His competitive approach to management tended to assume distortion and discounted the opinions of his advisers; he built a composite picture by collecting opposing views. In contrast, Truman's system underplayed competition and tended to overlook conflict. Yet, as the Steelman-Clifford incident reveals, coalitions did form and subtly shaped the President's decision-making process.

Neither competition nor conflict is intrinsically bad, but their existence must be recognized and managed. Truman's preoccupation with *the facts* diverted his attention from the contest below. His instincts, his understanding of personalities served as a check on his system, and as a result, he could gauge the men he was dealing with. Sizing them up shed light on the information they conveyed. Despite oversights, he maintained a fairly reliable flow of high quality advice. But the flow of information must be watched in both directions. Truman managed to maintain sufficient information *coming up* to make good decisions. But his preoccupation with making the decision and his policy of not interfering in a subordinate's sphere of action prevented him from *reaching down* the information network and properly monitoring the outside activities of his staff. These weaknesses would be evident in the events leading up to one of Truman's most far-reaching and controversial actions: the decision to invade North Korea.

Five years after the end of World War II, Communist forces invaded South Korea. For a time it seemed that the political structure of the world might be upended. The fear for many was that it might come to rest not on a balance of power but on a balance of terror.

On Saturday, June 24, 1950, the North Koreans crossed the

38th Parallel. The South Korean forces, caught wholly off guard, fell back in disarray. Over the next several days, more and more American (and eventually, United Nations') forces were committed in an effort to halt the North Korean momentum. Just when it seemed that the defending forces would be swept into the sea, General Douglas MacArthur's surprise amphibious invasion at Inchon reversed the tide. Now it was the North Koreans' turn to retreat.

MacArthur wanted U.S. and UN forces to cross the 38th Parallel, promising total defeat of the North and reunification of Korea if this were allowed. As he had throughout the emergency, Truman convened his advisers to consider MacArthur's request. Buoyed by the sudden successes of the previous weeks, the group (including Secretary of State Dean Acheson, the four ranking civilians from the Department of Defense, and the Joint Chiefs of Staff) met in an atmosphere of near-euphoric confidence—a marked contrast from the air of grim determination that had characterized their meetings in the weeks before. This day they shared a warm camaraderie as they gathered around the long mahogany table in the Cabinet room. MacArthur's proposals made sense, they concluded. It was time to draw the line and let the Communists know we meant business. Thus in consensus and with a cohesive sense of purpose, they ratified MacArthur's plans to press ahead.

Little did the members know how thoroughly this historic meeting and those that preceded it would be studied. Political scientist Glen Paige, whose revealing study of the group's first six meetings was based largely on interviews with its members, calls attention to the "intra-group solidarity" that evolved. "One of the most striking aspects [of these meetings]," he continues, "is the high degree of satisfaction and sense of moral rightness shared by the decision makers."[44] His observation is supported by the statements of participants, one of whom described the atmosphere in which major decisions were made as being "in the finest spirit of harmony I have ever known."[45]

There is much of Truman's style to be found intertwined among what has come to be known as the "Korean Decisions." His emphasis on solidarity, his determination to do right, and his preference for harmony left their imprint on the group and its discussions. Unfortunately, in this instance, Truman's style was out of step with the requirements of the situation.

Scholars disagree on the quality of the Administration's decisions made at the beginning of the Korean War. There is general consensus, however, that the discussions leading to the decision to cross the 38th Parallel were flawed. One weakness in these deliberations was simply that group harmony enforced unwarranted optimism. From his study of the records and from his retrospective discussions with Secretary Acheson, political scientist David S. McLellan has recorded that there was "something strangely unreal . . . about those meetings."[46] Part of the unreality stemmed from the highly cohesive relationships which Truman's reciprocal loyalty had built up with his advisers through the years. There is abundant evidence of this loyalty. The Joint Chiefs were so in accord with Truman that they earned from Senator Robert A. Taft the epithet "political generals."[47] Truman and Acheson likewise had a highly developed level of mutual respect and admiration. (Each has praised the other for being one of the truly great men to have filled his office.) There is nothing, of course, unreasonable about mutual respect between superior and subordinate. But to the extent that such admiration screens out objective treatment of the facts and the full range of alternatives, it undermines effective decision making.

There is evidence that such was the case regarding Korea. According to Irving Janis, whose insightful book *Victims of Group Think* documents the effects of group behavior on policy decisions at the time of the North Korean invasion, U.S. policy had been to prevent a pro-Communist government from conquering South Korea. But MacArthur's brilliant success, Janis concludes, led to an escalation decision and, implicitly, to a commitment to reunify North Korea and place it under control of the pro-American South Korean government. The policy switch from "containment" to "rolling back" was made in the face of repeated threats of military intervention by the Communist Chinese government.[48] These warnings had been explicit. For example, on October 1, 1950 China vowed that she would not stand aside if MacArthur crossed the 38th Parallel; a similar message was relayed to Washington by the Indian Ambassador to China. In addition, the CIA warned of troop movements and the capability of a Communist response. But the system counted upon the orderly flow of information up through channels, and since Dean Acheson guarded this particular channel and believed that China was bluffing, his interpretation became a basic assumption of U.S. policy.

At question here is not the decision to escalate per se (hindsight makes that task easy enough). More relevant is the criticism that policy makers had enough evidence to make them fully aware of the possibility of full-scale Chinese intervention. In the words of one analyst, "It was not the absence of intelligence which led us into trouble but our unwillingness to draw unpleasant conclusions from it."[49]

Truman's system depended upon information and advice; he did not get the full benefit of either. His group did not correct each other's oversights but rather reinforced them. This process is of particular interest because it occurred despite efforts by subordinates immediately below the policy level to press divergent opinions upon their superiors. Two such sources were Paul Nitze, head of the State Department's policy planning staff, and George Kennan, State's leading expert on the Soviet bloc. Both predicted a serious confrontation with China if MacArthur tried to occupy North Korea. Kennan describes himself as being "relegated to the sidelines, attending meetings in the Secretary's office but not those that took place at the White

House level."[50] Acheson, in a mood of confidence, did not invite these experts to brief the President or to develop a contingency plan based on their beliefs.

Acheson, the "funnel" of information, had become the "filter." Such is a hazard of the formalistic approach. And in Acheson's own views, as he hints later in his memoirs, this filtering had undesirable consequences.

As I look back, the critical period stands out as the three weeks from October 26 to November 17. Then all the dangers from dispersal of our own forces and intervention by the Chinese were manifest. We were all deeply apprehensive. We were frank with one another, but not quite frank enough.[51]

MacArthur launched his all-out drive to take North Korea on November 24, 1950. By 6:15 A.M. on November 28, General Omar Bradley, Army Chief of Staff, telephoned the President to tell him that MacArthur's forces were being attacked and driven back by an estimated 260,000 Chinese troops. Truman responded to the shocking news by promptly phoning his Secretary of Defense and Secretary Acheson. Evidently, they reassured him. "They all agree with me that we're capable of meeting this thing," he told his White House staff a few hours later.[52] Subsequently, he exhibited an extraordinary outburst of anger, not at his advisers or at MacArthur, but at newspaper publishers and Republican "vilifiers."

Years of anguish would follow before an end to the Korean War would be negotiated. In many respects the crisis had magnified the greatest weaknesses of Truman's system. His belief in "principals" was reinforced by advisers who held identical beliefs. Truman's experience suggests to us that a President cannot afford the comfort of such consensus. Empowered by this sense of rectitude, Truman tended to accede to, if not prod, his advisers in the direction they wanted to go. The links of his chain of command were thus welded shut—making them strong under tension but insensitive to outside and contrary advice. His system relied on what was coming up through the channels: it lacked a means to reach down and inspect for blockage.

In fact, Truman relied to the end on the counsel of his advisers. Richard Neustadt notes in *Presidential Power* that the President's advisers gradually came to agree among themselves that MacArthur's directives should be changed—and this meant a clash with the General. But each adviser had reasons of his own for not taking the problem to Truman: Acheson because he was already under fire from the Capitol, Marshall because he did not want to revive an old Army feud between himself and MacArthur. And as for "the President," Neustadt says, "[he] had little thought of overriding on his own, the tactical decisions of a qualified commander."[53] It was his advisers who pressed him to confront—and ultimately to dismiss—MacArthur. Nowhere do we see more clearly the degree to which Truman's assertive leadership style contained strong undercurrents of permissiveness and dependency.

Failures stemming from an elaborate information-gathering process are inherent shortcomings of the formalistic approach. But related to the legacy of Korea, and other Truman episodes, is a more subtle weakness which arose from Truman's personal traits. Truman was deferential to men he held in awe. His humility was gigantic. Five months after Roosevelt's death, he wrote to Mrs. Roosevelt, "I never think of anyone as President but Mr. Roosevelt."[54] Margaret Truman talks about instances in which "his humility almost got out of control, and he would begin talking about the possibility that there were other people in the country who could do the job of President a lot better than he was doing it."[55] Such self-doubt erodes command.

His tendency toward excessive humility led to a number of early problems with his Cabinet. Truman's inheritance of the Roosevelt Cabinet included a rich estate of egos. In time he planned to replace some members of the Cabinet. However, as a matter of public confidence, he accepted them all at the beginning, although it was not Truman's way to continue Roosevelt's methods—granting unclear charters, and preordaining himself as the highest court of appeals. "Instead," recalls one White House aide, "he delegated the work to the [Cabinet members], let them run their own shows and then backed up their decisions. This couldn't last long because the policy . . . developed little czars who considered themselves bosses within their own domains. It couldn't last without making Truman look like a Throttlebottom. And he was anything but that."[56]

Truman's humbleness invited such transgressions. The problem arose from misleading cues as to how he wanted people to utilize the "delegation" and "confidence" and "respect" he conveyed to them. He looked up to many of the Roosevelt Cabinet. But his respect carried with it a tone of permissiveness that tripped up some. When Truman telephoned Jesse Jones, the Federal Government's lending czar, to say that he had sent John Snyder's name to the Senate for confirmation as Federal Loan Administrator, Jones asked, "Did the President make that appointment before he died?"

"No," Truman replied curtly, "*he* made it just now."[57]

The downfall of Secretary of State Byrnes provides an embellished illustration of Truman's tendency to defer excessively to his advisers—then to have to bring them up short. Truman had held the brilliant and assertive Byrnes in awe from his first encounter with him in the Senate. Truman was aware that Byrnes had sought the Vice Presidency and had narrowly missed the mark when Roosevelt switched and appointed him instead. It was not Truman's way to hide his respect for Byrnes. In addition, he may have felt a certain degree of indebtedness to him. So, he installed Byrnes as Secretary of State, a post which Byrnes assumed with such independence from his chief that it appeared at times to be a separate branch of government! But rather than confront the problem, Truman remained so accommodating to Byrnes that he appeared to have dropped the reins of command.

The Byrnes episode came to a head in late 1945 when the Secretary went to Moscow for a conference of Foreign Ministers. Prior to his departure, Truman had sensed Byrnes' impatience. "When we sat in the Oval Office," Truman said later, "I could feel he was thinking that he belonged in the big chair instead of me."[58] At Moscow, Byrnes not only failed to keep his chief informed, but unilaterally reversed several policies that Truman had recently established. Adding insult to injury, Byrnes returned to Washington and proceeded to make arrangements for a coast-to-coast broadcast reporting on his conference—all this without first reporting to his chief. Truman seethed with anger. Yet his admonishment, when administered, was so gentle as to border on ambiguity. Calling Byrnes before him in the Oval Office, Truman *read* the following letter:

My Dear Jim,

I have been considering some of our difficulties. As you know, I would like to pursue a policy of delegating authority to the members of the Cabinet in their various fields and then backing them up in the results. But in doing that and in carrying out that policy, I do not intend to turn over the complete authority of the President nor to forego the President's prerogative to make the final decision. . . . I was completely in the dark on the whole conference until I requested you to come [here] and inform me. The communiqué [you framed in Moscow] was released before I ever saw it. . . . I do not think we should play compromise any longer. . . . I'm tired of babying the Soviets.[59]

Woven into Truman's handling of this episode are considerable insights into his character and style. First, Truman evidently had difficulty in adapting his preferred management style (i.e., delegation and back-up) to the greater complexities of Presidential policy making. In addition, he inherited advisers who had been schooled under Roosevelt's wholly different pattern of management. Another problem was that Truman's deference invited excesses; yet when a subordinate transgressed on his Presidential prerogatives, his pride was offended. A more commanding leader might have enforced his dominance in heated confrontation. But Truman's humility and tendency to avoid face-to-face conflict often caused him to administer a mild reproach when a full dressing-down was in order. In the Byrnes incident, Truman believed his letter placed the Secretary on notice. In fact, his reticence to confront Byrnes for thinly veiled insubordination only allowed the problem to fester. Truman could not easily bring himself to assert his role as a superior, but when subordinates transgressed his limits, he could fire them.

His personal style misled subordinates about how their relationship was to be defined. He also delegated more broadly and ambiguously than his decisional needs could tolerate, allowing subordinates wide latitude in what they *could* do—and just assuming they would know the proper boundaries. He was, in a sense, responsible for subordinates' misbehavior. He did not own up to this responsibility, however, but rather projected the blame on them "for not being loyal to him." His management style, shaped by the hierarchical imperatives of the army and the relatively simple relationships between a Senator and his staff, encountered real difficulties in coping with the more complex, shared power situations that arise between a President and his Cabinet.

The dilemma imposed by Truman's deference was to plague his years in office. He confided to Eisenhower in 1945 his willingness to step aside in 1948 should the General choose to run for President.[60] Later, as Truman became more comfortable in the Presidency, he grew to dislike Eisenhower—forgetting perhaps that he had invited the plague upon his own house. Virtually all the New Dealers he inherited from Roosevelt's Cabinet misread, and fell victim to, Truman's humility. Secretary of Commerce Wallace crossed the line early by telling Truman that he would be the President's "left hand in the Administration."[61] One by one they were dismissed: Morgenthau, Ickes, Wallace. In a sense, their passing was natural enough. Yet each departure was marked by a trace of misunderstanding. He was unable to explain how he wanted them to play their roles. Fundamentally, Truman relied on his concept of "loyalty" as a substitute for defining less ambiguously the norms required for his managerial approach. He gave subordinates more leeway than he should have or really wanted to, then when they grabbed the ball and ran with it, he got angry and considered them disloyal or worse. Nowhere were the consequences of this vague system of control more tragic than in the events leading up to the firing of Douglas MacArthur.

The MacArthur episode was a reenactment, in many respects, of the President's difficulties with Secretary Byrnes. But this time stakes were measured in military terms instead of the niceties of Washington protocol.

The President's problems with the General began to surface long before their final "summit" at Wake Island. All along there was the controversy about crossing the Yalu. Then MacArthur had issued several press releases in which he criticized the government for its unwillingness to use the Taiwan-based Nationalist Chinese in Korea. Now, as the Korean conflict deepened, it became essential for Truman to meet with MacArthur to ensure clear communications. MacArthur was waiting when Truman's plane set down on Wake Island at 6:00 A.M. on October 15, 1950. Truman was taken aback by MacArthur's casual wartime attire, which included an unbuttoned shirt and a battered cap. "I've been a long time meeting you," the President said, shaking hands. Reporters present noted that Truman did not act like a commander in chief greeting a subordinate. *The New York Times* described the encounter: "Truman [was] like an insurance salesman, who had at last signed up an important prospect . . . while the latter appeared dubious over the extent of the coverage."[62] Truman later admitted that he had not expected MacArthur to be friendly and was pleasantly surprised by his warmth. When MacArthur expressed regret for those press releases that might have embarrassed the President, Truman good-naturedly accepted his apology.

Here was Truman's opportunity for corrective action. But a lifetime of awe and insecurity are not set aside in a moment. Truman expected the General's loyalty—manifested in Truman's terms. In hindsight, MacArthur's easy apology was hardly an adequate substitute for getting down to brass tacks over Truman's expectations of how he wanted MacArthur to conduct himself as his subordinate. As is well known, MacArthur hardly "fell into line" after their meeting. Having been away from the United States for more than ten years, MacArthur was in important respects out of touch. His role as chief of the military government of Japan may further, though subtly, have contributed to these problems. Truman's challenge was in defining for MacArthur that the President would make the decisions, MacArthur present the choices (a chronic problem to be sure, but it is the responsibility of the Chief Executive). A larger man than Truman might have headed off this tragedy, but for all his courage and conviction, he essentially lacked the capacity to inspire and command. He was adept at sifting through information and making sound decisions, but when it came to the precarious game of harnessing the respect and loyalty of men, no measure of systemization would suffice. The raw, naked attributes of leadership and personal force were called for. Truman was lacking. So it was that MacArthur and Truman left Wake Island, each on a collision course from which neither would fully recover.

Men seek self-respect in hidden ways. On some private ledger a score is kept, hour by hour, day by day. For Truman, the struggle of his Presidency was forever to keep the accounts balanced. In this light, the firing of MacArthur may have been a lashing out, aimed at restoring a measure of self-assertion and self-respect. Truman realized that not only he but his advisers were aware of MacArthur's insubordination. His embarrassment was therefore public. Perhaps to some extent Mac-Arthur may have been a scapegoat and Truman's recourse may have exceeded the offense.

MacArthur was summarily dismissed in Korea. His return to the United States was accompanied by a public outcry unparalleled in the nation's history.[63] As for Truman, he never stopped fighting MacArthur and never stopped denouncing him. The reason, perhaps, is that Truman may have carried vague feelings of guilt and responsibility for allowing MacArthur to behave in a such a way that Truman had to dismiss him.

As the MacArthur incident dramatized, Truman's Presidency seemed to court controversy. His forays into the legislative arena were no exception. A Senate aide, describing Truman at the wheel of an automobile, provides an interesting insight. "He is the worst driver I have ever known. He always ignores the speed limits and he passes cars on curves and hills. You sit there praying you won't get killed."[64] The analogy is compelling. President Truman steered legislation from the White House with the same singleminded abandon. The result on most domestic initiatives was head-on collision. On September 6, 1944, just six months after taking office, he shocked Senate conservatives—who hoped for an innocuous President—with his highly progressive Economic Bill of Rights. Later came his Fair Deal legislation, a Social Security extension, and his anti-inflation program. All were blocked; worse, the Taft-Hartley Act and a tax bill favoring the rich were passed over his veto.

In February 1948 he once again revealed his talent for stirring up controversy. Without conferring with his Congressional leaders, Truman sent a ten-point civil rights message to Congress. He called for the strengthening of existing civil rights laws, a new law against lynching, establishment of a Federal Fair Employment Practices Committee, an end to Jim Crow laws in interstate transportation, the protection of the Negro's right to vote, and the eradication of the Oriental Exclusion Act of 1924. Southerners led the ensuing Congressional revolt. In the aftermath of their repudiation of Truman's program, *The New York Times* commented that the President's reputation for insisting on principles was certainly strengthened by his dogged but futile assaults on Congress. "Repeatedly," adds the *Times,* "he has insisted on legislation which, from a national point of view, could only be considered as an invitation to rebuff. . . . It is not unusual for a President to be rebuffed by Congress. What is a little unusual is for a Chief Executive, repeatedly rebuffed, to refuse to change his tactics."[65]

Truman's unproductive clashes with Congress did little for his national popularity. Yet Truman continued to feel that if Congress did not respond to his forthright appeals for reform, at least he had done his duty. We see again Truman's assumption that truth will stand on its own merits, that it is wrong to compromise or bargain. In hindsight, Truman's approach seems better suited to making Executive decisions than to advancing legislation.

Truman's adherence to principles worked all right in the decision phase of his managerial process; his downfall was in insisting on principles during the formulation phase of the legislative process. In contrast, Roosevelt's competitive approach, while weaker (or at least more circuitous) in decision making, was far more effective in advancing the President's legislative interests.

In his years in office, Truman made many tough decisions that have stood the test of time. If nothing else, they have exhibited staying power. In retrospect, his faith in the facts seems well supported. However, Truman's controversial actions frequently threatened to undo many of his major accomplishments. The setbacks to his domestic programs were actually less significant than they seemed at the time—in the long run the nation's remarkable postwar conversion made many of his domestic proposals unnecessary.

Truman was a man of the people, and yet he lacked the presence and the verbal gifts to communicate the significance of his actions to the nation. On the campaign trail, face to face with the crowd, he could establish rapport by roundly assaulting his opponents. But in an era of radio and nascent television, faced with issues too subtle for angry rhetoric, Truman was unable to cope.

If Presidential power is the power to persuade, Truman lacked that power. Constrained by his style, he tended to neglect this aspect of the Presidency. He had neither Churchill's vision and eloquence nor Roosevelt's charm. What dulled the edge of this remarkable and dedicated man was perhaps nothing more than honesty and simplicity. His attributes were thoroughly American. He identified himself with the people and yearned for acceptance by them. He was a man just like any other citizen—who got mad, made mistakes, enjoyed his family. There was no distance about him, no separation or intrigue, no majesty. Unfortunately for Truman, the President is expected to be different from everyone else. He sought the respect of the press and the Congress and the chieftains within the Executive branch, but his image was devalued by his very availability. They could not respect his lack of restraint and commonness.

Yet despite Truman's limitations, the judgment of contemporary historians is remarkably uniform and favorable. Perhaps hardheaded old Sam Rayburn characterized his friend in the White House best. "He was right on all the big things, wrong on all the little ones," he observed. "In spite of the fumbles of human frailty, the pettiness he often displayed, the impetuousness that often spoiled his aim, he impressed his image constructively and permanently on the history of his world."[66]

CHAPTER FOUR

EISENHOWER'S ORGANIZED ABSENTEEISM

TUESDAY, October 30, 1956, was, perhaps, John Foster Dulles' most agonizing day as Secretary of State. At eight that morning he hurried to his office in an effort to get a grip on the calamitous situation in the Middle East. Twenty-four hours earlier he had been stunned by the news that the army of Israel had invaded Egypt's Sinai Peninsula. This day he would have to struggle just to keep up with events. By early afternoon his characteristic poise and emotional resilience were wearing thin. He looked gaunt and drawn. He had already chaired five staff meetings that day, and was now reeling from the further news that Britain and France were about to attack the Suez and Nasser.[1] The white telephone, the direct line to Eisenhower, lay buried beneath the chaos of paper on his desk. What should the U.S. do? What would the Soviet response be? The questions were as intertwined as the tightening knot in his stomach. Yet the burden of decision was his to bear, practically alone. Such was the nature of his role in the Eisenhower Presidency; such was the condition of U.S. foreign policy in that cheerless autumn of 1956.

The Administration's handling of Suez captured the Eisenhower Presidency in microcosm. Eisenhower was often a hazy figure in the background of the decisions of his Administration; he delegated broad authority to his advisers and backed them up. Dulles was aware that Eisenhower would leave in his hands almost all of the direct and daily decisions in guiding the nation's response to the Suez crisis. "Dulles," in the words of one observer, ". . . was in the driver's seat as few other American Secretaries have been."[2]

A careful look at the sequence of decisions leading up to, and following, the Suez crisis sheds a great deal of light upon the policy-making process of the Eisenhower Administration. One of the most significant steps, deceptively innocuous at first glance, occurred on July 19, 1956 when Dulles informed the Egyptian Ambassador that the United States was withdrawing its financial support for the Aswan Dam on the Nile. Almost a year earlier, Nasser had shocked the NATO allies by announcing a major arms deal with the Soviets. This transaction, which raised the specter of a Russian presence in the oil-rich Middle East, had induced the United States and Britain to offer economic assistance for the Aswan Dam in hopes of heading off further Soviet influence. While evidently pleased with the offer, Nasser continued to enlarge his relations with Moscow. Later that year he recognized the Peking Government of China. In the United States it was felt that these actions flouted American prestige. Facing an election year and a Congress ill-disposed toward helping Egypt, Dulles contemplated withdrawing the U.S. offer. On July 16, Dulles informed the President of his doubts; Eisenhower shared his ambivalence but left the matter to Dulles.[3]

Thereafter, Dulles appears to have kept his own counsel. He did not summon his staff to discuss the issue. When the French and British Ambassadors called, he informed them that he was "dubious" about making the loan. Their response was to urge him to avoid an immediate confrontation. "To deny the loan," cautioned the French Ambassador, ". . . is a very dangerous action; it can affect the Suez Canal."[4]

On July 19, Dulles met with the Egyptian Ambassador. From

the records available, it appears that as the meeting began, Dulles had not yet decided what position the U.S. would take. But as the conversation progressed, Dulles, perhaps as a trial balloon, expressed several reservations about the loan. The Egyptian Ambassador, catching a hint of refusal, leaned forward in agitation. "Don't please say," he blurted out, "you are going to withdraw the offer, because . . ." (and he pointed to his pocket) "we have the Russian offer to finance the Dam right here in my pocket!"[5]

Dulles flushed in anger. "Well, as you have the money already, you can't need any from us! My offer is withdrawn!"[6] The Egyptian Ambassador, known for his sympathy to the United States, left, deeply upset.

One week later, Nasser expropriated the Suez Canal and thereby caught the United States wholly off guard. In Europe the surprise was accompanied by panic as Britain and France contemplated the approaching winter with their vital imports of oil in jeopardy. Nasser's move caught Dulles in Lima, where he was attending the inauguration of the new Peruvian President, Dr. Manuel Prado. Apprised of the situation by cable, Dulles telephoned Eisenhower and officials of State and the CIA. However, he decided not to return to the U.S. immediately, and the President did not order him back. In fact, Deputy Secretary of State Robert Murphy noted at the time that "the President was not greatly concerned."[7]

In Dulles' absence, Eisenhower found himself more immersed in the crisis than would ordinarily have been the case. A long cable arrived from British Prime Minister Anthony Eden, advocating "in the last resort, to use force" to regain control of the Canal.[8] Eisenhower's response was to dispatch Murphy to London with the brief instructions, "Just go over and hold the fort."[9] Murphy, arriving in Britain, learned of detailed French and British plans to invade the Canal Zone. Because Dulles was still absent, he cabled Eisenhower directly. Eisenhower cabled back the noncommittal reply that Dulles was returning from

Peru and would be continuing on to London.[10] Then the President departed for a three-day weekend in Gettysburg. Dulles arrived in Washington on the following day, convened a meeting at State and made a statement to the press outlining the U.S. position. Shortly before leaving for London, he phoned to brief the President in Gettysburg.

Throughout the next three months, Dulles struggled mightily to forestall military action against Nasser. Dulles proposed, and the British and French reluctantly went along with, two conferences between Britain, France, and Egypt aimed at bringing Nasser to terms. At each meeting Nasser proved intransigent. Since Dulles refused to attend either conference, the allied position was weakened by the evident absence of U.S. support. This situation was aggravated by several public statements by Dulles and Eisenhower which implied that the U.S. would not resort to force in the Middle East under virtually any circumstances. During this period, there appears to have been no discussion within the State Department or the National Security Council of alternatives to deal with Nasser. Obvious responses, such as a shipping boycott of the Canal, or a U.S.-assisted (or at minimum, tolerated) blockade, were available; yet in the voluminous records of the Suez crisis, these options appear never to have been seriously considered.

Frustrated by the United States' seeming indifference, Britain and France began to plan an invasion in secrecy. Meanwhile, as October progressed, Dulles fell ill and was eventually hospitalized for several days. Eisenhower thus found himself thrust more directly into the breach. He received a lengthy cable from Prime Minister Eden, again implying the allied intention of taking the Canal by force. Eisenhower replied by letter after a delay of ten days. Eisenhower's response was not only slow but vague. Sherman Adams quotes Eisenhower as saying, "I've just finished writing an answer to an informative cable from Eden . . . saying I understand and even sympathize with him on the problem he faces—but just hope he's figured out all the risks."[11]

Eisenhower's letter apparently left the British unsure of the U.S. stance, and they sought further clarification. British Chancellor of the Exchequer Harold Macmillan stopped by to pay a not-entirely-social call on his old wartime friend, the President. Eisenhower's comments on the Suez situation led Macmillan to report back that "Ike will lie doggo" if the invasion proceeds.[12]

On October 30, Israel, and subsequently Britain and France, invaded Egypt. Dulles had returned from the hospital and was on hand as the warfare erupted. Eisenhower, apparently willing to let Dulles call the shots, proceeded with plans to make his scheduled campaign trip to Texas. The trip was cancelled only after Adams informed him, "Foster would feel better if you're in town."[13]

From October 30 until a cease-fire was effected on November 6, and thenceforth until all armies were withdrawn six months later, the U.S. waged a campaign to force Britain and France to withdraw. The campaign was fought in the Security Council of the United Nations and with economic sanctions applied against the French franc and the British pound. There was painful irony in the United States' publicly taking sides against its allies, and this left scars on oldtime friends. On France's part, the government resolved to seek independent atomic power, according to C. L. Sulzberger of *The New York Times,* "so as never again to have to surrender to atomic blackmail as they had to when faced by the attitude of Moscow and Washington toward their national rights."[14] On Britain's part, Eden had indeed made a grave diplomatic error in not explicitly informing President Eisenhower beforehand of the planned invasion. But it seems equally proper to attach blame to the President for not being *absolute* regarding his attitude toward the employment of military force.

Could military action have been avoided? Shortly after the invasion Eden had telephoned Eisenhower and proposed flying to Washington to speak with him. Eisenhower readily agreed.[15] But his advisers at the State Department felt otherwise: their consensus of opinion was that the visit was premature and should be discouraged. Eisenhower acceded to their wishes, but unhappily. According to Sherman Adams, "[He] understood the State Department's thinking and accepted its decision, but he accepted with reluctance and impatience." "He told me," Adams continues, "[that] turning down Eden's request for a personal talk did not seem the right thing to do. He felt this was no time to be concerned with appearances and propriety."[16] We can speculate that the U.S. would not have been as affronted by the allied invasion if Eisenhower had talked with Eden.

For the United States, it had been from start to finish an episode in improvisation. Dulles was undeniably in an embarrassing position, having led the President to believe that the situation would not explode. When it did, Dulles' reply was, "I really don't know how much we can do. Every day that goes by without some outbreak is a gain, and I just keep trying to buy that day. I don't know anything to do but keep improvising."[17] It was perhaps with precisely these tactics in mind that the *New York Herald-Tribune,* not known for undue harshness toward the Eisenhower Administration, ran an editorial with the heading, "Too Little and Too Late." The editorial deplored the Administration's policy as

a series of improvisations and inconsistencies. . . . The State Department was well aware before the summit meeting in Geneva that Nasser would seek arms and economic assistance where he could find it. The United States merely dawdled. . . . The manner of the American reversal on Aswan was brusque, and there was obviously little preparation for a counter-stroke. . . . The [U.S.'s actions toward the allies] have inspired naturally enough great bitterness in both Great Britain and France. . . . It is essential now that the United States should think through a policy on the Middle East.[18]

The policy never emerged.

In unraveling the Suez crisis, we must first examine the extraordinary relationship between Eisenhower and Dulles. In Sherman Adams' words, "During the six important years that

John Foster Dulles served as Eisenhower's Secretary of State, there was never much doubt about who was responsible for the foreign policy of the United States. Eisenhower delegated to Dulles the responsibility of developing the specific policy, including the decision where the Administration would stand and what course of action would be followed in each international crisis."[19] Eisenhower, of course, was well aware that his own approach to foreign problems was more conciliatory than Dulles', "[but]," according to Adams, "[he] deferred to the tougher stand of Dulles."[20]

Thus it was that Dulles, with the mandate of the President, received virtually exclusive and absolute command over every policy, every decision, and every action that concerned foreign affairs. Dulles guarded these prerogatives rather closely. From time to time, Dulles found in his domain such men as Harold E. Stassen, Special Assistant in charge of disarmament, C. D. Jackson, Special Assistant responsible for Cold War psychology, and Nelson A. Rockefeller, who was Special Assistant for Latin American affairs. According to Sherman Adams, "Dulles watched these specialists intently, and, at the first sign of what he suspected to be a possible threat to the tight and straight line-of-command between himself and the President, he straightened it out himself . . . [and] did not hesitate to take it to Eisenhower."[21]

Dulles' success in consolidating the foreign policy machinery under him simplified things for Eisenhower: Dulles alone was the man whom the President could turn to.[22] But the costs, as suggested in the Suez episode, became substantial when Dulles the adviser became Dulles the advocate. In the Suez crisis, Dulles clearly became the adherent of a particular approach. Other perspectives and other policy options were ignored.

There are two ways in which a Secretary of State can advise a President. One way is to state the problem, the facts, and the alternatives. But Ike was discomfited with messy choice. His personal requirements dovetailed with Dulles' own preference to identify not just the options but the *solutions*. Thus the second way, Dulles' way, was to study the problem, recommend a course of action, and support that recommendation with arguments.

Despite the dependence of Eisenhower upon Dulles, the President and his Secretary achieved a delicate accord in their relationship. Never forgetting the fate of Secretary of State Byrnes, who had failed to keep Truman informed, Dulles religiously kept the President briefed. He busied himself in his own fashion with the education of the President in foreign affairs. Eisenhower was, in the words of one observer, "exceptionally reliant on this process and . . . had to be sedulously briefed in the simplest elements of fact and interpretation."[23] Dulles ordinarily called Eisenhower at least once every other day. He had immediate, round-the-clock access and was the only Cabinet member who could speak with the President at the White House without a witness being present.[24]

Dulles was "well prepared" (as the President would often say); but the question is, "Well prepared for what?" What if Dulles was wrong, got angry, lost his head, got out of step with the march of events? Dulles' primacy in foreign affairs deprived Eisenhower of access to alternative viewpoints. This shortcoming plagued the Suez decisions and as we shall see proved costly in a number of decisions made by the Administration.

Through the prism of the Suez affair one may observe the cardinal elements of Eisenhower's *formalistic* approach: his reliance upon a pyramidal flow of information, his massive delegations of authority, his drive toward conciliation, his tendency to vacillate on tough decisions, and the absence of thoroughgoing deliberations in formulating policy. Let us examine these characteristics and their consequences one by one.

Few things were more prominent during Eisenhower's Presidency than his appetite for orderly administrative machinery. Throughout the campaign of 1952 he had vowed to "clean up the mess in Washington." Once in the White House, his responsibility was clear: to remedy the disorganization and in-efficiency of the Executive branch. With all the dedication of a pharaoh, the new President set out to construct an organizational pyramid to accomplish this task. Unlike his Egyptian counterparts who used slaves and stone, Eisenhower used paper, sign-off chits, councils, regularized meetings, and last but not least, a strict chain of command built upon specialists with assigned responsibilities.

Eisenhower adopted his system from the Rockefeller Committee's recommendations on how the Executive Office of the President should be organized. His chain of command for all domestic matters flowed through the Assistant to the President, Sherman Adams; below were the various staff components—the secretaries to the President, the Special Counsel, administrative assistants, and the special assistants—all nominally under Adams' supervision. The pattern closely resembled a staff organization in the military, where all information funnels through a chief of staff and the commanding officer expects his staff to present him with a recommended course of action, not simply the facts and the alternatives. There is little doubt that Eisenhower's years in the army had led him to expect the same approach in the White House. "The organization plan must make it plain to everybody," he said to Sherman Adams shortly after taking office, "that I am looking to you to coordinate this office."[25]

While Eisenhower was evidently concerned with the structuring of his system, he remained steadfastly aloof from the process that selected the people to man it. Of the aides Eisenhower brought to the White House staff—James C. Hagerty, his Press Secretary, Emmet John Hughes, his chief speech writer, Thomas E. Stephens, Secretary to the President, and General Wilton B. Persons, who handled Congressional relations—only Persons was a long-time friend. Eisenhower had met the others for the first time during the campaign.

Eisenhower evidently viewed the manning of the system as

less important than "the system" itself. He directed his old friend General Lucius D. Clay to screen and *select* candidates for the Cabinet.[26] Interestingly, Eisenhower did not as a matter of principle, "offer anybody a job personally." According to Sherman Adams, "It was wrong, he felt, to put a person in the embarrassing position of being forced to say 'No' to the President of the United States, and of course, it was also embarrassing for the President to have his personal requests turned down."[27] So the advisers in charge of the selection process made the choices for him, bringing such men to Washington as Charles E. what's-good-for-General-Motors-is-good-for-the-country-Wilson as Secretary of Defense and George M. Humphrey as Secretary of the Treasury. Virtually all of these men were close to the President in age, had a similar intellectual bent, and had been executives of large companies. Insofar as Eisenhower was concerned with their personal traits, one observer comments that "[he] liked men around him who were confident and cheerful and who gave evidence of knowing the job at hand and not bothering him with detail."[28] There was not in these criteria the makings of much grist for debate and conflict; instead, homogeneity was sought as if it were glue to hold the system together. Eisenhower recruited men not for their élan or brilliance but for their capacity to function like "standardized units" in a synchronized chain of command. In some respects, this way of choosing shows a certain wisdom. Eisenhower's practice of delegating large amounts of authority required that subordinates behave true to the boss' intentions. The price was that aides who were prone to behave with such reliability were often, by nature, unexplorative individuals not inclined to embark on new initiatives.

Eisenhower expected his Cabinet members to be almost completely responsible for their departments. Although Secretaries officially had a right to call upon the President, few felt free to do so. The President made his preferences clear soon after the Inauguration. When his Secretary of Defense, Charles Wilson, called for his advice on a decision he was about to make, the President admonished him: "Look here, Charlie, I want *you* to run Defense. We can't *both* run it. And I *won't* run it. I was elected to worry about a lot of things other than the day-to-day operations of a department."[29]

Eisenhower's formalistic system aspired toward machine-like precision; this required not only reliable engineers but an apparatus in which they could operate. An important device for achieving order in decision making was the Cabinet meeting, which became a unique instrument under Eisenhower. As President-Elect he had been astounded to learn that the principal executives of government had, by tradition, gathered only sporadically and usually without any preconception of the business to be considered. To correct this anomaly, Eisenhower instituted regular weekly meetings, created the post of Cabinet Secretary, and arranged for an official agenda and discussion papers to be promulgated beforehand. In an effort to head off discrepancies between decisions and departmental performance, Eisenhower had his Cabinet Secretary meet with key assistant secretaries after Cabinet meetings to assign specific responsibilities for implementation. Every several months, a Cabinet meeting was slated as "Judgment Day"; there each Secretary revealed how much (or little) he had done.

An observer looking over the White House after Eisenhower's first year in office could not help but be impressed with its Spartan orderliness. In a real sense, the former General viewed his Cabinet members as theater commanders. He invested them, like field generals, with broad responsibilities and expected them to take the initiative. He let them choose their own assistants and he resisted party pressures to man the departmental posts on a patronage basis. He defended his department heads' latitude of conduct. When Attorney General Herbert Brownell leaked the appointment of Governor Earl Warren as Chief Justice to a few newspapers, he defended him against resentful papers not privy to the news. When Secretary of Labor James P. Mitchell endorsed a strong equal employment opportunity bill, Eisenhower stated that the Secretary was entitled to his views even though he himself felt otherwise.

Delegation of responsibility and the Presidentially enforced autonomy of Cabinet members undoubtedly spared Ike much of the heat of agency operations. Thus Cabinet members became the sole authorities in their respective domains. As we have seen in the Suez affair, this made it next to impossible for the President to prevail against their judgments. Secretary of Treasury Humphrey's power in the Administration came in no small measure from Eisenhower's early pronouncement that "George is synonymous with money! If it is a question of money, then you must clear the policy with George."[30] Accordingly, Humphrey's deep convictions about having a balanced budget determined many of the Administration's policies: Humphrey weighed in against the Aswan Dam for fiscal reasons, undercut proposals for foreign aid to developing nations, reduced by half the military research and development appropriations requests, and (as a result of these cutbacks) played a role second only to Dulles in trimming back the U.S. defense budget until the national posture was almost wholly reliant on massive retaliation. Perhaps the most striking example of Humphrey's influence occurred in 1957 when he attacked the President's budget "as having a lot of fat in it . . . and . . . requiring taxes . . . that would curl your hair."[31] These remarks were made on the very day the budget was submitted to Congress! Amazingly, Humphrey had cleared his statements beforehand. At that time, Eisenhower's Budget Director, Percival F. Brundage, cautioned Humphrey against allowing a wedge to be driven between the Secretary and his Chief. But Eisenhower demurred; others nodded their heads in agreement, and on that amicable note, Humphrey received endorsement for his divisive mission. The incident was to cause Eisenhower considerable grief. In characteristic fashion, he respected the positions of both sides and vacillated for several months in the embarrass-

ing chasm between his budget and the attacks of the economiz-
ers. The Democratic Congress watched with amusement and
asked at one point for the President's clarification on *which* of
the many proposals represented the Administration's request.[32]
Not until it appeared that the new fiscal year might begin with
no budget, did Eisenhower become desperate enough to clarify
the Administration's stance and prod Congress into action. The
incident was richly revealing of the man and his methods.

No discussion of Eisenhower's delegations to Cabinet members would be complete without mention of his Secretary of
Agriculture, Ezra Taft Benson. More than the rest, Benson did
not fit the "standardized" Administration mold. Moreover, as
is suggested by his long record of mishaps in office, the system
seemed to have had no effective way of dealing with him. Benson's abrupt downward adjustments in the farm subsidy program registered his rare and repeated gift for stirring up a
ruckus. Although many demanded his resignation, Eisenhower
would bravely endorse his actions.[33] Benson was also given to
introducing legislation to Congress without first getting White
House clearance. He persistently pursued his own course, ignoring Adams and the Administration's command structure. "When
I pointed this out to him," Adams commented, "Benson did not
seem to be greatly disturbed."[34]

We have thus far described an elaborate pyramid, manned
by individuals with wide discretionary powers. This autonomy,
as noted, contributed from time to time to Presidential head-
aches. Nonetheless, the overall impression is one of smooth—if
not distinguished—performance. Part of the reason the system
worked, as mentioned earlier, may have been because of the
remarkable homogeneity of the men who ran it. Also, Eisenhower called meetings to tie the system together, and these Cabinet meetings merit particular attention. Sherman Adams said:

Eisenhower never made a policy decision on an important domestic
issue until after his course of action had been talked over and sup-

ported in a Cabinet meeting. . . . The President encouraged . . .
opposition to his own views in Cabinet meetings.

"I have given way on a number of personal opinions to this gang,"
he good-naturedly remarked one day. [But] it was more or less understood that he preferred to have an objection . . . brought up
before the assembled Cabinet rather than in a private discussion
in his office. He took pains to see to it that such disagreements were
fully aired and ironed out.[35]

When Eisenhower felt secure in the position that he—or more
correctly, the Administration—would take, he would conclude
the discussion with something like "Well, I guess we'll all get
behind the thing unless I hear something to the contrary."[36]

A careful reading of Adams' portrayal of Cabinet meetings
reveals an important aspect of Eisenhower's approach. While
his Cabinet met and deliberated, one gets the impression that
it tended more to "join" in the consensus than actually create it.
The Cabinet was not truly a sharp instrument of decision. For
the most part, the courses of action presented there had been
staffed out long before. The meetings were frequently accompanied by formal presentations and illustrated with charts,
slides, and films. The Secretaries, perhaps taking a cue from the
President, generally went along. As a result, many observers
and some Cabinet members believed the meetings were a waste
of time and too prone toward generalization. Secretary of Labor
James P. Mitchell was frustrated by Eisenhower's requirement
that each Secretary brief the others at Cabinet meetings. "I
would get up there," Mitchell recalls, "and talk about what we
were doing over at Labor . . . and it was clear that people like
Dulles and Charlie Wilson could care less. But Ike insisted, like
a General calling all his field officers together to ensure a common goal."[37]

At these meetings Eisenhower would periodically expound
on such issues as the fundamental struggle between totalitarian-
ism and democracy or the burdens of military preparedness ver-

sus the domestic requirements of the state. Occasionally, he would look around the table and say, "If anyone has any ideas, for God's sake, don't hold them back."[38] Typically, no one had much to say.

As difficult as these discussions were—often as inconclusive as academic seminars—they played an important role in Eisenhower's scheme of governance. They fixed occasions for the exchange of ideas; they brought the Secretaries into contact with one another, and this, in itself, helped preserve the Administration's homogeneity of viewpoint. Eisenhower's philosophic digressions, often tangential to the matter being discussed, permitted, if nothing else, the periodic reinforcement of his values and his goals. While he did not try to manage his Cabinet members and their agencies, he appears to have tried to shape their attitudes and thus their choices, their horizons, and their pace. His methods call attention to the subtle nuances of management that more direct approaches often ignore.

One drawback, however, was that Eisenhower's fondness for the conference method of coming to a decision frequently led him to put a large number of issues, some of them close to burning hot, into the cool hands of the Cabinet. Their deliberations were invariably slow and often tainted with unreality. Insofar as the process worked, it entailed risks that were succinctly described by Henry A. Kissinger nearly a decade before he would join the White House staff himself:

The committee system not only has a tendency to ask the wrong questions, it also puts a premium on the wrong qualities. The committee process is geared to the pace of conversation. Even where the agenda is composed of memoranda, these are prepared primarily as a background for discussion, and they stand or fall on the skill with which they are presented. Hence, quickness of comprehension is more important than reflectiveness, fluency more useful than creativeness. The ideal "committee man" does not operate with ideas too far outside of what is generally accepted. Thus the thrust of committees is toward a standard of average performance. Since a complicated idea cannot be easily absorbed by ear—particularly when it is new—committees lean toward what fits in with the most familiar experience of the members. They therefore produce greater pressures in favor of the status quo. Committees are consumers and sometimes sterilizers of ideas, rarely creators of them.[39]

There were other problems too. Having granted his Secretaries broad authority, few could resist guarding their prerogatives against encroachments. Agriculture Secretary Benson's autobiography reveals the lengths to which Cabinet members went to win a point of particular importance to their departments—through behind-the-scenes negotiations or elaborate presentations designed to simply overpower the opposition.

Had the behind-the-scenes intrigue ended there, it probably would not have been too damaging to the President. More serious were major transgressions involving conflict of interest and scandal. Conflicts of interest tend to thrive under conditions where authority is delegated broadly. Both Truman and Eisenhower—and, as we shall later see, Nixon—delegated in this fashion and were plagued by problems when this power was abused. While the scandals of the Truman Administration were more numerous and more publicized than those of the Eisenhower Administration, there were nonetheless scandals enough to be embarrassing. Secretary of the Air Force Harold Talbott and several officials in the General Services Administration became deeply implicated in conflicts of interest. The Talbott case caused the President a good deal of personal discomfort. Although he and Talbott were not close friends, they had come to know each other well and had played bridge together in the White House. When Talbott came to Washington, he retained his partnership in his New York engineering firm. Within months, he began writing letters on Air Force stationery and making phone calls in the interest of getting business for his company. The ambitious Secretary was apparently successful in bringing a number of firms into line. During his first two years at the Pentagon, he received $132,032 in profits from his company.[40]

Another instance of wrongdoing involved Peter A. Strobel, Commissioner of Public Buildings for the General Services Administration, who retained his 90 percent ownership of his New York company. Strobel and his boss, the administrator of the General Services Administration, both resigned after having admitted that they allowed political favoritism to enter into the award of certain contracts.[41]

By far the Eisenhower Administration's most embarrassing conflict of interest case was the Dixon-Yates episode which involved the financing of a privately owned steam plant in the Tennessee Valley. Starring in a double role was Adolphe H. Wenzell, consultant to the Bureau of the Budget and, in private life, a vice president of the First Boston Corporation. The stakes were extraordinarily high—$107,250,000 was needed, to be supplied from private sources but insured by the government. Predictably, First Boston was selected to be the financial backer; later it was learned that Wenzell had been party to both the recommendation that the steam plant be built with private capital and to the arrangements for financing.[42]

Conflict of interest was only a part of the Dixon-Yates controversy. Politically, it was overshadowed by the resistance of the Democrats to the whole thrust of the Dixon-Yates legislation, which sought to dismantle the government-funded Tennessee Valley Authority, a major New Deal program, and restore the hydroelectric projects in the area to the domain of private capital. As Congressional interest rose, Eisenhower's administrative machinery left him helpless and exposed. He found himself making untenable statements. First he denied any wrongdoing whatever on Wenzell's part and charged the Democrats with malicious innuendo. The facts, he said, would be completely open to the public and he directed the Bureau of the Budget—the principal agency involved—to provide a complete record. "It is all yours," he told assembled reporters. But when the curious sought the "complete record," they were handed scraps and rebuffs from a defensive BOB. Once more, the President's help was sought. In a voice almost trembling with irritation, he said the press would be shown "every document which is pertinent to the thing." Speaking on his own authority, he assured reporters that Wenzell "was never called in or asked a single thing about the Dixon-Yates contract."[43] Later, when Wenzell's involvement was publicized, the President was deeply embarrassed. It reflected on the integrity of the Administration. But a year later when he was asked again about his promise for a complete record, he replied, "I don't intend to comment any more at all . . . I don't know such details as that."[44] Finally, on July 11, 1955, Eisenhower cancelled the Dixon-Yates contract.

What went wrong? If Dixon-Yates had been unique in the Eisenhower Administration, one might attribute it to poor communication and bad breaks. But followed by such incidents as the Suez crisis and contradictory pronouncements on the 1957 budget there were indications of more basic shortcomings. Fundamentally, Eisenhower's elaborate system functioned to perpetuate his unawareness. In no recent administration were so few decisions made by the President. The parceling out of tasks to departments and committees and task forces, the delegating of authority to advisers, the President's insistence upon unanimity before decisions reached him—all served to limit his role to veto and ratification, with ratification the rule. "Amid the mechanical apparatus," the London *Economist* observed in a study of Eisenhower's methods, "the presidency is insulated from the information and pressures which stimulate imagination, feed inspiration, foster insight and develop sensitivity."[45]

The most elaborate piece of Eisenhower's management machinery was the National Security Council. He relied heavily upon this body, was briefed daily by its Secretary, and met with the full Council at least twice a month. Perhaps more than any other body, the NSC felt the full impact of Eisenhower's reforms. First, he established the position of Special Assistant for National Security. Second, the NSC was formally given its own staff—called the Planning Board—to define policy issues to be placed before the Council. In theory, at least, the Council's meetings were designed to operate in a semijudicial manner: an agenda was presented and its highlights summarized by a member of the Planning Board. NSC members could then comment on the issues. At the conclusion of the process, Eisenhower, who usually remained silent during the discussion, would make his decision.

Inevitably, informal practices of the Council members and the NSC staff began to erode the theoretical ideal of how the NSC should operate. Council members would try to keep controversial items off the agenda by coming to agreement beforehand. Moreover, Eisenhower's high regard for the NSC made attendance at its meetings a status symbol. Attendance at meetings grew to fifty or sixty people, and these oversized sessions cut down on the free flow of discussion. Secretary of State Dulles, in particular, would refuse to talk openly if he felt too many outsiders were present.[46]

Beneath the surface of this formidable order was a curious irony. Eisenhower, who had run for President vowing to clean up Truman's "mess," had instituted a system embarrassingly similar to (and more elaborate than) the one he was committed to eradicate. While he had campaigned against Truman's "ends," he was largely unaware of Truman's "means." He was preoccupied, at the time, with what seemed to be the endless blunders and embarrassments of the Truman Administration. The flaw in Eisenhower's thinking was in not recognizing that means frequently shape ends; that even the Supreme Commander of the largest and most complex military operation in history could not entirely surmount the hazards of the managerial system he would create. Ironically, and with considerable pride, Eisenhower installed his formalistic system of management. It resembled Truman's in form, but went considerably beyond it in refinement.

The relationship between a President and his closest advisers is a window to understanding his personal needs. If FDR used Harry Hopkins as an operative and an informant, and periodically as a vent for Presidential frustration, Eisenhower used Sherman Adams as a protector and a shield. He placed Adams at the apex of his system and designated him "Assistant to the President." Adams has written of his formal role, "Eisenhower simply expected me to manage a staff that would boil down, simplify, and expedite the urgent business . . . and keep as much work of secondary importance off his desk as possible."[47] Eisenhower believed that any issue, no matter how complex, could be reduced to its bare essence. He insisted that his aides distill involved documents and complex issues into one-page summaries. "If a proposition can't be stated in one page," he declared, "it isn't worth saying."[48]

Throughout his professional life, Eisenhower made it a matter of principle to keep his desk clear. Suddenly as President, he was engulfed by a Niagara of paper and urgent requests. He turned to Adams to stem the flood. When a visitor or official sprang a new proposal on Eisenhower, he was prone to say, "Take it up with Sherman." If a paper came to him, he would look first for the approving sign of, "O.K., S.A."[49] If it was missing, he was sure to ask, "Has Governor Adams approved this?" Thus, Adams became the linchpin in Eisenhower's interlocking system and his power was vast. His scope of authority was remarkable—all White House staff specialists dealt through him on an informal basis, and so did the Cabinet, Congressmen, governors, and others outside the Executive branch.

Adams provided an interesting contrast to his boss. As Supreme Commander, Eisenhower had learned that he needed a tough, hard-nosed chief of staff to provide a cutting edge to his own more easygoing manner. As President, he sought a similar arrangement. Eisenhower chose Adams as a sort of one-man peace-keeping constabulary who would keep the noise level down and resolve conflicts with rugged firmness. Adams found this role a comfortable one, although it occasionally brought him into the crossfire of Cabinet members. One day when arguing a point, a Secretary snapped, "Are you telling me I cannot see the President?" "No sir," replied Adams, "but if I had a matter of this kind to settle I'd do it myself without involving the President."[50] The Secretary settled it himself. It took a while for Cabinet members to accept Adams as the spokesman of the President's position. "But," in Adams' words, "after I had served a year as his assistant, the President himself, at least, felt that I had reached that position."[51] Near the end of his tenure, when two Cabinet members couldn't come to terms, Adams told them bluntly, "Either make up your minds or tell me and I will do it."[52]

Eisenhower's positioning of Adams made him a ubiquitous and controversial influence. At fifty-four, Adams was sinewy and quick. He took a sixteen-hour day at the White House in stride, saw scores of visitors, and made as many as 250 phone calls in the course of a day's work. Calling in a petitioning official, he would say abruptly, "State your business."[53] He was notorious for his monosyllabic responses. "No," he would tell a caller bluntly and hang up the phone. His curtness carried a price tag that could be registered in his accumulation of enemies over the years. His downfall in 1958, resulting from having received gifts from his old friend Bernard Goldfine in exchange for favors at the Securities and Exchange Commission, revealed the number and passions of his antagonists.[54] In contrast to the carryings-on of some of Truman's aides, Adams' indiscretions seemed slight. But more significant than the offense was the attack on Adams' role of substituting for the person of the President. Adams was hounded out of office as much for this reason as for the specific sin of aiding Goldfine. His downfall provides a grim case study for those who might aspire to become a President's alter ego. It is worth noting that Eisenhower's Vice President evidently did not draw these same conclusions. Richard Nixon, having observed the Eisenhower process, installed an identical arrangement a decade later and, as if guided by the same relentless plot, witnessed his chief of staff, H. R. Haldeman, fall victim to the same trap. This time, however, the transgressions were of Constitutional proportions.

Adams' role provides considerable insight into the personal needs of his boss. Since Eisenhower disliked reading, Adams saw to it that long documents were summarized in one-page reports. The President complained in his memoirs that he received from Dulles alone in the six years prior to the Secretary's death, "a stack of cables and memoranda more than four feet high."[55] Using a little arithmetic, this comes down to reading a stack eight inches high a year, or well under an inch a month—hardly overwhelming! Eisenhower's dislikes did not end there. According to Adams, he had a similar aversion toward writing, and seldom exchanged written memos with either Cabinet members or his staff. He preferred to get his information from talking to people directly. He disliked the telephone, and the only person who got away with using it frequently was Dulles.

The way Eisenhower chose to have information given him restricted considerably the amount of intelligence he actually received. And while Adams assures us that the President "liked to hear things in person," it was Adams' practice, each day, to review the long list of those wishing to see the President and "boil it down to a handful of eligibles."[56] "[On these]," says Adams, "I sought the President's preferences."[57] Eisenhower's opportunities to "hear things in person" were thus rather sharply limited.

For Adams, at least, accessibility was not a great problem. He recounts:

I never had the slightest hesitation in interrupting Eisenhower at his desk, or after work, for a decision that took only a brief "Yes" or "No." Whether he was at his desk or taking a swim in the White House pool or even, on occasion, in his bedroom, I was expected to come in when and if I decided it was necessary. Needless to say, the reasons for disturbing him in his private residence had to be urgent indeed. I remember that once when I needed a decision on an appointment I went out on the back lawn, where Eisenhower was practicing golf shots. Dulles was already there ahead of me on a related errand. The President saw me coming and with a simulated sigh said, "Look, Foster, here comes my conscience!"[58]

Eisenhower asked Adams to attend all important meetings, and this in Adams' view "was next to impossible [given that] I had too many telephone calls, too much paper work, and too many appointments [of] my own, as well as a White House staff to supervise."[59] Nonetheless, Adams apparently performed all his functions to Eisenhower's satisfaction—including sitting in on his share of meetings each week. There, too, Adams' influence was pervasive. On many occasions, Adams recalls, "I listened until I thought the meeting had outlived its usefulness, and then I arose as a broad hint that the participants do likewise. Invariably they did."[60]

Assembling these reports, a picture begins to emerge of a curiously passive President. Herein lay the greatest difference between Eisenhower and his predecessor. While both Truman and Eisenhower respected staff machinery and utilized what we have called the formalistic approach, Truman's machinery was geared as an aggressive apparatus for acquiring and conveying information to the top: in contrast, Eisenhower arrayed his staff machinery like a shield. Truman wanted alternatives to choose from; Eisenhower wanted a recommendation to ratify. When Ike could not work through his set procedures, or when the shield failed him, or when his associates quarreled or confronted him with a difficult choice, he grew disheartened and angry.[61] Members of his staff learned to cater to his moods. When the President was perceived to be "unhappy," his schedule was rearranged and lightened.

Dwight David Eisenhower's strongest stands were frequently *against* taking a stand. This posture had its roots deep in his past. Eisenhower, like Truman, was the product of a lower middle class family that lived in near poverty. Both men, in fact, lived close to one another—Independence (Missouri) and Abilene (Kansas) are no more than 150 miles apart. Both were brought up in a stern semi-Fundamentalist Protestant tradition. From this background emerged men of straightforward integrity and personal honor. Both were essentially nonideological and nonintellectual; both were instinctive pragmatists. But there the similarities end. Truman was schooled in hard knocks and haberdashery. Eisenhower's learning came from "making do"—first in the structure of his large family and later in the programed existence of the army.

Young Ike was the third of seven boys in the family and consequently took a lot of abuse from his older brothers. His mother permitted it, feeling that young boys needed to get anger out of their system. His father was not a strong figure and was away working much of the time.

Once, when told he could not join his brothers trick-or-treating on Halloween, Ike pounded his fists bloody on a tree trunk. The incident, he recalled later, taught him that "I had expressed resentment, and only damaged myself."[62] Here is perhaps our first glimpse of Eisenhower's capacity for self-denial, a trait that would have an important effect on his professional life.

Dwight Eisenhower learned early that getting along meant going along. He followed his older brothers through high school; they were the initiators and he was a member of their team. Two interesting events in his boyhood foreshadow his behavior in later life. The first took place while he was in elementary school. A fistfight was instigated by a stronger opponent. The two lads slugged it out for two hours, and although Ike was getting the worse of it (his face was swollen beyond recognition), he hung on until his opponent lost interest from sheer exhaustion. The second event, a fight of grimmer sort, took place while he was in his teens. A leg infection developed into blood poisoning. Day by day as it worsened, Ike's fever rose and the pain grew unbearable. Finally the doctor announced he must amputate the leg. Young Ike insisted on fighting it out without the operation. Miraculously, even though the infection had spread to his thigh, it suddenly receded. Throughout life, Ike's form of fighting was, in a sense, passive. When challenges confronted him, he took them on and surmounted them, but he was rarely the aggressor.

Eisenhower was an average student in school. His mind, like his father's, was orderly and logical. He had a passion for facts and was frustrated by subjects which he perceived as ambiguous and ill-defined. Ike's most outstanding characteristic, most observers seem to agree, was his friendliness. Everyone liked Ike because Ike liked everyone. He radiated sunniness and optimism.

Throughout Eisenhower's life, events had a way of coming to him. Unlike his brothers, Ike had no idea of what he wanted to do after high school. He went to work and helped support his older brothers who were in college. One day, Ike, who was good at math, was asked by a friend to help him prepare for the West Point entrance exam. Ike agreed. In the process, he learned a lot about the Academy; his friend, catching Ike's kindling interest, persuaded him to give the exam a try. Although he had never considered the army as a career, it offered, at that moment, a concrete option among ambiguous alternatives. He took the test and passed it. On June 1, 1911, he entered West Point as a cadet.

Eisenhower was a middling performer at West Point. As before, his greatest strength was in getting along. Because he had worked for two years after high school, he was older and more mature than most of his peers and he adapted easily to a routine that was grueling for many. His strongest performances were on the football field. There Eisenhower was his most assertive self and he excelled until permanently benched by a knee injury. But above all, he was a popular, regular guy, fun to be around and not in the least conceited.

After West Point, Eisenhower moved through a sequence of

staff jobs. It is difficult to interpret what occurred in the twenty-nine years that lay between his graduation from West Point in 1915 and the massive job he undertook as Supreme Commander in Europe in 1944. His biographers describe these years as ones of steady ripening, years filled with accomplishments each more stunning than the last. It is possible that all of this is true. But a close look at the record reveals the period as a relatively undistinguished one. Eisenhower was moving from one routine assignment to the next—now to a small command, next to coach football, then to teach for a few years, and so forth. In each post he settled into his comfortable role as "the-guy-who-could-get-along-with-people." While former classmates Omar N. Bradley and George S. Patton, Jr. were learning about battle from firsthand experience in World War I, Eisenhower was running a tank training camp. He attended to the details, the tanks kept running, and the men liked him. But as would occur repeatedly throughout his life, events came to call—this time in the person of General Fox Connor who took a liking to the good-natured junior officer.

In 1922 the General arranged for Eisenhower to accompany him to Panama and serve as his Executive Officer at Gaillard, a jungle post on the Canal. There he assumed responsibility for the Twentieth Brigade—a ragtag outfit with lax standards of conduct and poorly maintained facilities. Eisenhower discovered his new boss to be a tough taskmaster and a hard driver. Inevitably, as second in command and as executor of the General's wishes, Ike soon came to be viewed in much the same light as his boss. As Executive Officer, Eisenhower supervised all administration and training. The General explained in detail just what kind of outfit he wanted and then sat back with a critical eye to see if Ike could carry it out. It was something to watch. Making few allowances for the torpid climate, Ike saw to it that the camp grounds were restored, the lawns trimmed, regulations obeyed, and that all of the General's directives were complied with immediately and completely.[63]

Gaillard was one of the few times in Ike's life when doing his job meant being unpopular. But his great gift—then, before, and later—would be working effectively on a team, following the lead of others, and carrying his share of the load. In the years between wars, Eisenhower moved through a progression of assignments, attending the war college and serving for a time as an aide to General Douglas MacArthur. As World War II began, Eisenhower moved into planning assignments. The time was propitious for his talents.

For the American military, the name of the game throughout World War II was welding the Allied fighting forces into a cohesive unit. In General Marshall's view, Eisenhower had the attributes that were needed. Immediately after Pearl Harbor, Marshall, as Chief of Staff and architect of U.S. military strategy, transferred Eisenhower to the War Plans Division in the Office of Chief of Staff and set him to work out a plan for a cross-channel invasion.

Then came the test. In 1942 Eisenhower commanded the Allied forces in "Operation Torch," the North African campaign. Until that time, he had spent only nine months in a command appointment in his twenty-seven years in the army. Nevertheless, Eisenhower distinguished himself in the new job. He found that his team skills were more important than the professional abilities of the soldier. Others could—and did—provide expert and experienced leadership on the battlefield.

Soon events catapulted Eisenhower into an even larger role—as Supreme Commander of the Normandy invasion. Chester Wilmot in *The Struggle for Europe* writes:

In the role of Supreme Commander [Eisenhower showed] himself to be the military statesman rather than the generalissimo. . . .

Eisenhower was conscious of his lack of experience in the tactical handling of armies, and this gave him a sense of professional inferiority in dealing with men like Montgomery and Patton who had been through the mill of command at every level. As a general rule, he tended to seek the opinions of all concerned and to work out the best compromise. When he could gather his commanders and advisers around the conference table, he had a remarkable capacity for distilling the counsel of many minds into a single solution, but, when his commanders were scattered over France, he was open to persuasion by the last strong man to whom he talked.[64]

It seems fair to say that the very qualities that made Eisenhower a successful Supreme Commander prevented him from becoming a great battlefield general. His great talent lay in holding the Allied team together, and in reconciling the interests of different nations and services. This was a particular asset in planning the Normandy invasion. But once the troops hit the beach, Eisenhower's conscientious tolerance and inclination to compromise became liabilities. The occasion called for a decisive man—even at the price of occasional rigidity. What was needed was a general with a bold plan, who knew what was essential and who had the will to impose his ideas without regard for personalities or public opinion. But Eisenhower's drive was toward cooperation. In war, and later in peace, he sought to integrate divided positions; sometimes he fell between the stools.

Despite shortcomings, Eisenhower performed admirably in Europe. He had all the attributes of a champion—modesty, a commanding presence, and the title of Supreme Commander. The American press made him a folk hero during the war; he enjoyed friendly relations with reporters and was able to take them into his confidence. How different it would be in the Presidency. He was heard to complain once, "Some of these guys aren't reporters at all—they sound more like district attorneys."[65]

Ike was weak in fluid situations. His career had been built upon a philosophy of "getting along"; his logical mind was not quick to react to fast-moving, unstructured problems. As we have seen, Eisenhower hated to make enemies and in an effort to avoid doing so, tended to insulate himself from conflict. Unfortunately, the Presidency is a focal point of divergent interests and conflicting priorities. Yet even in that office, the avoidance of conflict appears to have been one of the most central of Eisenhower's personal requirements. He hated confrontations and there is virtually no record of his having a sharp clash with anyone during his eight years in the White House. When Secretary of Labor Mitchell became engaged in a public dispute with Secretary of Agriculture Benson over migratory farm labor policy, Eisenhower never stepped in. Benson enlisted the growers to publicly support his position; Mitchell appealed to organized labor. "But Eisenhower," according to one official involved, "acted like he was never aware. He didn't call in the warring principals, he simply avoided the whole unpleasantness."[66]

Eisenhower was equally diffident when conflict was aimed directly at him. Sherman Adams tells of the time when Senator Taft exploded in anger at the President in full view of his assembled Cabinet. The scene was in the Cabinet room several months after his first Inauguration. Eisenhower had just broken the bad news to Taft that the Administration would not be able to balance its first budget. According to Adams:

Taft heard the President out in grim silence and listened impatiently to further explanations from [Budget Director] Dodge. . . . Then Taft exploded . . . [in the worst] emotional outburst against the President that I saw in all my six years in the White House. . . . Taft [lost] control of himself, pound[ed] his fist on the Cabinet table and shout[ed] at the stunned President, who was sitting opposite him.[67]

Senator Taft told Eisenhower with great heat that all he had done was to perpetuate deficit spending on the same scale as the Democrats. Silence filled the room. Eisenhower bent forward and was visibly upset. Some intervening small talk on the part of his aides helped to ease the situation. Lamely, the President explained that the budget was necessary because of increasing Cold War tensions.

Why had Eisenhower stoically endured Taft's affront? He told Adams later that he had held back his anger because one should "never lose [his] temper except intentionally."[68] Whatever his rationale, such denial was present throughout his eight years in office. When Joseph McCarthy abused him, he turned the other cheek: "I will not get into the gutter with that guy." Ducking the politically crucial decision of who should replace Robert Taft as Majority Leader of the Senate, he said, "I want to say with all the emphasis at my command that this Administration has absolutely *no* personal choice for a new Majority Leader. We are not going to get into *their* business." When Congress defeated his programs, he dismissed the matter as the fault of "those damn monkeys on the Hill." He would stay out of it. When asked if he felt attacked by the press, he replied, "Listen! Anyone who has time to listen to commentators or read columnists obviously doesn't have enough work to do."[69] When someone irked him, his practice, he said once, was to "write his name on a piece of paper, put it in my lower desk drawer and shut the drawer."[70]

When Senator John Bricker proposed the "Bricker Amendment" to limit the President's treaty-making powers, Eisenhower responded with patience and persuasion, and continued to consult with the proponents of the amendment. "It is not possible to attack Congress and conciliate at the same time," he said. He continued to seek a compromise. "I don't know any other way to lead," he confessed to one aide.[71] But his conciliatory posture gave the appearance of irresolution and beset his efforts to find a middle ground. He told his Cabinet that he wanted to simultaneously protect the President's prerogatives but also to relieve the legitimate fears of those supporting the amendment. One White House aide recalls:

The President spent pained months—and the Cabinet hours beyond number—trying to avoid what Eisenhower glumly called "a head-on collision over this darn thing." One week, the Cabinet merely groaned at the dilemma; another they [enlisted Secretary of Treasury Humphrey to try and] deter his friend Bricker from his cause; yet another week, they . . . set up . . . the "Bricker Commission"— in the hope that all Bricker wanted was something big in public with his name on it.[72]

In his efforts to conciliate, the President invited Bricker over for a friendly chat. Sherman Adams recounts that Eisenhower "felt that the differences between himself and Bricker . . . were largely in the wording of the resolution. Always ready to mollify a dissenter, the President gave Bricker a friendly hearing. The warm and sympathetic tone of the talks gave Bricker the impression of more willingness to compromise than Eisenhower intended."[73] Subsequently Eisenhower found himself in the predicament of having agreed to more than Dulles was willing to permit. At a Cabinet meeting soon thereafter, Dulles stated bluntly that the Administration's policy was fuzzy. The President defended himself, saying that he had told Bricker he would go so far and no further. Dulles retorted, "I know, sir, but you haven't told anyone else."[74] In the final days of debate, the President sent the Republican leadership a letter opposing the amendment. His intervention was perilously late; the amendment was defeated by only a very small margin. Eisenhower considered Congress "politics," and for that matter, the entire process of orchestrating influence (which is what politics is all about) as something beyond his ken.

Eisenhower's discomfort with conflict, his dislike of "politics" came inevitably to be reflected in the machinery he managed. His formalistic system of management, intrinsically prone to isolate the decision maker, was in a sense refined to make that isolation more complete.

Power is not fixed in the Presidency: boldness and clarity of purpose are the currency of strength; willingness to compromise a sign of weakness. Eisenhower with his immense popularity could easily have gone to the people about the Bricker affair; in 1952 he had carried thirty-nine out of forty-eight states. But Eisenhower did not see the people as an instrument of Presidential power. He didn't particularly *care* about power— he wasn't just bipartisan, he was apolitical. He strove for a national consensus, not for a realignment of the Republican party. His harvest of popularity was great—in a love affair with the American public that persisted to the end. But as for consensus, measured in the tallies of Congress, he got little. Ironically, he stumbled on the same situation that beset Roosevelt in his second term. Like Roosevelt, Ike weakened his party by virtue of having bipartisan support. His problems were compounded because he showed no interest in power and made no attempts to wield it, which was not the case with FDR. Eisenhower was unwilling to exploit the media to mobilize public support for his priorities; nor did he strive to exploit his popularity to influence Congress.

Eisenhower's handling of the Bricker Amendment would be repeated in a rather lengthy list of other muddled incidents. Early in his first term, a proposal for cooperative U.S.-Canadian action on the St. Lawrence Seaway was advanced. The matter was discussed at a Cabinet meeting and Secretary of the Treasury Humphrey opposed outright Federal funding of the project on the basis of the cost. Eisenhower agreed. Later, Humphrey and Attorney General Brownell urged the President to take a strong position in favor of funding the project with private capital. Ike equivocated. As time wore on the Canadian government threatened to build the seaway by itself. Congress was now prodded into action and a bill committing U.S. financing was introduced. Still, Eisenhower remained "troubled" by the project.[75] As the bill gathered momentum in Congress, the Administration decided to take a stand against it. Then, a month later, the President reversed his position, stating that the Administration would support the bill because the seaway was advantageous to national security. His announcement was nearly an afterthought as the bill passed Congress virtually without opposition. Ironically, the President took considerable pride in the project and adopted it as a landmark of his Administration.

On a host of other fronts, Eisenhower's performance was marred by equivocation and misunderstanding. The events leading up to his sending Federal troops to Little Rock is a case in point. Eisenhower had taken a far from clear position on civil rights prior to the Little Rock incident. A year earlier, the Administration had submitted its civil rights bill to Congress, but subsequently the President told the press that he did not agree with all aspects of it.[76] At a press conference in July 1957, Eisenhower said, "I was reading part of that bill this morning, and I—there were certain phrases I didn't completely understand. . . . I would want to talk to the Attorney General. . . . Naturally, I am not a lawyer."[77] Later in July, almost as if to invite the worst, he told reporters, "I can't imagine any set of circumstances that would ever induce me to send federal troops . . . into any area to enforce the orders of a federal court because I believe that the common sense of America will never require it."[78] In August, it appeared as though the President's civil rights bill was going to go down the Congressional drain. The Administration's slowness to rescue it enlarged the impression that it had only lukewarm support. The stage was set for Little Rock.

On the week following Labor Day in 1957, the President and Mrs. Eisenhower left Washington for the naval base at Newport, Rhode Island, for a few weeks of rest. The President liked the golf course there, and the cool weather and the unhurried atmosphere of the commandant's residence. On the same day that Eisenhower flew north, Governor Orval Faubus of Arkansas took an important action in his state: he called out the National Guard, ostensibly "to prevent racial violence." In a *de facto* sense, his action halted the planned integration of Little Rock's schools.

Attorney General Brownell immediately dispatched a Federal investigating team. Faubus responded with a telegram to

Eisenhower; he complained about the intrusion and requested a personal conference with the President. After conferring with Brownell, Eisenhower agreed to meet with Faubus on the understanding that Faubus would commit himself in advance to observing the law. Faubus' reply arrived at Newport the afternoon of September 12. The President was just starting a round of golf, and according to Sherman Adams, "Hagerty brought the wire to him as he was holing out on the first green. They sat down together . . . and drafted a reply."[79]

As arranged, Faubus arrived at Newport on Saturday, September 14. It is not known what transpired between the President and the Governor since they met privately for the first twenty minutes. Eisenhower apparently sympathized with Faubus' dilemma, being torn as he was between the Federal law and the political imperatives of a Southern state. Attorney General Brownell also spoke with the Governor at Newport and stressed the necessity of upholding Federal law. Faubus remained silent. But on returning to Arkansas, he proceeded to bar desegregation and based his actions on his impression that Eisenhower was favorably disposed toward giving Little Rock "a one year cooling-off period."[80] The President, still in Newport, learned of this on September 16. On that same day, as Negroes attempted to enter Little Rock High School, a riot began in which a number of blacks and whites were injured. Chagrined, Eisenhower asked Brownell what could be done by the Federal Government to cool off the crisis. Brownell answered, "Nothing."[81] Two days later, still in Newport, the President signed an Executive Order authorizing the "use of U.S. armed forces to remove obstructions" in the riot-torn city. Then he flew to Washington to address the nation from the White House, "partly," according to Sherman Adams, "because of the broadcasting facilities there and partly because he felt it inappropriate to deliver such a serious and important message from vacation headquarters."[82]

So it was that Federal troops came to preside over the integration of Little Rock High School. Faubus was stunned; the nation was surprised. Some wondered if the incident might have been avoided if the Administration had conveyed its commitment to the court order from the start.

There was a similar cast to the Administration's conduct on the foreign policy front—fuzzy positions, vacillation, and the impression that important decisions were being made in a seat-of-the-pants fashion. In this respect, Eisenhower's brand of formalism fell below the norm. Ordinarily, the formalistic approach with its elaborated staff system enhances the thoroughness of policy analysis. But Eisenhower's detachment and his uncritical acceptance of practically anything his top advisers proposed, weakened his machinery by virtue of the laxity of his standards.

Illustrative of his system's potential—and its ultimate shortcomings—was the Administration's handling of its national defense strategy. Eisenhower, following Dulles' lead, had deeply committed the nation to a deterrence strategy of massive retaliation. However, in 1955, the President commissioned the Gaither Committee which submitted a secret report on national security and confronted the Administration with a serious challenge to its previously held assumptions about defense. In a carefully reasoned analysis, the report questioned the survivability of the Strategic Air Command (SAC) and argued persuasively that America's second strike force could not survive a nuclear attack: it called for an acceleration of the intermediate range missile program, favored dispersed missiles in underground sites that could survive attack, stressed the need for a U.S. capacity to fight limited wars, and concluded that Administration proposals to spend $40 billion on Civil Defense blast shelters should be relegated to the lowest priority. Here were policy recommendations of the highest importance, which were certainly topics that could be understood by a President with Eisenhower's vast military experience. Yet when Dulles voiced his opposition to the report, Eisenhower seemed hesitant to act on it. Paradoxically, Eisenhower, the military man, was unable to seize the initiative; his successor, John Kennedy, would. The Gaither Report became, in fact, the forebear of U.S. defense policy under Kennedy. For the Eisenhower Administration, it was another example of promise unmet and potential unrealized.

There was more to come. When the Soviet Union launched *Sputnik* in 1957, Eisenhower tried to comport himself as a busy man reluctantly looking up from his evening newspaper and shrugging his shoulders. His Defense Secretary called it a "nice technical trick."[83] Adams disparaged the achievement as "an outer-space basketball game."[84] Only gradually would the full impact of this accomplishment sink in upon the nation. More serious for its immediate consequences was the U-2 incident in 1960. Only fourteen days before a long-planned summit conference of the Big Four in Paris, a CIA reconnaissance plane was shot down over Russia. The Administration's response followed the murky pattern of earlier crises; bad judgment and incoherent action converted misfortune to disaster. First, the Administration asserted that the plane must have been on a weather flight and the State Department solemnly avowed that no American plane had ever been deliberately dispatched across Soviet borders. Two days later, confronted with Soviet proof of the American lie (in the form of the pilot, Francis Gary Powers, who had apparently been telling them all he knew), the Administration acknowledged the incontrovertible. But again, the State Department explained that no such flights were "authorized" by anyone in Washington. Then the White House, fearing charges by the Democrats of outrageous negligence for allowing "unauthorized" flights over Russia, decided to head off such criticism. Eisenhower assumed full responsibility for the flights and termed them "a distasteful but vital necessity to penetrate Soviet military secrecy."[85] Across the globe, Khrushchev, who had been for months walking a tightrope with his Politburo for responding to American peace overtures, was now embarrassed. He vindicated himself at the Paris Summit Conference by berating the President. The U.S. suffered a loss of face. The Summit Conference was in a shambles—and with it, one of the few original initiatives of the Eisenhower Administration.

Not all of Eisenhower's efforts turned out badly and the exceptions merit close attention. In 1953 Eisenhower gave a speech entitled "The Chances for Peace." It was notable for two reasons: first of all, because of its statesmanship during a particularly frosty period of the Cold War, and secondly, because Eisenhower had contributed the principal ideas of the speech himself. Ordinarily his speeches were not reflections of his own thinking. When the time was viewed as opportune for a speech, Adams solicited ideas and drafts were prepared. Eisenhower was not involved until a final copy was ready and a tentative date for delivery was worked into his calendar. However, following Stalin's death in 1953, Eisenhower seemed genuinely moved to action. Calling in his speech writer Emmet Hughes, he said, "Here is what I would like to say. The jet plane that roars over your head costs three-quarters of a million dollars. That is more money than a man . . . is going to earn in his lifetime. What world can afford this sort of thing? We are in an armaments race. Where will it lead us? . . . Couldn't . . . we offer . . . another road?"[86]

From this conversation, the idea for a speech advocating a "peace offensive" was born. The President seemed unusually committed to it. Hughes, hoping to keep it alive, arranged a meeting the next day with the President, Secretary Dulles, CIA's Allen Dulles, and C. D. Jackson, his Cold War adviser. Secretary Dulles, says Hughes, contributed a "dry and dubious acquiescence."[87]

With Eisenhower's support, Hughes pushed ahead, determined to guard his project from "the ambushes of policy debate and bureaucratic scrutiny."[88] Working closely with Eisenhower, he hammered out a speech. When it was circulated, the State

Department announced that it doubted the need for any speech. Others treaded water. Ordinarily the idea would have died there because Eisenhower usually acquiesced in the face of opposing counsel. But on this occasion, the idea survived—largely by dint of Eisenhower's own commitment to it. The speech was delivered on April 16, 1953, and received national and international attention. It emphasized U.S. interest in peace and asked for a similar statement of Soviet intentions. Thereafter, "keeping peace alive" became a major priority for Eisenhower. This interest led to the Open Skies proposal, which was made at the Geneva Conference in 1955, Khrushchev's visit to the United States, Vice President Nixon's visit to Russia, the Atoms for Peace plan, and the ill-fated Summit Conference in Paris following the U-2 incident. Regrettably, Eisenhower's labors toward peace fell with the same crashing finality as the U-2.

There are two interesting afternotes to Eisenhower's "The Chances for Peace" speech. Sherman Adams tells us, "It was the most difficult speech that Eisenhower ever delivered."[89] The President interrupted a golfing vacation in Augusta to work on the address, and up to the last moment was not sure whether he should go through with it. He suffered a stomach upset the day of the speech, and told Adams later, "[I] had no recollection of what [I] was saying toward the end of the speech."[90] "Nonetheless," Adams adds, "a few days after he returned to Augusta, he was out on the golf course with Senator Taft in the best of health."[91] The second afternote comes from Emmet Hughes, who recounts the White House staff's reaction to the speech. No credit was given. Their comments focused entirely on the public relations benefits. One aide said, "I think it's pretty obvious what we need. One speech isn't enough. We've got to follow up. We need *another* speech. Only this one has to do for us in *domestic* affairs what we've just done in *foreign* affairs. If we could just get the same sex appeal into this other speech as there was in yesterday's . . ."[92]

The peace episode provides a glimpse of what the Administration might have been. It also contains a dramatic message for those who aspire to command. Presidential leadership is more, far more, than acting out a titular role as head of government. It requires personal involvement and exacts personal costs. For a number of reasons discussed in this chapter, Eisenhower sought to defray those costs by shifting the burden to his system. Perhaps for him, the personal costs were too high. His evident nervousness and upset before delivering "The Chances for Peace" speech may have simply been more than he was willing to endure. Insofar as he wished to take subsequent initiatives, the same system that he had created to carry him tended, in subtle ways, to resist him. His reward system, for example, clearly worked against change. Emmet Hughes' rewards for his efforts on "The Chances for Peace" speech were meager: his access to the President did not change, Eisenhower did not bestow on him special thanks or prominence, and other members of the White House staff viewed the speech as a routine event. These nonrewards had the effect of reinforcing the status quo. Former *Life* publisher C. D. Jackson encountered a fate similar to Hughes'. Jackson found himself struggling up a mountain of resistance in getting his bold foreign aid programs past Humphrey and Dulles. Jackson left after a year; Hughes followed him. But Eisenhower fought few battles. Perhaps he did not need scrappy lieutenants.

Eisenhower's second peace initiative was the Open Skies proposal, and it gives us another perspective on the ways in which his system resisted change. Sometime in 1954, after his "The Chances for Peace" speech, there are indications that Eisenhower began to resist his singular dependence on Dulles in the foreign policy area. Perhaps hoping to make further peace initiatives, and knowing Dulles would not be sympathetic, he elevated Nelson Rockefeller, previously his adviser on Latin American affairs, to a new post as Special Assistant for Russian-American relations. With Presidential blessing, Rockefeller organized a large staff and moved them into seclusion at the

Marine base at Quantico, Virginia, away from Dulles and the State Department. Sherman Adams recounts that "the air of secrecy around the Rockefeller operation . . . made Dulles apprehensive. 'He seems to be building up a big staff,' Dulles said to [Adams] one day. 'He's got them down at Quantico and nobody knows what they're doing.' "[93]

Here we catch a glimpse of a very different Eisenhower, acting, it would seem, in the manner of FDR. He wanted a kind of advice that he could not get from Dulles and therefore set up a separate and competing advisory unit to get it. For a time, it worked. The Rockefeller panel, after studying recent breakthroughs in aerial reconnaissance photography, concluded that these techniques would permit the U.S. to obtain adequate intelligence of Russian military movements from the air. They proposed, as a result of the findings, that the major powers open their skies to aerial photo reconnaissance to assure each other and the world that they were not preparing for a surprise attack. Now Eisenhower was confronted with a dilemma: on one hand was Rockefeller with his bold Open Skies proposal, on the other was Dulles with his skepticism. Should he stick with "the system" or go with the plan?

Eisenhower liked the idea but he did not make a quick decision on whether or not he would offer it to the Russians. He went over the pros and cons . . . with the military leaders and with Dulles, who was skeptical of its chances of acceptance by the Soviets. When the Geneva meeting opened, the President still had not made up his mind about when, how or if he would make the proposal.[94]

Differences between the formalistic and competitive approaches involve much more than the way in which people are organized. There are enormous differences in the demands upon the time and attention of the President. As we shall soon see, Eisenhower underestimated what it would require of him personally to keep the Rockefeller plan alive. For two long days, the President muddled through the Geneva Summit with no clear statement of the U.S. position. At the end of the second day, he called a private meeting of his advisers and decided to go ahead with the plan. When he unveiled it publicly the following day, the Russians were taken by surprise, and some say, suspected that it was a propaganda stunt. Nonetheless, the Open Skies initiative was a major triumph for the United States and the "spirit of Geneva" was acclaimed around the world. Regrettably, the promise of Geneva dissolved in subsequent meetings between Dulles and the Russians later that year.

Ostensibly the demise of the "spirit of Geneva" resulted from negative Russian response. But in terms of this inquiry, it is profitable to examine the Administration's failure as well. Owing to Eisenhower's indecisiveness about whether to introduce the plan, there was little opportunity for the U.S. to lay the necessary diplomatic groundwork with the Soviets. Surprising them with the plan may have caused them to react defensively. Tracing the matter back farther, Eisenhower's indecisiveness resulted from the lack of unanimity among his advisers. Dulles, in particular, was unhappy with the arrangement, and according to Sherman Adams, equally unhappy with Rockefeller's growing influence.

Rockefeller's influence with the government depended on a close relationship with the President. After the heart attack, which struck just two months after Geneva, access to the bedridden President was sharply restricted. Secretary of State Dulles could see the President, Rockefeller could not, and the latter's influence fell accordingly.[95] With Rockefeller in mind, Dulles said to Adams shortly after the President was hospitalized, "There might be certain people outside the government who would try to set themselves up as authoritative spokesmen for the President on various public issues." The best way to prevent this, Dulles went on, was to reinforce Adams' position "as the sole official channel . . . between Eisenhower and the world outside."[96] "In insisting upon having me with Eisenhower," Adams adds, "Dulles was once again vigilantly protecting his own position as the maker of foreign policy."[97]

Eisenhower had created his system to carry the load and it worked best when he let it. Once ill, his will to make peace was no match for the machinery he had set in motion. A fundamental axiom of organizational life is that a peripheral adviser such as Nelson Rockefeller cannot offset a Dulles *unless* the President takes it upon himself to reward his less accessible advisers with special attention. Even in the best of circumstances, Eisenhower was ambivalent about investing the time and energy necessary to sustain countervailing counsel. Once hospitalized, this function was totally abdicated. Eisenhower became captive to the advisers who manned the "gates." So effective were these barriers that Rockefeller was unable to see the President from the time of his attack on September 24 until December 5! In the meantime, Dulles had held his "discouraging" talks with the Soviets and the "spirit of Geneva" was broken. Rockefeller resigned on December 31, 1955.

Eisenhower constructed a massive system, and like all large organizations, it took on a momentum of its own. Like a large vessel underway, it became difficult to change its course. Periodically, as we have seen, Eisenhower wanted to pursue the albatross of peace. To do so required the capacity to zig and zag off the established course of Administration policy. The tragedy for Dwight D. Eisenhower was that however harshly he shifted the tiller, he could not—given the short span of his attention—alter the Administration policies in a lasting way. Eisenhower tried, through Rockefeller, to utilize competing ideas and safeguard his options with an auxiliary channel of advice. Such a safeguard is a sensible hedge against one of the major shortcomings of the formalistic approach. But it is not enough just to *install* a safeguard; it must be *maintained*. Such maintenance demanded firmness and endurance on Eisenhower's part, but his grasp remained hesitant and his commitment piecemeal.

Eisenhower's handling of the Lebanese crisis provides a third illustration of an exception to his usual management approach. It was a curious incident—almost, it seemed later, contrived. Ostensibly it demonstrated that Ike could move decisively. The incident is perplexing because, while street fighting did occur, and U.S. assistance was requested from the Lebanese President, there really was no "crisis." Eisenhower, in a wholly uncharacteristic move, summoned Dulles and told him what he planned to do. Dulles supported him fully. Next he called in Congressional leaders and told them he was sending in the Marines. He did. The intervention proved as open and shut as an amphibious exercise off Camp Pendleton, California. The Marines went ashore—no shots, no casualties—and left quietly after several weeks. Had it been a show of force to underscore U.S. commitment in the Middle East? Was it inspired by the President's efforts to redress past lapses in his command? We can only speculate. Sherman Adams offers this appraisal:

It was my own feeling at the time that sending the Marines to Lebanon, like sending the soldiers to Little Rock, was a frustrating and unhappy experience for Eisenhower. In both instances he was keenly sensitive to the critical repercussions that followed. Looking back on both decisions with the benefit of hindsight, he probably underestimated the effect of his action at Little Rock and overestimated the gravity of the Lebanon situation and the effects of his intervention in that Middle East brushfire.[98]

There was an air of national hibernation as the Eisenhower years wore on. Part of the difficulty was that increasingly Eisenhower's being "out of touch" was compounded by his being "out of Washington." Barely a month after the Inauguration, he made his first trip to the Humphrey estate in Augusta, Georgia, for four days of golf; the Suez crisis found him on vacation in Gettysburg; virtually all the decisions and all the communications with Faubus that led to the crisis in Little Rock were made, as has been noted, on a golfing vacation in Newport. Even at the White House, relaxation was important to Eisenhower. Adams states "that he was always hopeful . . . that if he could get his work cleared away early in the day, he might find time late in the afternoon to get out of doors on the golf course or with a Number 8 iron on the back lawn of the White House for the fresh air and exercise that he so vitally needed."[99]

On August 5, 1955, Eisenhower departed for a vacation in Denver at a golf course near Lowry Air Force Base. He enjoyed his days there, taking pride, according to Adams, in the fact that he had to "work for only an hour or so at his office at Lowry in the morning and [could then] spend the rest of the day playing golf, fishing, painting or playing bridge."[100] He felt healthy and played 27 holes on many days.

The days slipped into weeks and the weeks to seven as the vacation continued past September 23 with no sign of ending. When asked if he was getting a good rest, Eisenhower replied, "Well, I sure am. They hardly let me do any work at all."[101] But a slight note of acerbity had begun to mar the chorus of praise as editorials queried whether the country could be run without a President. Eisenhower, almost entirely shut off from the world (he had long since substituted a condensed media briefing for reading the newspapers), probably was unaware of the criticism. But events would soon silence the critics. On September 24, Eisenhower suffered a heart attack and was hospitalized for two months. During that time, his Cabinet reportedly met and functioned "as usual" with no power plays or interruptions of routine.[102]

One strength, at least, of Eisenhower's formalistic system was that it could function effectively without him. The machinery had been geared to carry the weight. Long before his heart attack, Eisenhower had fretted in the harness of the Presidency. He disliked its heavy schedule of work, the voluminous stacks of reading, and the endless queues of visitors. "When does a man get a chance to think around here?" he complained to his staff after his first month in office.[103] "Getting time to think" gradually became the rationale for his delegating so much responsibility. The result, inevitably, was a gradual diminution of command. "Let's face it," Senator Everett M. Dirksen commented once, "Eisenhower did not know much about what was going on during his Administration. He would call a group in—let the others do most of the talking—he used to sit. and doodle for about two hours and then he would say, 'Okay, boys, who is going to carry the ball?' It was frightening—Eisenhower's lack of knowledge of what was taking place and the things he didn't know about the United States Government."[104]

Following his heart attack, Eisenhower's isolation advanced another notch. One official close to the White House describes the evolving situation:

The process had been cumulative since the heart attack. Then there were massive delegations [of authority]; which simply followed the existing lines to Adams and on down. Those delegations were administered by men who told each other [and themselves], "don't bother the boss," "can't do this to him now." But the less he was bothered, the less he knew, and the less he knew, the less confident he felt in his own judgment. He let himself grow stale. . . . That made the delegations irreversible. It made him cling the tighter to the judgments of the people already around him. The less he trusted himself, the more he *had* to trust them. And they thought the way to help him was to "spare" him. A lot of this was very well intentioned.[105]

It is interesting that in his first six weeks of convalescence after the heart attack, Eisenhower was given no newspapers at all. It was held that he would find them disturbing. For some it was remarkable that a President, well enough to oil paint and to work crossword puzzles, should be less agitated when deprived of newspapers than when given them. Most public men would suffer more from *not* knowing what was happening in the world than from knowing.

It is sad that a man of such enormous popularity did not accomplish more. Many of the domestic problems that the nation would face in the 1960s—the unrest of the blacks, the decay of the inner cities, hard-core poverty—were all there bubbling beneath the surface. But their existence went largely unrecognized by the Eisenhower Administration. Yet had the President noticed, he might not have considered them his concern. And had he been concerned, his system probably would not have had the creative ideas to cope. There was no tension there, no rub, no friction. The "peace initiative," regrettably, was to be the rare initiative. Truman had been thwarted on the beachheads of Congress but nonetheless launched an ambitious legislative program. Eisenhower was content to captain the ship of state in a sea of deadening neutrality. His wish to avoid conflict and ambiguity and the sheer mass of his administrative machinery held the nation dead in the water. Gradually, the major initiative of reform shifted to Congress where an aggressive Senator named Lyndon Johnson was building an impressive record. But perhaps after the Depression, the New Deal, World War II, the Fair Deal, and Korea, there was a need for a decade of tranquillity. If that was the case, Eisenhower's particular system made it possible.

CHAPTER FIVE

KENNEDY'S GAMBLES
ON GROUPTHINK

I$_N$ THE early hours of June 6, 1961, John F. Kennedy sat in his shorts in the dim cabin light of *Air Force One*. His historic meeting with Nikita Khrushchev was over. He had gone with great hopes—of lessening tensions in Berlin, of forestalling the resumption of nuclear testing. Now these hopes gave way to gloom. His thoughts were troubled. Khrushchev had been intransigent—at times, bullying. The President's eyes were red and bags had formed beneath them. He shifted uncomfortably in his seat to ease the nagging ache in his back, occasionally reaching down to rub the spot, as if that action would dispel it.[1]

He wondered what would follow. Yet, it was invaluable, he thought to himself. He had met his man, studied him carefully during the long hours of negotiations. He sensed now, more clearly than ever before, Khrushchev's toughness—and vulnerabilities. Ahead lay some difficult days for the United States. But for John F. Kennedy, this long night gave him time to think and gather heart for the trial ahead. Now, knowing Khrushchev, he could work in the cool atmosphere of reality which he preferred. In those quiet hours of June 6—unmarked by crisis, unnoticed by history—John Kennedy puzzled his problems and searched for answers.

One measure of greatness is the willingness of some men to

gather the full measure of their resources and expend them, knowing in advance that they will be consumed beyond their limits. Inevitably, this is an inner trial—unheralded and drawing deeply on inner strength. For those who have known it, crisis itself is an anticlimax—a public manifestation of the struggle that has gone before. Perhaps John Kennedy, some time after the abortive invasion at the Bay of Pigs—possibly that night returning from the summit with Khrushchev—faced that inner trial. The future was grim, but not hopeless, he may have decided. Somehow he would face the fire and make it through. Imperceptibly, the line graph of his Administration's fortunes, which had plunged during the Bay of Pigs episode, had bottomed out and begun to trend upward.

On August 2, 1944, Joseph P. Kennedy, Jr. was killed on an experimental bombing mission off the coast of France. His death brought a whole set of complex forces into motion which were to shape the destiny of a future President. It now became inevitable that Jack would enter politics. "It was like being drafted," he confided years later. "My father wanted his eldest son in politics. 'Wanted' isn't the right word. He *demanded* it."[2] In 1946 John Kennedy ran for Congress.

It is unclear how willingly John Kennedy accepted the mantle of his fallen brother. "I'm just filling Joe's shoes," he told campaign workers in a moment of discouragement. "If he were alive, I'd never be in this."[3] Nevertheless, this campaign was to be the first of many. The battle was uphill and before it was over it would draw upon the drive and discipline that he had until then held in reserve. He was, in many respects, an unlikely candidate: twenty-eight years old, shy, gaunt, and unassertive. He had lived much of his life in the shadow of Joe. An unflinching rivalry had developed between the two young boys—and Jack, as the smaller and less developed, always lost. The intensity of this competition was sharpened by Mr. Kennedy's belief that his children should be competitive with one another: tennis matches became matters of personal honor;

touch football was fratricidal. "They are the most competitive and at the same time the most cohesive family I've ever seen," said a long-time family friend. "They fight each other, yet they feed on each other."[4] Here were the makings of Kennedy's later style, a peculiar blend of brotherhood and conflict that would carry into his Presidency.

Throughout prep school and college, Joe, Jr. led the way. He was a top student and an excellent athlete; Jack fell short of his mark. Jack's performance at Choate and Harvard was spotty. His senior honors thesis was published and became a best-selling book; but this achievement, like others, was diluted by his father's influence. Mr. Kennedy had arranged for its publication. Jack drifted after college—a trip to South America, enrollment at Yale Law School, a brief stint at the Graduate School of Business at Stanford. Following World War II, he tried his hand again at journalism, but his deliberate prose and factual reporting drew minor reviews alongside the sensationalism of the Hearst syndicate.

Accompanying these developments were Kennedy's recurrent bouts with illness. As a boy, he endured scarlet fever and appendicitis and almost died of diphtheria. A series of jaundice attacks postponed college for a year and a back injury sustained while playing football at Harvard cast an unremitting shadow of pain upon his life. The ramming by a Japanese destroyer of his famed PT-109 aggravated the back injury and his ensuing narrow escape from the Japanese left him further weakened with malaria. Upon discharge from the Navy in 1944, he spent months recuperating in Chelsea Naval Hospital. Shortly thereafter, the rigors of political life accelerated the wear and tear on his fragile body. As a Congressman on a tour of Asia, his colleagues feared for his life when he developed a temperature of over 106 degrees and had to be rushed to the military hospital in Okinawa. In his uphill contest for the U.S. Senate in 1952, he drove himself relentlessly as he crisscrossed Massachusetts. He hated to appear on crutches, and he was frequently in pain. By 1954 he was so crippled by pain that he had to undergo delicate, risky spinal surgery. Two operations were in fact necessary; the second brought him perilously close to death. Twice the last rites were administered. He survived, but the pain remained. It would accompany him to the Presidency along with other health problems—an adrenal deficiency and chronic stomach trouble, which caused him to eat carefully and often. His aide Ted Sorensen has observed that he never complained about his pains or imagined new ones, "yet he used (and carried with him about the country) more pills, potions, poultices and other paraphernalia than would be found in a small dispensary."[5]

Hardship carves itself on character. By his mid-twenties, John Kennedy had been shaped in important ways by fraternal competition and nagging illness. The presence of pain, the prospect of death had taught him to stand outside himself, to detach his emotions from his physical ordeal in order to concentrate on external events. Robust determination and a steely self-discipline had overgrown his fragile frame. He had learned something of that intriguing quality—courage—about which he would write his Pulitzer Prize winning book, *Profiles in Courage*.

John Kennedy may not have had his heart in his first Congressional contest. But once having won, his resources became enlisted in the office. After his first term, Kennedy ran for another. Following his second term, Kennedy set his sights on higher office, whatever that might be. He embarked on an exhausting schedule of weekend speaking engagements that brought him state-wide attention. In 1952 he ran for the Senate and won decisively against his firmly entrenched opponent, Henry Cabot Lodge. Eisenhower had inundated Adlai Stevenson in Massachusetts by 208,000 votes and the Republicans had also swept the State House. Like a sapling left standing among uprooted oaks, Kennedy was suddenly the dominant Democrat in his state.

Despite Kennedy's public image, he was far from the sunny,

gregarious type who lived a life of grace and adventure. "Actually," says one close observer, "he [was] a serious, driven man, about as casual as a cash register, who enjoy[ed] the organizational, technical parts of politics [far more than] the stumping."[6] For his wife Jacqueline, the talk of her husband as a glamour boy was "nonsense." "He has a curious inquiring mind that is always at work," she said.[7] Jackie knew all too well. In 1956, after he lost the Vice Presidential nomination, he departed to join his father on the Riviera, leaving Jackie to have her first child in Newport. Afterwards, in Georgetown, he resumed his furious pace and enjoyed little personal life. He was always restless and hated to waste time. When he awakened, he would shave and read a magazine while bathing. He was a voracious reader, consuming material at twelve hundred words a minute. "Young man in a hurry," one journalist called him.[8] Sometimes his friends feared that he was too much in a hurry—that his periodic illnesses were his body's way of saying "stop."

It seemed to the public that John Kennedy was following a course as natural as that of a river to the sea when he stepped into the White House as the thirty-fifth President of the United States. But what seemed to be a natural progression for the wealthy Senator from Massachusetts had been a very long journey of the spirit. He had not only weathered the journey but had grown from it. This capacity to learn under stress, to gain from hardship, would remain one of the most interesting aspects of his Presidency.

President Kennedy's managerial approach lay midway between the polarities of Eisenhower and Franklin Roosevelt. "I want to be in the thick of things," he said, and sought to carve out a commanding role in the conduct of the office.[9] He aimed to ensure his centrality, but sought to avoid the jagged methods and din of turmoil of FDR's White House. Roosevelt's demands for primacy, he felt, overburdened the Chief Executive; needed was a way of being informed without becoming inundated, of ensuring diversity without unleashing divisive forces among his staff. In short, Kennedy sought quality decisions that were at the same time implementable. He recognized that to achieve this he needed organization, but he would not go to Eisenhower's structured extremes. He rejected Ike's pyramidal organization but brought the semblance of a system to his staff by organizing it like a wheel, with himself at the hub and the spokes connecting him to his individual aides. Kennedy wanted to be more in touch with the facts upon which decisions were based than Eisenhower or Truman had been. To achieve this, he needed colleagues to help him collect information, test alternatives, and make decisions. Teamwork became the critical factor, and through trial and error, it would set the theme of the decision process during Kennedy's thousand days.

Kennedy's collegial approach relied upon several operating principles. First, it was person-centered to a greater extent than had been the case with Roosevelt, Truman, or Eisenhower. It is not that these former Presidents lacked able, or loyal, and congenial advisers, but Kennedy was dedicated to finding more men with all these qualities. In doing so, he was willing to set aside a long-standing tradition of making appointments to repay political debts. "I don't care whether a man is a Democrat or an Igorot," he said to his talent scout, Clark Clifford, "I want the best fellow I can get for the job."[10] Onto his White House staff he took old-time associates like Theodore Sorensen and Kenneth O'Donnell, but there were new faces also—men he had gotten to know during the campaign, like McGeorge Bundy and Arthur M. Schlesinger, Jr. It was in the process of selecting Cabinet officers that Kennedy's commitment to talent was brought most sharply into focus. In Kennedy's view, the key posts were Defense and Treasury. In manning each, he invested an unconscionable amount of time. First he had Clifford and his brother-in-law Sargent Shriver reconnoiter for likely candidates; then he pared down the lists of names. After talking once, twice, even three times with the candidate himself—on one pretext or another—he made his selection. Robert S. McNamara and C. Douglas Dillon were chosen in this manner.

Kennedy's choice of Douglas Dillon as Secretary of the Treasury illustrates in several respects the sensitivities underlying his selection process. First, Kennedy was willing to invest literally days in selecting Dillon from a half-dozen qualified alternatives, including Averell Harriman and Senator Albert Gore of Tennessee. Secondly, Dillon was a Republican, yet the President-elect discounted that, saying, "Oh, I don't care about [that]. All I want to know is: is he able? and will he go along with the program?"[11] Dillon was afforded the "full treatment"; Kennedy cross-examined him on his views and sought to learn about his character and commitment. In this latter regard, Kennedy steadfastly cast aside the traditional posture of a President granting his distant blessing upon preselected appointees; rather, he was a full-fledged and discerning participant in the process. He wanted talent, he wanted men he could work with, and above all he wanted men of integrity who would stand up for their ideas. By and large, he got such men—in Arthur J. Goldberg, Secretary of Labor, and Adlai Stevenson, Ambassador to the United Nations, among others.

Kennedy wanted to direct foreign policy. For this reason, he did not want a well-known figure like J. William Fulbright or Averell Harriman or Dean Acheson to be Secretary of State but rather an easygoing person with whom he could get along. Dean Rusk, the chairman of the Rockefeller Foundation, fit the bill. Kennedy hired Rusk at their first meeting, contrary to his usual selection process. Curiously enough, his choice came back to haunt him. Rusk, unlike Kennedy's other advisers, was reluctant to take a strong position and seemed overly dependent on the system. Near the close of his third year, both the President and his brother Robert were talking with intimates about the possibility of a new Secretary of State.[12]

Diversity through the choice of men with conflicting views was the second operating principle of the Kennedy Administration. To balance Dillon's conservatism, he manned his Council of Economic Advisors with men like Walter Heller—exponents of the new economics. Kennedy sought to bring talent and complementary outlooks together. After the fiasco at the Bay of Pigs, Kennedy replaced CIA Chief Allen Dulles with John McCone, an extremely conservative near-reactionary Republican millionaire from California. The liberals in the Administration were appalled, but Kennedy wanted a different point of view—as well as a proven doer and an activist who could cut through the flabby bureaucracy. Kennedy summoned McCone to the White House on the pretext of discussing nuclear testing. After sizing him up during a two-hour conversation, he invited him back and abruptly offered him the job.

Kennedy wanted men of diverse opinions on his staff and he encouraged them to speak out frequently; when he found them in accord, he played devil's advocate to see if he could take the opposite side of a question and support it with logic. He valued dissent, and one aide has said, "in fact, anyone in the small group around him [was] expected to disagree, and disagree loudly if he felt so disposed."[13] Schlesinger comments that people sometimes wondered why he kept men like Curtis LeMay, who occasionally seemed to be entirely out of sympathy with him, on the Joint Chiefs of Staff. In Kennedy's opinion, "it [was] good to have men like Curt LeMay and Arleigh Burke commanding troops when you decide to go in. But these men aren't the only ones you should listen to when you decide whether to go in or not. I like having LeMay head the Air Force. Everybody knows how he feels. That's a good thing."[14]

Kennedy built overlap into his staff assignments to ensure a diversity of viewpoints. Shortly after the election, when Richard Neustadt was given a transitional assignment that infringed upon the broader charter of Clark Clifford, Neustadt tactfully asked how he should "relate" to Clifford. "I don't want you to relate," Kennedy replied quickly. "I can't afford to confine myself to one set of advisers. If I did that, *I* would be on *their* leading strings."[15] In a similar move, Kennedy assigned Paul Nitze and Adlai Stevenson parallel tasks in laying out Administration foreign policy options. This irritated Stevenson, "but

Kennedy," according to Schlesinger, "in the mood of FDR, did not intend to confer on anyone the exclusive rights to advise."[16] Unlike FDR, Kennedy expended considerable effort in soothing the conflicts of his own creation. He placated Stevenson by stating, in effect, that he looked forward to receiving both reports.

Similarities to FDR's approach, although with marked differences in outcome, have perplexed many observers of the Kennedy Administration. His White House contained a goodly share of egotists, yet there was little evident friction. Sorensen was policy adviser and speech writer, Pierre Salinger was Press Secretary, McGeorge Bundy was head of the NSC staff, Arthur Schlesinger and Richard Goodwin were recruited as all-purpose assistants, Laurence F. O'Brien was assigned to Congressional relations, Kenneth O'Donnell was designated Appointments Secretary, and David Powers was added to chase down loose ends. Titles were purely nominal, for given Kennedy's collegial approach, he was prone to give any and all assignments to the first aide he encountered. Furthermore, he injected himself at any point along the decision-making spectrum from problem-selection to final judgment. Whereas Eisenhower wanted decisions brought to him for approval, Kennedy wanted problems brought to him for definition—well in advance of the final decision itself. Eisenhower wanted a tightly worded consensus placed before him, Kennedy eschewed consensus; he wanted to know a problem's facets and its possible solutions.

Illustrative of Kennedy's intervention into the problem-solving process was his handling of his scientific advisers and his ultimate decision to put a man on the moon before 1970. Earlier Presidents had been awed by their scientific counsel; Roosevelt deferred to Vannevar Bush, Eisenhower deferred to George Kistiakowsky. For Kennedy and his scientific adviser Jerome Wiesner it was another matter. When Kennedy was urged by Wiesner to play down the Soviet success in placing a man in orbit around the earth, Kennedy would have none of it. He recognized that Americans might prefer to rationalize the event. But unlike Roosevelt, he did not move with the tide; through his own actions he sought to bring the nation to face its shortcomings. In a similar vein, Kennedy challenged his scientific advisers' views on the resumption of atomic testing. Disconcerted with the unanimity of opinion and quickness of response, he insisted that Wiesner convene a group of atomic specialists who were not part of the Administration. The group was to include both hawks and doves. Many heated deliberations led him to conclude that there were only marginal strategic advantages in matching detonations with the Russians. Only after the USSR had detonated its thirtieth nuclear weapon in 1961 did Kennedy change his mind—this time more for political than military reasons.

In these and other decisions, Kennedy profited from diversity, the third major principle of his Administration. The glue that held these centrifugal forces together was Kennedy's particular ability to smooth over rifts and draw his team together. Here lay an important difference between his results and Roosevelt's. "Contrary to [the] Roosevelt fashion," said Sorensen once, "[Kennedy did not] encourage conflict and competition among and between his staff and Cabinet."[17] There was "rapport between the President and his staff. Our role was one of building government unity rather than splintering responsibility." Sorensen continues, "He was informal without being chummy, hard-driving but easy-mannered, interested in us as people without being patronizing. . . . He treated us more as colleagues or associates than employees."[18] Kennedy encouraged diversity of views but not interpersonal rivalry and competition for influence.

Intuitively perhaps, Kennedy perfected a number of tactics in his skillful juggling of personalities. First of all, he was accessible. "You've got one of the most accessible Presidents in history," one Cabinet member said. "I must talk with him in person or on the phone twenty times a week," said another Secretary. "I don't hesitate to call him if something important comes up—even at night or on Sunday," said another.[19] Maxwell Taylor, his Chairman of the Joint Chiefs of Staff, echoed a similar refrain, "You might have to wait until late in the night, but if you sent word that you needed to see the President, you got to see him."[20]

Kennedy enforced his accessibility not only through his evident personal receptivity, but through the ingenious expedient of a "two-door" policy in his office. Schlesinger explains:

He was infinitely accessible to his Special Assistants . . . while Ken O'Donnell guarded the main entrance to the Presidential office with a wise concern for the President's time and energy, Evelyn Lincoln [his personal secretary] presided over the other with welcoming patience and warmth. For the half hour or so before luncheon and then again the last hour of the afternoon, the door between Mrs. Lincoln's office and the President's room was generally ajar—a signal to the staff that he was open for business. Once one put one's head in the door, he was beckoned in; then the report was made or document cleared briskly across his desk. Everything was transacted in a kind of shorthand.[21]

Through this procedure, key advisers like Bundy and Sorensen could carry out their work without colliding with the hard-minded O'Donnell.

There were, of course, inevitable clashes among this driven and talented staff. According to Sorensen:

His staff, to be sure, was neither as efficient as we pretended nor as harmonious as he thought. Failure of communication appeared more than once. A degree of envy and occasionally resentment cropped up now and then. A group of able and aggressive individualists, all dependent on one man, could not be wholly free from competitive feelings or from scornful references to each other's political or intellectual backgrounds. But Kennedy's personal interest in his aides, refusal to prefer one over another, and mixture of pressure and praise achieved a total command of our loyalties.[22]

Kennedy's sensitivities, perhaps acquired from family scraps and from having endured the bullying of his older brother, tended to quickly pick up the hurt feelings that surfaced. When Sorensen was teased for having so over-identified with the President that he was sublimating his personality, Kennedy told the staff to lay off. When he sensed that some of his aides viewed Arthur Schlesinger with ill-concealed disdain, he went out of his way to bolster Schlesinger's bruised feelings. Schlesinger notes:

[T]here had been predictions of conflict between [Sorensen and Bundy]. Sorensen, it was supposed, having had a monopoly of Kennedy for so long, would not easily relinquish him to other hands. I myself had been warned that, in entering the White House, I would be plunging into a ruthless scramble for access and power. But this did not seem to be taking place—and, indeed, the Kennedy White House remained to the end remarkably free of the rancor which has so often welled up in presidential households. One reason . . . was that the President handled the situation with effortless skill, avoiding collective confrontations, such as staff meetings where everyone might find out what everyone else was up to. He tactfully kept the relations with his aides on a bilateral basis.[23]

Outwardly, Kennedy's White House had a *form* very much like Roosevelt's—the President serving as chief of staff, emphasis on generalists, ad hoc assignments, and so forth. But the differences were to be found in the relationships of his advisers. "Each man could and did assist every other," one said.[24] Sorensen talks about "equal stature, equal salaries, and equal access to the President."[25] In earlier chapters we have observed that access and influence play an inordinate role in the reward system of the White House. Roosevelt managed them to induce competition. Kennedy, Sorensen's remarks suggest, managed access to promote equality and teamwork. Roosevelt's availability was there one minute, gone the next; he used it as a gambit of competition or to bolster an aide who was on the brink of quitting. In contrast, Kennedy broadened the White House reward system, permitting his staff to obtain credit and recognition for their accomplishments. "He was a secure President; unlike Roosevelt or Johnson, he did not begrudge his men their press clippings. When the press made much of McGeorge Bundy's importance, Kennedy commented dryly, but not angrily: 'I will continue to have some residual functions.' "[26]

Kennedy delegated authority to his staff with little fear that they would thwart his interests. First, he always maintained contact with outside points of view; second, he could rely on his brother Bobby; and most importantly, he inspired loyalty and could trust his men. With the exception of Schlesinger and Bundy, all of his principal White House aides had been with him since 1952. He bound men to him in generally lasting relationships. "The fact that all his major aides were still with him when he was killed contrasts rather pointedly with the turnover on Lyndon Johnson's staff despite the fact that Johnson showered gifts, praise, and dinner invitations on his aides, and Kennedy did none of those things."[27] He commanded their respect as an intellectual equal: he was curious, he was real, and he was challenging. "One man who served both Presidents recalls: 'I must have had dinner with Johnson a hundred times, and if you told me Sorensen never once had dinner with Kennedy, I'd believe it. Kennedy was more reserved . . . he never asked you for anything, but he got absolute loyalty.'"[28]

Kennedy's men could count on his support in time of trouble. Sorensen recalls:

When Arthur Schlesinger was under fire for calling a columnist an "idiot"—when Dick Goodwin was accused of meddling in diplomacy—when Pierre Salinger's trip to the Soviet Union was under attack—when hard-working Bundy, Rostow, Galbraith were maligned as "the dancing professors"—and when Walter Heller, Stewart Udall, Willard Wirtz, Arthur Sylvester and many others were assailed for mistake or misstatement—the President took pains to reassure each of us in private and, if asked, to defend us in public.[29]

At one time or another he defended them all when it would have been politically wiser to have remained silent.

The fourth principle of Kennedy's system of management was his drive for the facts. He had a keen nose for detail that took him into the interior of problems. Although interested in general principles, he pressed toward the edge of action. He had, a colleague said, "a highly operational mind."[30] Policy separated from operations was, in his view, meaningless. His desk was "piled high with reports and memoranda," one observer states. "The remarkable aspect was that he read them closely and could reach into the pile, and pull out a memorandum and resort almost instantaneously to a paragraph to make a point or raise a question."[31] Kennedy liked the press and kept up with what reporters were writing. His staff had to do the same. He reviewed his Cabinet members' most troublesome mail and worked with them personally on knotty problems. "President Kennedy," an adviser once said, "is a desk officer at the highest level."[32] There were risks and dangers in such involvement, as we shall see. But the benefit was that advisers were forever kept alert to critical details.

"He refused to take the chance that his subordinates were screening out criticisms, alternatives or information on his or their errors," Sorensen commented, ". . . he made certain that he had the final decision on whom he would see and what he would read."[33] After the Bay of Pigs, Bundy's "situation room" had teletypes installed receiving copies of every important cable moving out of State, Defense, and the CIA. Kennedy once stated his philosophy this way: "I sit in the White House, and what I read . . . and see is the sum total of what I hear and learn. So the more people I can see, or the wider I can expose [my mind] to different ideas, the more effective [I] can be as President."[34]

Kennedy was a memo man. Throughout the day he would dictate into a portable unit beside his desk. Toward evening, Mrs. Lincoln would rescue the transcripts for typing. They were terse messages, sometimes only a sentence or two long. He savored the craftsmanship of frugal, pungent language and occasionally thumbed through Churchill to get inspiration from the master memo man of the century.

Kennedy disliked meetings and kept them as brief as the subject permitted; many lasted no more than fifteen minutes and few ran over an hour. The larger they were, the more likely to elicit his nervous fidgeting. While he relied considerably on Cabinet officers as individuals, he convened the Cabinet only six times in three years. "Cabinet meetings," he once told a friend, "are simply useless. Why should the Postmaster sit there and listen to a discussion of the problems of Laos?"[35] He wanted his meetings honed to the edge of action. He kept them short and to the point.

Kennedy's information system encompassed not only his everyday machinery but auxiliary channels as well. His ingenuity was manifest in choosing the latter—maintaining direct lines of communication with Ambassador John Kenneth Galbraith in India and personal relations with English Ambassador David Ormsby-Gore and a number of heads of state. He was in touch with Henry Kissinger at Harvard, with Joseph Alsop and Clark Clifford in Washington, and with others across the nation. Yet clearly, the most important back-up source of information was his brother Bobby. It had taken courage to appoint him to the post of Attorney General. But when the Cuban invasion crumbled, the President realized the need for an independent set of eyes and ears. Bobby was summoned to inquire into the cause of the bungling. Thereafter, he was a mainstay of the decision process. More than the Attorney General, he became the President's alter ego, confidant, counselor, and troubleshooter. Above all, he could be counted on to disagree— to "talk back" when others might withhold their views in the President's presence.

The four basic features underlying Kennedy's collegial approach evolved gradually in time. Near the close of his third year, he had come a long way from where he started. Long ago, it seemed, he had roamed around the West Wing on his first day in office, poking his head in doors, pressing buttons on his desk, and designating a space for his personal secretary, Evelyn Lincoln. His immediate moves were to establish his staff system and dismantle Eisenhower's ponderous committees within the Cabinet and the NSC. After the Inauguration, Bundy slaughtered the NSC committees right and left and compressed the remains into a flexible NSC staff. These were the golden days: Kennedy was everywhere and perpetually accessible. His system was in place.

But was it a system—or just a retinue of good fellows masquerading as an organized staff? The Bay of Pigs invasion, occurring barely two months after the President's Inauguration, required a close reexamination of the process. Kennedy's collegial approach, as we shall see, developed slowly and like an exotic sports car, demanded constant tuning and occasional re-engineering.

The Bay of Pigs invasion plans were well in motion when Kennedy entered office. The CIA leadership—Allen Dulles and his second in command, Richard Bissel—were committed to the project both personally and organizationally. As they presented the plans, they seemed, in Arthur Schlesinger's words, "less analysts than . . . advocates."[36] Another aide said, "Allen and Dick didn't just brief us on the Cuban question, they sold us on it."[37]

It wasn't that simple. Two days after the Inauguration, Kennedy—along with Sorensen, McNamara, Bundy, and Rusk—was given a detailed briefing on the proposed invasion by Allen Dulles.[38] During the next eighty days, the core group of advisers repeatedly discussed the plan informally and in meetings with the Joint Chiefs of Staff. In giving their full approval, the President and his advisers assumed that a brigade of Cuban exiles could secure the beachhead without U.S. air support, that they would be supported by the Cubans once ashore, and that the United States would not be implicated in the attack. These assumptions, which hindsight brutally revealed to be false, passed through the Kennedy system unchallenged. Why? There appear to be several reasons, not the least of which was the euphoria of the New Frontier. There was an air of invincibility, captured in part by the words of a Justice Department official with whom Robert Kennedy discussed the CIA plans on the day the invasion was launched: "It seemed that, with John Kennedy leading us and with all the talent he had assembled, nothing could stop us. We believed that if we faced up to the nation's problems and applied bold, new ideas with common sense and hard work, we would overcome whatever challenged us."[39] A second reason behind approval for the plans was an unchallenged assumption that there was unanimity among the advisers. In Schlesinger's words, "Our meetings [took] place in a curious atmosphere of assumed consensus."[40] Interestingly, at meetings confined to just State Department officials, Rusk asked penetrating questions that frequently reexamined the U.S. position.[41] But at the White House meetings, Rusk remained on the bandwagon, only occasionally offering a gentle warning about avoiding excesses.

One danger of the collegial approach is that in building cohesiveness, it is all too easy to build a *closed* system of mutual support. This takes on more serious overtones when one member of the group takes it upon himself to enforce consensus and police those who deviate. This, in fact, occurred during the Bay of Pigs deliberations. When Schlesinger presented his violent objections in memo form to the President, Robert Kennedy took him aside and delivered a stern lecture. He said, "You may be right or you may be wrong, but the President has made his mind up. Don't push it any further. Now is the time for everyone to help him all they can."[42] Later, when Roger Hilsman at State got wind of the adventure, he asked Rusk's permission to allow Cuba experts in the State Department to scrutinize the plan. "I'm sorry," Rusk told him, "but I can't let you. This is being too tightly held."[43] Rusk's stance was ironic since advance news of the invasion was being leaked to the press. After the fact, Sorensen concluded that men in the State Department as well as those on the White House staff "entertained [doubts] but never pressed, partly out of fear of being labelled 'soft' or undaring in the eyes of their colleagues."[44] Such is a risk of the collegial system.

Thus, team consensus developed—blind to the tactical assumptions of the invasion and ignoring important strategic questions which the invasion raised. It should be acknowledged that hindsight makes criticism easier. Our concern, however, is less with the outcome and more with the process that permitted it. At the core of the process was Kennedy himself. Kennedy had raised more skeptical questions than anyone else. But at each meeting, instead of opening up the agenda to permit a full airing of opposing views, he allowed the CIA's representatives to dominate. He allowed them to refute immediately each tentative doubt. Senator Fulbright, who violently opposed the plan, was invited to one meeting and delivered a strong argument against the project. Yet Kennedy, instead of following up on Fulbright's questions, asked each person around the table to state his final judgment.[45] In retrospect, the President's demand that each person commit himself to a final position contributed to a stultifying consensus. No one among his brandnew team of advisers wanted to be the first to appear chicken and say no.

Kennedy blundered badly in the Bay of Pigs affair, and in taking full public blame he was probably doing what was right as well as what was administratively proper. Kennedy was deeply affected by his failure. He recognized the need to staff out the facts far more carefully—and if possible, to require incontrovertible evidence on key points. He had always trusted people more than institutions, but now he recognized how an agency's specialization and its rivalries with other departments could narrow its point of view. A President could not depend, he concluded, on one channel of information for critical facts. He realized that Bundy's vastly scaled-down NSC was almost too small a group to ensure full coverage on important choices. He was also determined to enlist more outside advice to catch his blind spots. He recognized, too, the importance of looking at the big picture, and not just at the tactical issues of the moment—to question the basic strategy, and morality, of a project.

Kennedy commissioned his brother Robert and General Maxwell Taylor to thoroughly investigate the Bay of Pigs affair. Based partly on their recommendations, he introduced several subtle but important changes into his decision-making process. First, he thereafter required his advisers to take the role of "generalists"; they would participate as critical thinkers, *not* as spokesmen from their respective agencies.[46] Second, he charged his team with examining policies as a whole, and made the group collectively responsible for its product.[47] Third, two men whom the President trusted most—his brother Robert and Theodore Sorensen—were given the special role of watchdogs. They were told to pursue ruthlessly every bone of contention, to criticize superficial analysis, and prevent oversights from being swept under the rug. Robert Kennedy accepted this role avidly, barking out sharp and sometimes rude questions; at times he paid the price of becoming unpopular.[48]

A final change in Kennedy's decision-making process involved the group atmosphere itself. Remembering the stifled meetings of the Bay of Pigs experience, Kennedy now insisted that sessions be frank and freewheeling and that the usual rules of protocol be suspended. Formal agendas were avoided and outsiders were invited in to ensure fresh points of view. To encourage critical thinking, Kennedy frequently formed subgroups to staff out opposing positions, later bringing them together to debate and cross-examine one another.[49]

With substantial changes to his decision-making apparatus in place, Kennedy confronted his next crisis in Berlin. The Berlin crisis of 1961 began to take shape following Kennedy's meeting with Khrushchev in Vienna. Kennedy had hoped for an open dialog; instead, he found the Chairman to be tough and bullying. "[It was] the roughest [meeting] in my life," Kennedy told *New York Times* reporter James Reston.[50] Khrushchev had presented an ultimatum: his missiles would fly and the tanks would roll unless Berlin was reunified under Soviet terms. Afterwards, former Ambassador to the Soviet Union George F. Kennan said, "Kennedy [was] bested by Khrushchev at the Vienna summit. I think Khrushchev thought this [was] a tongue-tied man who's not forceful and who didn't have any ideas of his own. He felt he could get away with something."[51]

Eventually, Berlin came to dominate his thoughts. Fearing another blunder, he perhaps overreacted, driving himself and his advisers to spend time on the tiniest details. "It was as if the President was a desk officer, and the Secretary of State his assistant," said one onlooker. But when questioned about spending too much time on Berlin, the President answered, "better too much than too little."[52] Kennedy commissioned a task force under Dean Acheson to independently analyze the Berlin situation. Acheson's hard-line analysis prescribed the strengthening of the American presence in Berlin and the development of contingency plans should the access to West Berlin be blocked. Opposed to this view were "soft-liners"—among them, Ambassadors Averell Harriman, Llewellyn Thompson and Adlai Stevenson, and in the White House, Theodore Sorensen. These men felt the Soviets had understandable security concerns in Berlin and that there was room to negotiate.[53]

One of the burdensome demands that the collegial approach can impose now confronted Kennedy—the dichotomous alternatives of his teams' invention. He was left to decide. The evidence suggests that he did not on this occasion achieve an intellectual fusion of ideas but rather a compromise. "Kennedy attempted to mediate the debate between his two schools of advisers. . . . [He] accept[ed] most of the positive recommendations of both schools and reject[ed] their negative ones."[54]

He accepted Acheson's recommendation for developing a contingency plan and augmenting U.S. forces stationed in Europe. He also endorsed the soft-line proposals that negotiations be attempted with the Soviets, with attention given to their problem of refugee outflow into West Berlin.

The solution was not a bad one, but it did not anticipate one likely scenario: What would the U.S. do, short of a military response, if provoked by the Soviet bloc? When Chairman Walter Ulbricht of East Berlin halted the refugee flow by erecting a temporary wall across major access roads into the West, the Administration was caught off guard. This was a most predictable provocation, given the East's problems. Yet it had not been anticipated. Not until four days later did the Western allies make a public protest and Kennedy dispatch 1,500 troops down the Autobahn to West Berlin to confirm that access rights were unabridged. Later, he sent Vice President Johnson to the city.

Kennedy's handling of the episode merits satisfactory but not outstanding marks. Some felt his edginess and piecemeal strengthening of the armed forces in Berlin invited the Soviet moves.[55] His system had demonstrated its capabilities to analyze alternatives, but it was less effective in developing a full range of options. The President's personal shortcoming was in not pushing his advisers hard enough to anticipate the contingencies. They had failed to recognize that their most difficult problem would not be military threat but limited provocation.

The Laotian crisis confronted Kennedy with a soon-to-be-familiar scenario of Cold War problems. Involved were treaty commitments, crumbling Southeast Asian allies, and impossible military logistics. The situation in Laos had deteriorated for several months following Kennedy's inauguration. By April 1961, the Royal Laotian Army was in disarray, with the Communist Pathet Lao pursuing them in determined assault. Kennedy's handling of this situation revealed a steady accumulation of experience since the Bay of Pigs. Kennedy and his advisers searched for hard facts upon which to base a judgment.

The situation continued to worsen. Kennedy's military advisers began to argue that nothing short of putting American forces into Laos could save that landlocked republic. McNamara was immediately dispatched to Saigon to meet with top U.S. officials. After hearing their plans to bomb the Pathet Lao on the Plain of Jarres and airlift in American troops, McNamara said, "Let me play the devil's advocate: if we intervene in Laos, if we overfly North Vietnam, will the Chinese let us do it? What will Hanoi do?" Then he leaned back. "Now let's get down to it." He waited. What ensued was one the longest silences McNamara had ever witnessed. "They had all been pushing hard," comments one analyst, "but they had given little or no thought to what the other side might do. Now they had no answers, nothing to say."[56]

McNamara's findings troubled Kennedy. In particular, he was annoyed because he felt the military was not being candid, that they were building a record for the invasion and putting the onus on him. Perhaps drawing upon the lessons of Cuba and Berlin, he sought other alternatives and searched for a more limited response than outright U.S. intervention. The answer came from Averell Harriman who, as Roving Ambassador, had been asked by Kennedy to ascertain from Khrushchev if Laos was worth war. "Why take the risk?" was Khrushchev's response. "It will fall into our lap like a rotten apple."[57] Harriman's meeting with the Chairman led to reevaluation and ultimately to meetings with the Laotian neutralist leader, Souvanna Phouma, in New Delhi. In Geneva, the Administration ultimately hammered out a set of accords with the Communists. This initiative was accompanied by a show of force. U.S. Marines were stationed in Okinawa and Japan for possible contingencies in Southeast Asia, and a televised Kennedy briefing to the nation committed the U.S. to Laotian neutrality. Thus, the Kennedy Administration worked out its response to the crisis in Laos. The President would say later that the Bay of Pigs had saved the U.S. from going to war in Laos.[58]

Those who watched John Kennedy during the Bay of Pigs and again on October 16, 1962, found him a far different President on the second occasion. He knew that the men around him—both civilians and military men, and the top rung of the CIA—were all men he had worked with before. He knew their style and they knew his. Bob Kennedy was in this crisis from the beginning, and so were Sorensen, Rusk, and McNamara. "On the very first morning," said one aide intimately connected with the crisis, "the President gathered all the threads together in his hands and he held them. Kennedy kept in touch with each man and made certain that each man kept in touch with him."[59]

The Cuban missile crisis has been reported extensively and need not be detailed here. In terms of Kennedy's developing collegial style of management, his handling of the crisis revealed significant improvement in the quality and reach of his system.

Kennedy's initial remarks to Adlai Stevenson reflected the immediacy of the crisis. "We'll have to do something quickly," Kennedy said. "I suppose the alternatives are to go in the air and wipe them out or take other steps to render the weapons inoperable."[60] Kennedy's statement also suggests what the U.S. response might have been if his system had not been in place. In fact, there were considerably wider "alternatives."

Faced with the reports of intermediate range offensive missiles in Cuba, Kennedy's first directive was for more photographs—to verify their presence and determine the state of completion of the missile sites. Simultaneously, hand-picking men he could trust, he convened his Executive Committee. The Ex Comm, as it was later called, met for five continuous days of deliberations. He instilled in them a strong sense of collective responsibility. When General David Shoup, Commandant of the Marines, said, "You're in a pretty bad fix, Mr.

President," Kennedy replied, "You are in it with me."[61] Instead of urging his advisers to focus on the air strike option he favored, he emphasized the need to canvass alternatives. Early in the discussions, Robert Kennedy had asked, "Surely, there was some course between bombing and doing nothing."[62] In response to this prod, the Ex Comm broadened the spectrum of options to ten: (1) do nothing, (2) exert diplomatic pressure on the Soviet Union, (3) arrange for a Kennedy-Khrushchev summit, (4) warn Castro to split off from the Soviet Union or face annihilation, (5) set up a blockade to prevent further shipments of missiles, (6) bombard the missiles with pellets to rend them inoperable without causing casualties, (7) surgical air strike on the installations with a warning to avoid injuring Cuban and Soviet personnel, (8) surgical air strike without warning, (9) massive air strike against all military targets in Cuba, (10) launch an all-out invasion of Cuba.[63]

The Bay of Pigs made clear that a key lesson of crisis management is to widen the community involved. Kennedy had this in mind when selecting the original members of Ex Comm, and as a double check invited outsiders Stevenson and Acheson in after several days of discussions. Kennedy also consulted with Ambassador at Large Llewellyn Thompson and Ambassador to France Charles E. Bohlen. When the President attended, his skepticism and disregard for traditional deference to military judgments contributed to the openness of the debate. He also took pains to call on men in secondary positions—such as Paul Nitze and George Ball—to obtain their views and to promote open exchange. It has been said that group members changed their minds on vital issues more than once, among them President Kennedy, who gradually changed his mind about the air strike and began to favor the blockade.

From the various accounts of the thirteen days, it is apparent that the members not only vigorously disagreed but resisted pressures to reach a premature consensus. "By and large," says political scientist Irving Janis, "the members of the group proved to be extraordinarily successful in retaining their critical resources as independent thinkers."[64] After several days, the debate centered on two alternatives, the blockade and the air strike. Kennedy asked spokesmen of the opposing sides to write up their positions. When a subsequent Executive Committee session became deadlocked, Sorensen said he would draft speeches on both proposals (one favoring blockade, the other favoring bombing) to sharpen the focus on the specific issues. Sorensen recounts:

Back in my office, the original difficulties with the blockade route stared me in the face: How should we relate it to the missiles? How would it help get them out? What would we do if they became operational? What should we say about our surveillance, about communicating with Khrushchev? I returned to the group later that afternoon with these questions instead of a speech; and as the concrete answers were provided in our discussion, the final shape of the President's policy began to take form. It was in a sense an amalgam of the blockade—air-strike routes; and a much stronger, more satisfied consensus formed behind it.[65]

Sorensen's statement underscores the subtle dividends of Kennedy's brand of management. Fundamentally, while valuing open confrontation on difficult issues, he rewarded teamwork more than the point of view that won. Perhaps Kennedy's personal attention and equitable reward system bestowed upon his advisers a quieting sense of personal worth and security. Surely Sorensen's behavior in this episode is a significant departure from that of any adviser in Roosevelt's time. Sorensen apparently felt little need to "perform" by bringing back a polished speech or striving to remain the "final word" before the President's. Instead, he returned to the Ex Comm to *share* his questions rather than to *defend* his answers. His use of the term "amalgam" in his characterization of the final position adopted is also of interest. The Cuban missile crisis, while a special case in some respects, is noteworthy because of what *didn't* happen. In the main accounts that have been written of life in the Kennedy Administration, the terms "win" and "lose" are conspicuously absent. Somehow, Kennedy's management style tamed conflicts and achieved a fusion of individual ambition and collective purpose. The focus was always on the problem and its resolution.

The President recalled later that "[from] the beginning there was a sharper division . . . this was very valuable."[66] In planning for the Bay of Pigs invasion, his advisers had spoken virtually with one voice; now he spurned unanimity. Moreover, in contrast to the Berlin decisions in 1961, he pressed his team beyond simply articulating sharply conflicting alternatives. Eventually they forged a limited response that left a door open for escalation. "[Kennedy] approved a view that [all] his advisers had reached," said one participant. "The process was not a series of conflicts but an exchange of ideas developing a rolling consensus."[67] Perhaps the ultimate triumph of Kennedy's system came in the final hours of the crisis. Despite the pressures upon him and the seemingly thorough explorations of the Ex Comm, he still kept his channels open to alternative points of view. This enabled British Ambassador David Ormsby-Gore to suggest that Khrushchev had hard decisions to make and that every additional hour might make it easier for him to climb down gracefully; why not move the U.S. blockade closer to Cuba and give him more time? Kennedy accepted this proposal —and then fought his obdurate Navy to have it implemented. Subsequently, cables—one "hard line" and one "soft line"—were received from Khrushchev. At Robert Kennedy's suggestion, the President responded to the positive overtures of the "soft line" cable. The outcome is well known. But somewhere among the tributes to this victory mention must be made of a managerial system that had played its part to the fullest. During the course of four crises, Kennedy's collegial approach had matured. In the Cuban missile crisis it met the test.

We have not thus far dealt explicitly with the costs of the Kennedy system. Dean Acheson captures one drawback, complaining that the "discussions within the Executive Committee after a couple of sessions seemed to be repetitive, leaderless, and a waste of time."[68] Acheson, accustomed to the single-mindedness of Truman's judicial approach, was uncomfortable in a less structured discussion. (It is possible, too, that Truman's approach gave Acheson more influence as he was one of Truman's most persuasive senior advisers.)

Acheson's complaint, however, illuminates a clear drawback of teamwork: it takes time. Had the President only hours to decide, his system might not have served him so well. Acheson also calls attention to the fact that the process of teamwork is sometimes frustrating. One cost of broad and sustained debate is the wear and tear on team members themselves. The absence of clear, directive leadership also breeds anxiety. One senses this in the various accounts of the participants in the crisis. This is in pointed contrast to the comfortable sense of unanimity and mutual support that emerges from descriptions of the decision-making process that accompanied Truman's involvement in the Korean War. (It might be argued that some measure of anxiety is both legitimate and desirable in a decision of this nature.)

Despite frustrations, the Ex Comm functioned effectively, in large measure because of Kennedy's personal skill in carrying out his role. It is highly significant that Ex Comm's conflict was substantive, not interpersonal. (Imagine the result if Hopkins, Corcoran, Moley, and Hull had been convened for this purpose under FDR's direction!) Clearly Kennedy's choice of men and his day-to-day handling of them laid the foundation for their effectiveness in the crisis.

Another facet of Kennedy's skill, as demonstrated during the crisis, was his self-control. Facing a missile threat of considerable urgency, he exercised discipline over both tendencies for premature action as well as his own preset preferences for an air strike: he charged the Ex Comm with generating new alternatives as well as selecting the best one. Curiously, Kennedy from time to time throughout his career was accused of being overly detached and lacking in conviction. Perhaps what might be weaknesses in some circumstances were precisely what was required to make Kennedy's decision process tick. "A basic check [upon the system]," one participant in the crisis has stated, "was the President's cool, almost detached personality which helped to prevent the growth of emotionalism that could distort perceptions."[69]

When working, Kennedy's decision-making machinery was extraordinarily effective. But the costs of maintenance were high. An interesting illustration of these benefits and the personal costs is suggested by reviewing Kennedy's handling of the unfolding drama in Vietnam. By mid-1963, Kennedy was a very different President with a very different sense of confidence. He was more sure of himself and his team, and more dubious about the wisdom of heavy-handed responses in foreign affairs. Kennedy considered Berlin his biggest problem; Vietnam was a troublesome back-burner issue. But the problem in Southeast Asia refused to go away. As the situation in Saigon deteriorated, it became evident that the Diem regime was in trouble. Kennedy's bureaucracy was divided: the military favored supporting Diem with advisers and weapons, while the civilian intelligence sources reported a steady deterioration of confidence in Diem and subversion in the countryside. Kennedy was uneasy about the use of force on Diem's behalf. Wanting more reliable information, he dispatched McNamara to Saigon on several occasions. He gave encouragement to Roger Hilsman, Director of Intelligence and Research at the State Department, who was a long-time critic of the military's Vietnam estimates.

Signals that a decision point was approaching over the Diem situation, sharpened the bureaucratic strife. Even Kennedy's mastery of the information channels could not altogether offset the in-fighting. When Hilsman submitted a devastating report challenging the military's projections of progress in Vietnam, McNamara confronted him and succeeded in putting the lid on further State Department appraisals of Pentagon statistics.[70]

On another occasion, Kennedy requested Hilsman to compose a cable asking for data. The wording of this request conveyed the President's doubts about the progress of the war. Replies from the field were received. Ambassador Henry Cabot Lodge's assessments were thoroughly pessimistic, although a cable from General Paul Harkins was remarkably upbeat. "In it," recounts a White House reporter, "puzzled White House aides found a reference by Harkins to an outgoing cable of General Maxwell Taylor's [then Chairman of the Joint Chiefs of Staff]."[71] Tracing down the cable to the Pentagon, the aides uncovered a remarkably revealing message from Taylor to Harkins "explaining just how divided the bureaucracy was, what the struggle was about, saying that the Hilsman cable did not reflect what Kennedy wanted, that it was more Hilsmanish than Kennedyish, and then outlining which questions to answer and precisely how to answer them."[72] That Kennedy's aides exposed the caper reflects a strength of the collegial system: an open, inquisitive staff, in touch with the President and his interests, succeeded in this instance in heading off a clear effort to warp the information system. Kennedy, incidentally, summoned Taylor to his office soon thereafter for a private talk.

A major price of the collegial approach is its demands upon the decision makers' energies and attention. These are limited resources, and Kennedy, viewing Berlin as his *big* problem, perhaps did not have a great deal of residual energy to invest in staffing out Vietnam. He tended to it periodically, sending McNamara on fact-finding visits and encouraging opposing viewpoints, such as those of Hilsman and Lodge. (These appear to have been primarily exercises of the left hand, however.) As noted earlier, a shortcoming of the collegial approach is its requirements for direction—and when that is lacking, the system tends to coast. So it was when Kennedy reached his final decision to support a coup against Diem. Kennedy had solicited the views of his top advisers (some of whom were not in Washington at the time). Their unanimous opinion was to support a coup and a cable was sent to Saigon to that effect. "But when the principals gathered in Washington," continues one source, "there were second thoughts among some of them, particularly as each learned that some of the others had misgivings."[73]

Now, when some of his closest officials began reneging on [the] cable, Kennedy blew up. He was furious at some of them for waffling, and furious at [others] for having been so sloppy as [not to have staffed it out], in a rare and very real burst of presidential anger he looked at them and said, the voice very cold, very distant, that there had been some doubt about the cable, that it might have been precipitous. Fortunately, it was not too late to change. "Do you, Mr. Rusk, wish to change?" "No." "Do you, Mr. McNamara, wish to change the cable?" "No." "Do you, General Taylor, wish to change the cable?" "No." "Do you, Mr. McCone, wish to change . . ."[74]

In one sense, the President's anger was justified. But anger directed against backsliding can undermine the integrity of a decision-making system. For reasons of pique, Kennedy shut off dissent about the planned coup against Diem. Perhaps regarding the entire matter as a secondary issue, he simply lacked the energy to roll up his sleeves and plunge himself and his advisers into a full-fledged analysis of the problem. Subsequently, there was abundant debate after the Diems were deposed and the situation worsened in Vietnam. Regrettably, Kennedy did not live long enough to give the matter his full consideration, and his successor would pay the price. Lacking Kennedy's drive for the facts and ability to distance himself and nurture a thoroughgoing discussion, Lyndon Johnson would rely far more on his advisers' judgments and pursue a single-minded course of intervention.

Kennedy's approach worked increasingly well as his term wore on—particularly when applied to policy decisions and when limited to his circle of advisers. He encountered more difficulty, however, in extending his managerial grasp to the

Executive branch. Having whipped the apex of his system into shape, formidable challenges lurked at the base of the federal pyramid. The early crises of his Administration instructed him in the idiosyncrasies of bureaucracy. During the Cuban missile crisis, the weekly routine built into the reporting procedures of the CIA and the Air Force delayed for a week dissemination of the vital information on the missile build-up. Later in that episode, bureaucratic reflex seemed at play in the Air Force's advocacy of a so-called "surgical" air strike option—but with targets included that went far beyond the missile installations themselves. A cleaner surgical strike was in fact possible, but plans for it had to be dragged out of the Air Force. The Navy, too, had stubbornly resisted moving the blockade closer to Cuba. Only a Kennedy confrontation with the Chief of Naval Operations, Admiral George Anderson, had brought compliance. Kennedy recognized that these organizations were attuned to fighting wars rather than to the nuances of nuclear diplomacy. Each service had simply tried to do its part in terms of what it best knew how to do.

"Though [Kennedy] was well aware of the problems within the Executive domain," Schlesinger stated later, "I do not think he had entirely appreciated [their] magnitude."[75] The problems of the Presidency had been growing insidiously since Roosevelt's enlargement of government under the New Deal. Roosevelt believed that he could not fight the Depression through the departments of Agriculture, Labor, Commerce, and the Treasury (or, later, fight the war through State, War, and Navy). He therefore bypassed the traditional structure and resorted instead to the expedient of creating emergency agencies that were set up outside the Civil Service and staffed from top to bottom by men who believed in his policies. This worked well in the 1930s. But Roosevelt left his successors a much bigger government, and in due course, the iron law of organization began to transform what had served as brilliant expedients for FDR into dead weight.

Nowhere was Kennedy's frustration more manifest than in his dealings with the Department of State. His consuming interest in foreign affairs and his avowal to be his own Secretary of State practically guaranteed his early collision with the denizens of Foggy Bottom. "Damn it," Kennedy said once after months of repeated frustration, "Bundy and I get more done in one day than they do in six months at State." "The State Department is a bowl full of jelly," he told a reporter in the summer of 1961. "It's got all those people over there who are constantly smiling; I think we need to smile less and be tougher."[76] State's creaking machinery seemed to have been stuck in reverse for over two decades. Franklin Roosevelt and Cordell Hull had started the Department's descent—Roosevelt because he had bypassed State using special assistants like Hopkins and Welles; Hull because he was not temperamentally able to deal with the subsequent decline in department morale and initiative. Then the McCarthy era took its toll. When Kennedy returned old hands like Harriman and Kennan to office after the Inauguration, they were startled by State's deterioration in the decade since they had been there.

From Kennedy's point of view, State—the most recalcitrant of the bureaucracies he had inherited—moved like a glacier, marking progress, it would seem, to the pace of geologic time. Many of the problems unquestionably stemmed from genuine bureaucratic paralysis. But in addition, the President and his agency were separated by markedly different time frames. Kennedy was a creature of politics. He was attuned to the rapid changes in national and international thinking. Moreover, like many of his predecessors, he had come from Congress, where accomplishment is measured in terms of votes made or bills passed. Kennedy said, "It's a tremendous change to go from being a Senator to being President. In the first months it's very difficult."[77]

Kennedy never really succeeded in managing State, although he sought to penetrate it by reaching down through the hierarchy to lesser levels. He dictated sub-Cabinet appointments, designating an Assistant Secretary, an Undersecretary, and the Ambassador to the United Nations. When these measures failed to secure the desired responsiveness, he and his aides began to deal directly with second- and third-echelon subordinates. In a year-end television interview in 1962, he was asked, "Is it true that during your first year, sir, you would get on the phone personally to the State Department and try to get a response to some inquiry that had been made?" "Yes," Kennedy replied, "I still do that when I can, because I think there is a great tendency in government to have papers stay on desks too long. . . . . After all, the President can't administer a department, but at least he can be a stimulant."[78]

Using his White House staff as emergency repair crews, he sought to keep the departments in order. "[But] with such solid mandates," notes one observer, "the White House staff at times became over-exuberant."[79] After six months, Kennedy was forced to retrench somewhat. "The White House staff," Kennedy directed," "was not to interfere in the operations of departments or agencies."[80] The ruling was apparently triggered by a quiet crisis in the State Department's Inter-American Division. For several months the post of Assistant Secretary of State for Inter-American Affairs lay vacant, creating a power vacuum into which the President's staff quickly moved. This aroused bitter resentment among State Department career men.

Kennedy's failure with State was largely a failure of his managerial approach. His efficacy within his immediate circle of advisers depended on fluid assignments, an open exchange of conflicting points of view, and lastly, his skill at smoothing over potentially destructive rifts and instilling a sense of teamwork among colleagues. The first two elements of his style could be—and were—thrust upon the bureaucracy; but the latter, owing to the limits of the President's personal reach, could never be. Kennedy's violation of the chain of command

and encouragement of deviant outlooks within the agencies had the effect of inspiring power plays and bureaucratic politics, which, all in all, probably undermined Administration control. Inadvertently, Kennedy had installed a competitive approach. The result was that civil servants within all levels of the bureaucracy now found it advantageous to scramble for the President's ear. One high-level civil servant, who worked under both Kennedy and Johnson, said:

> There was a lot of strife under Kennedy, and a lot of personality conflicts too. Still, a person working in the Executive Branch could write a paper and be sure he could get it read by one of Kennedy's Special Assistants. There was a lot of opportunity for access. His aides didn't all think the same either, if you couldn't get to one, you could usually persuade another to give you a hearing. If your ideas were good, so much the better; and if your proposals were lousy and people didn't like it, in contrast to the later Johnson years, you didn't get punished. They didn't blackball you.[81]

Here was the two-edged impact of Kennedy's managerial approach. Unquestionably, it opened up the pores of agencies and gave some civil servants a sense of excitement and opportunity. But its effect on orderly bureaucratic machinery was disruptive. Hindsight suggests that Kennedy's approach was not successful with State, that he left it weakened and as unresponsive as it was before. But bound as he was to one approach, he remained committed to reaching out and taking the initiative. "My experience in government," he once said, "is that when things are noncontroversial, beautifully coordinated and all the rest, it must be that not much is going on."[82] One of his most successful burrowing tactics was to ask the departments to supply his office with biweekly reports on current problems and impending decisions. In this way he sought to inject himself into problems before they crystallized and to reinforce his policy that he was available to officials several rungs down. Prime Minister Harold Wilson once spoke of Kennedy's tactics of getting in on emerging questions by, "holding meetings of all relevant ministers at an early stage before the problem gets out of hand; that's one of the techniques the world owes to Kennedy."[83]

Interestingly, Kennedy's most lasting impact upon the bureaucracy occurred not where he had most fully exploited his own techniques but rather where he had adopted a wholly different formalistic approach. In dealing with the Department of Defense he delegated wholeheartedly to McNamara, much as Eisenhower might have done. McNamara, in turn, relied on procedures and a new control system, called Planned Programmed Budgeting, to enforce the Administration's priorities. The Kennedy-McNamara success was a significant accomplishment. The Defense Department had already thwarted, exposed, and broken a succession of able men. "This place is a jungle, a jungle," McNamara cried in his first weeks.[84] But McNamara believed that the way to manage the Pentagon was through a new theory of control, "conceiving his responsibilities," writes Schlesinger, "not as that of a judge, reviewing and reconciling recommendations made to him by the services, but of an executive, aggressively questioning, goading, demanding and leading."[85] McNamara's problems at first seemed insurmountable—especially as the new Administration introduced added tension in the defense establishment by shifting its national defense strategy toward a balanced posture of nuclear and conventional forces. Eisenhower had geared the Pentagon to an all-out nuclear response. But even on this front, the Kennedy Administration feared the nation was grievously exposed. Missile development lagged, and the major strike force depended upon SAC bombers, which were highly vulnerable if the Russians attacked first. On the conventional side, only eleven out of the fourteen army divisions were ready for combat. If, in these circumstances, even ten thousand men were sent to Berlin or Southeast Asia, it would deplete Kennedy's strategic reserve.

Jungle training was nonexistent, tactical air power was weak, and over three-quarters of the Air Force bombers were 1955 planes with no all-weather capability. This was hardly reassuring, given the possibility that the Air Force might be called to provide air support in a monsoon-plagued nation like Laos.

For McNamara, the problem wasn't simply one of grabbing the reins. Changing defense requirements meant a major shift in the allocation of resources and major changes in strategy. Such reforms flew directly in the face of two decades' worth of each-service-gets-its-share defense planning.

McNamara enlisted tough, able assistants. Charles Hitch and Alain Enthoven were recruited from Rand; their techniques of planned-programmed-budgeting launched what has since been called the McNamara revolution. Such reforms encountered vigorous opposition. The services had abundant contacts in Congress and were quick to enlist them to the cause. Leaks were numerous, and although rarely traceable, had a persistent tendency to cast the military in the best light.

Kennedy relied on subordinates to handle the problems of Defense far more than he did with the problems of State—perhaps because of his confidence in McNamara. Abiding by his principle of "people," he supported McNamara and got very rough with those who thwarted him. He transferred out his first JCS Chairman, General Lyman L. Lemnitzer, and replaced him with more responsive Maxwell Taylor. He refused to re-appoint Admiral Anderson for the customary second year as Chief of Naval Operations. Curtis LeMay was replaced. These actions sent shock waves through the five-sided bastion on the Potomac. The President wanted loyalty and a closing of the Pentagon's back door to Congress. He never got it all, but the transgressions became infrequent and discreet.

Beyond the reaches of the Executive branch, Kennedy had his ups and downs. As a public figure he commanded unparalleled attention from the press. He introduced the live, televised press conference and was generally liked by the news corps. He cared a great deal about his relations with the media, reading a half-dozen newspapers a day and startling columnists from time to time with a personal telephone call made to register his comments. Yet his understated manner and his self-deprecating wit may have detracted from his impact on the media. Kennedy had a keen sense of the public pulse—and he was far more daring than FDR in taking the initiative in shaping public opinion. But unlike FDR, he was no spellbinder. When he held the nation in rapt attention during the peak of the Cuban missile crisis, many felt he missed an opportunity by not exploiting the millions of listeners with a major address on foreign policy. Instead, he delivered a terse message that Khrushchev had agreed to remove the IRBMs. On the other hand, JFK fully recognized the need to educate the public and enlist its support behind his controversial shifts in defense posture and foreign policy. At this, he was strikingly more successful than Truman, for example, who made his decisions and let the chips fall where they may.

Kennedy's greatest impact on the nation—and quite possibly a lasting one—was less by word than by example. The phrasing of his Inaugural may remain with us, but what brought power to these phrases was Kennedy's personal example. His wit, his grace, his integrity, stood him well with his countrymen. In the short space of three years, with the minimum of preaching and emotional appeal, he managed to touch millions of private lives. Among his achievements, he helped the nation see itself with new eyes. He set a new standard of professionalism for the Presidency.

Kennedy's nemesis was Congress. There, the fundamental tenets of his approach were ill fitted to the task at hand. Kennedy, the President who employed detachment to explore alternatives and accommodate conflicting views, never mastered the Hill. Kennedy's understated tone, his reluctance to bully, to buy votes with patronage and favors, to exploit personal weakness and coerce, all diluted his leadership. And perhaps more fundamentally, he didn't want to get his hands dirty in the bargaining. When his minimum wage bill came up for vote in the House, it was defeated by a 186/185 vote margin. Significantly, the reason why the measure was defeated was because ten liberals from the industrial states of the North —ten members who were in favor of the bill—were in Washington that day, even in the Capitol area, but did not come to the floor for the vote. "It was not conspiracy," said a House leader, "it was laziness. Three were even in the House restaurant drinking beer during the vote."[86] The burden of carelessness rested not just upon the Congressmen but upon the Administration. Kennedy's famed attention to detail seems never to have been engaged when it came to twisting arms and hustling Congress.

There were successes like the Trade Bill, which was significant despite serious compromises on the floor. But by and large, Kennedy's legislative leadership was lackluster. Many of his proposals to Congress that were not acted upon—including Medicare, federal aid to education, a Department of Housing and Urban Development, manpower training, and the relief of poverty—laid the groundwork for the Great Society. Ironically, Kennedy's assassination created the national sense of urgency that was lacking during his incumbency. Lyndon Johnson would capitalize upon these currents and transpose the Kennedy proposals into law.

For John Kennedy, two personal concerns were salient: courage and death. Of courage, his record must speak and it will be weighed by history. Of death, Jacqueline Kennedy once observed that "the poignancy of men dying young haunted him."[87] And on Cape Cod, in October 1953, returning from his honeymoon, he read his young wife what he said was his favorite poem. She learned it by heart for him, and he used to have her say it. It was Alan Seeger's "I Have a Rendezvous with Death."[88]

> It may be he shall take my hand
> And lead me into his dark land
> And close my eyes and quench my breath . . .
> But I've a rendezvous with Death
> At midnight in some flaming town,
> When Spring trips north again this year,
> And I to my pledged word am true,
> I shall not fail that rendezvous.

CHAPTER SIX

JOHNSON'S TYRANNY
OF PERSUASION

One day in the fall of 1966, Lyndon Johnson summoned two of his top advisers to the White House. He was in a black mood. The war in Vietnam was going badly; public opinion polls were registering serious disenchantment. As Secretary of Defense Robert F. McNamara and Ambassador W. Averell Harriman entered the Oval Office, Johnson rose and began to pace menacingly. His advisers were uneasy; they knew from past experience that he was tormented by the deteriorating situation, and that one way or another, they would be made to share in his vexation.

Johnson shifted his anger from man to man and hammered away at their vulnerable points. He berated McNamara for his ineffectiveness because he did not get a defense appropriation through Congress and intimated that he himself would probably have to go to the Hill to get it done. Next he challenged Harriman, implying that he was losing his grip on foreign affairs and might not be of use to the Administration in the future.

One could gauge from the tension in the room that Johnson was pushing each man to the brink. McNamara's sense of duty and competence was challenged; Harriman's political judgment was questioned and his continuing influence placed in doubt.

It would be difficult to imagine themes more threatening to the reputations and identities of these two men.

At the core of the process was fear. Lyndon Johnson knew it well. But from the anguish of his own experiences had come the insight that now permitted his mastery of other men. He had discovered early in life that the cornerstone of most men's pride and self-respect is their own self-image. If that self-image is shaken, powerful restorative forces are mobilized. With uncanny accuracy, Johnson had developed an instinct for the essence of other men. Armed with his powerful rhetorical style and forceful presence, he could question, threaten, and push a man dangerously close to that point all men fear—where pride and self-respect vanish. He was aware that the magnification of self-doubt creates a deficit in a man's self-image and he exploited this now in taunting his advisers. He knew from experience that this would drive them to even greater efforts to redeem themselves in his eyes—but more importantly, in their own. Such was the chemistry of human bondage, Johnson style.

Few questions have aroused more speculation than those endeavoring to "explain" Lyndon Johnson. What brought him to the top? What contributed to his problems in the White House? Important clues to this puzzle are scattered along Lyndon Johnson's past. The most important stem from his childhood.

Lyndon Baines Johnson was born on August 27, 1908. From the outset, he was deprived of some of the love and acceptance in infancy that contribute to security in early life. His parents bore bitter burdens: each had sought more from life than it had yielded. By the time of his birth, each was resigned to the corrosive despair of having traveled too far to turn back, yet with painful awareness of dreams unrealized. For each, in his own way, Lyndon became the channel for frustrated hopes.

Political scientist Doris Kearns has written that Sam and Rebekah Johnson were in many respects polar opposites.[1]

Rebekah, accustomed to the niceties of life, had been in her third year of college when her father's fortunes took a sudden and irreversible turn for the worse. Perhaps it was partly out of necessity that she consented to become the wife of Sam Johnson, a rowdy politician from the South Texas hill country. Before the wedding flowers could wilt, the new couple were confronted with harsh realities that neither could wholly accept. Sam found that to provide for his young bride he must give up his first love, politics, and with it his seat in the Texas legislature. Rebekah soon discovered that his boasts of fortunes to be made on speculative deals in cotton were as shallow as the Pedernales in summertime. Sam was—and would remain—essentially penniless. The wedding ring became a link in a chain that bound the town-bred girl to Sam, his politics and coarse manners, and to the primitive two-room cabin in Johnson City.

In his effort to support his wife and son, Sam had to spend a great deal of time away from home. Besides working the hard soil of the farm, he traveled widely to buy and sell cattle and cotton and to see prospective customers about real estate. He found the monetary return minute for the time involved. Lyndon's earliest memories include one occasion when his father was gone and only he and his mother were home. He remembers his mother on a dark night pumping water from the hand pump on the back stairs and crying. Lyndon, as small as he was, reassured her: "I'll take care of you, Mama."[2]

Rebekah may have nurtured a healthy dose of self-pity, but with steely determination she set out to squeeze from her scorched and poverty-worn world an existence that might permit her to mold her son into something neither her husband nor her father had ever been. Her young son was made to know that he must bear her aspirations. The family talked openly of Lyndon becoming "a United States Senator before he was forty."[3] Throughout his first five years, young Lyndon was held fast within his mother's influence. During his father's long absences and repeated setbacks, Rebekah embarked on a "headstart" program designed to take him to the top. By his second birthday, he knew the alphabet, by three, the Mother Goose rhymes plus a repertoire from Tennyson and Longfellow. And from his mother's driven efforts to make him someone great, the young child learned that his role must be to *act* great—to behave in a manner that would fulfill his mother's expectations of him—regardless of the fears and insecurities he might hold within. Thus it was that Lyndon developed and retained through life a sense of being loved not for himself but for his ability to take charge of things and to perform. Herein lay the chemistry of a precise tension which would persist.

Rebekah's prodding, the love she held out for her boy but with strings attached, served to push her son to the edge of performance. Once, for example, Rebekah not only coached her son for a school recitation contest, but as an extra prod to Lyndon, coached a neighboring immigrant boy who had a thick German accent. To Lyndon's deep shame, the German boy won, perhaps driving him to work harder next time. On another occasion, after losing an important debate in high school, so deepfelt was Johnson's self-reproach that he went to the bathroom and vomited.[4] In college his mother would occasionally make a day-long trip by car to coach him for crucial examinations.[5] The push was always there, along with subtle undercurrents: Was he really good enough? Was he really working hard enough to justify her sacrifices? Lady Bird recalls that even as a U.S. Senator, his mother's frequent visits heightened tensions in the home. "She found ways to remind Lyndon of bitter memories in his past," Lady Bird said.[6] These taunted him for his inadequacies.

Children, when tormented by painful factors in their environment, endeavor to control the source of hurt. For Lyndon, the hurt came from seeking love, only to find that the strings attached often placed it beyond his grasp. Psychological survival required that he forever strive to discipline his need for love in order to bear the disappointment of not getting it. It also required that he learn to control his relationship with his mother by staging performances in order to satisfy her aspirations. (By first grade, he was already telling teachers and playmates that one day he would be President of the United States.) The common theme was *control*—over self and others. Control was the mechanism through which he could create a sense of self-sufficiency and repress his painful dependency. These strivings would follow him through adulthood and leave their imprint on his Presidency.

At the age of five, at a time in life when the search for role identification is most determined, young Lyndon executed a complicated shift: his efforts to live up to his mother's ideal remained, but increasingly he sought to emulate his father. Lyndon's broadening orientation was partly the outgrowth of developments in his parents' marriage. After six years of struggle, Rebekah and Sam had reached a denouement: each partner was now resigned to their enormous differences, but little love or communication remained. Sam, after years of trying to "make good" in his wife's terms, largely gave up his search for fortune and with it much of the traveling that had consigned the young boy to his mother's influence. Sam was home more and he invited his coarse and boisterous friends to the house. Soon he resumed his involvement in politics. For Lyndon, the search for a self-image was realized by adopting the mannerisms of his father. "Lyndon was so much like his father," a friend commented once, "that it was humorous to watch. They sort of looked alike, they walked the same, had the same nervous mannerisms, and Lyndon clutched you just like his daddy did when he talked to you."[7]

As Lyndon adopted the outward vestiges of his father, tensions developed between his new-found self and the earlier ideal of his mother. Was it possible to integrate the contradicting attributes of polar opposites into his single mind and body? Lyndon did just that, somehow imprisoning their warring

forces within him. The contradictory images of Sam and Rebekah would surface throughout his career. His relationship
with his mother remained tense. Henceforth, he would perform
to many of her standards—often seemingly overstating his dedication to her. Any rebellion he manifested was expressed in
peripheral ways: an antipathy toward intellectuals (which she
had represented), his refusal to read books (despite childhood
precocity as a reader), the adoption of his father's coarse manners—belching, obscene humor, scratching himself indiscreetly
(behavior which had offended his mother during his childhood).

Ten-year-old Lyndon went campaigning with his father in
1918. He saw how Sam recruited support with vague intima-
tions of patronage, handshaking forays, and oratory filled with
anecdote. In the process, Sam counseled his boy, "If you can't
come into a roomful of people and tell right away who is for
you and who is against you, you have no business in politics."[8]
After the election victory, Sam often brought his son to Austin
and the boy would stand next to his father's desk in the Legislative chamber. Here he learned the ropes, and the legend of
Lyndon Johnson began.

It is said that legends are fact embroidered by fiction. For
Lyndon Johnson, an important discovery was that fiction could
create the fact. As a young child he had been made to value
achievement. But the problem was how to measure it—on his
mother's terms, his father's, or his own? Rebekah measured
success in the hard currency of accomplishment. Sam applied
a more personal gauge, one that would influence Lyndon considerably. Sam had spent a lifetime running one step ahead of
collapsing fortunes; by necessity, he counted his accomplishments in terms of the transient impressions he could make on
other men. His tools were bluster and bluff: with them he
created the dignity that otherwise eluded him. Sam was known
to go to considerable lengths to maintain a false front. For example, an item appeared in the Blanco County newspaper at

his instigation. This exercise in self-aggrandizement featured the Johnsons as among the most "prominent [citizens of] Johnson City . . . [with] . . . one of the largest and best-kept farms in the section."[9] An additional means of padding his image came from his choice of associates. A fellow legislator in the Texas House recalled Sam's escapades with rich lobbyists during legislative sessions. "He seemed thrilled to be in contact with anyone rich."[10] Sam was the master of pyramiding an image on a shoestring. Hyperbole was his estate; with it he could perpetuate his standing—not only among his fellowmen but before the mirror in the morning.

Through the myriad incidents of childhood, young Lyndon could not help but be imbued with these values. Once, as a teen-ager, he drove his father's car off a bridge while drinking. Lyndon subsequently ran away rather than face the consequences. When his father tracked him down by phone, Lyndon did not receive the reproaches he had feared but rather a surprising invitation. Sam had traded in the old car for a brand new one; now he wanted Lyndon to pick it up and drive it home. "There's one other thing I want you to do for me," Sam said. "I want you to drive it around the courthouse square, five times, six times, nice and slow. You see, there's some talk around town this morning that my son's a coward, that he ran away from home. Well, I don't want anyone thinking I produced a yellah son, so I want you to show up here in that car and show everyone how much courage you've really got . . . O.K., son?"[11] The issue, of course, was not one of courage but of saving face. Courage was unnecessary since Lyndon had already been forgiven. Whatever the discrepancy between the boy's own fears and feelings and his parents' expectations, he learned to straddle both. Saving face, creating a fictional form and inflating one's image to fill it, became his parameters of social exchange.

After high school, Lyndon embarked upon an interlude of independence. He hitchhiked to California and back, spent his time in sundry menial jobs by day and drinking and brawling by night. Once, when he came home cut and bleeding, his mother sat on his bed and wept that the son for whom she had sacrificed so much was turning out to be a bum. After three years of this existence, Lyndon had enough. With his parents' help, he was enrolled in the small Texas State Teachers College at San Marcos.

Biographers have taken at face value incidents in Johnson's early manhood that extol his powers of persuasion. For the wary, there remains the question of where the man leaves off and the myth begins. From the outset, Lyndon had an enormous advantage over his peers at San Marcos. He was older, stronger, infinitely more experienced in the ways of the world, and deeply committed to making something of his life. Sam's tutelage had expanded Lyndon's powers of communication, and firsthand exposure to the Texas legislature endowed him with political maturity well beyond his years. From this perspective, it is not surprising that Lyndon Johnson took the sleepy college campus by storm. For a short time, he overawed the president and installed himself as his executive secretary. Soon, however, the president eased him into a less visible position. Simultaneously, Lyndon moved toward domination of campus politics—child's play for a lad who had grown up under the tutelage of his father. But in the retelling of the tales, a legend was in the building. Johnson had learned that people yearn for the extraordinary—and that a facsimile, reasonably presented, will be grasped as the real thing. This lesson would be put to use in Washington.

On November 29, 1931, Lyndon Johnson became the Congressional secretary of a Texas Congressman. From that day forward, he would totally identify with politics. Johnson may have been a new hand in Washington, D.C., but no sooner had the lanky Texan crossed the threshold of the Capitol than he acted like he owned the place. His techniques for instant friendship moved into high gear—handshakes, jokes, first-name intimacy, arms around shoulders and laughter—made him an old-timer with his fellow aides after the first night. Outwardly, Johnson was affable and open, he would lend people the shirt off his back. But privately his calculating ambition was rarely disengaged. "He stuck closely to those who he believed could teach him the Congressional ropes in a hurry."[12] During lunches in the Capitol cafeteria, Johnson always managed to put his hour to double purpose. "When the gang met, Johnson always rushed to the front of the group with his tray, collected his meal on the run, dashed to a big empty table and gulped his food before the others arrived. With his lunch out of the way, he was now free to pump the others about their work."[13] A Congressional press secretary who observed it carefully concluded, "This skinny boy was as green as anybody could be, but within a few months he knew how to operate in Washington better than some who had been here twenty years."[14]

Johnson quickly recognized a need to learn not only from his peers but from his seniors. A key element in his evolving strategy was to adopt "Daddys." He established filial relationships with experienced Congressmen from whom he could learn much and whose successes he wished to emulate. Johnson was adept at identifying with others, adopting their traits and learning their methods. His "Daddy" approach worked, partly because he was skilled at it and partly because his earnestness was flattering to his tutors. Few rejected his apprenticeship. Congressman Sam Rayburn was among the first, and perhaps the most influential, of Johnson's "Daddys."

Johnson's tenure as a Congressional secretary gave him his first real taste for administration. After a year on the job he persuaded his boss that he needed assistance. Two junior aides were recruited. He was a difficult master. He expected his subordinates to work nights and weekends, and he lost his temper frequently. Their fate was similar to that of all who would follow them. Throughout his career, Lyndon Johnson tended to view aides as extensions of himself; he drove them as ruthlessly as he was driven. He won begrudging respect from subordinates but rarely earned their affection.

The legend of Lyndon Johnson was advanced another notch when he learned that his peers had a club—called the "Little Congress." "How was the leadership selected?" he inquired. "Through seniority," was the reply.[15] Lyndon's discerning eye was quick to recognize the shakiness of the command of this near-defunct organization. There was a notable absence of members at meetings and the leadership seemed remote and isolated. For Lyndon Johnson, such sleeping opportunity compelled conquest. Organizing the nonattending members, he simply showed up with his slate on election night and had himself voted into office. "Who's that guy?" the defeated Speaker bellowed. "He comes to one meeting and takes over."[16] In actuality, the contest was a pushover. But it contributed to Johnson's image. The story lent itself to retelling and with it came the speculation that Lyndon Johnson was a man on the move.

After four years as a Congressional secretary, Lyndon Johnson fell from grace. His incursions upon his Congressman's authority had long since violated discretion. Now he was bluntly dismissed. It is not known how Johnson took this setback, but it quickly worked to his advantage. Within a year he returned to Washington—this time as a Congressman.

Johnson campaigned for Congress brazenly designating himself as "FDR's protégé." The voters were impressed and apparently the White House played along. Even after victory, Johnson found he could trade on his contrived status in Washington. While his contact with the President was minimal, innuendo permitted him to impress colleagues and bureaucrats. He cornered a remarkable share of New Deal funds for his district.

In his management of his own staff, Johnson remained as driven as ever. One observer recalls that "he visualized every day as a special crash program."[17] He burned off geysers of energy and revealed a persistent talent for generating ideas that consumed his efforts and his staff's. Once, for example, he sent a personal letter to every graduating high school student in Texas.[18] He was forever setting up filing systems or embarking on emergency projects. But behind the consuming energy were childhood fears: "Every job I've had is bigger than I am," he once confessed to Lady Bird, "and I have to work twice as hard as the next man to do it."[19]

No element of the House is more obdurate than the traditions of seniority. Even Lyndon's drive and impatience could not overcome them. Uncomfortable standing still, he began to seek other outlets after his first term. In 1940 he entered the race for U.S. Senate and was narrowly defeated. Subsequently, he sought a position on the Democratic National Committee and on FDR's White House staff. Again, he was odd man out. His interest in the House rekindled for a time in 1943 when he was named chairman of a Congressional subcommittee investigating naval wartime procurement. He embarked on this assignment with zeal, recruiting the largest subcommittee staff in Congress, and privately conceding his intent to compete with Senator Truman's famous wartime investigations. But the harvest of Johnson's investigation was meager. Fundamentally, he lacked the patience and exactitude for careful investigatory work. His methods of management tended to distract his staff rather than focus them. He had a remarkable ability to memorize material at first hearing, "but unless he had the opportunity to [use it] within a week," said one close friend, "his mind erased it entirely."[20] Thus, while he was capable of commanding detail as a temporary expedient of control, he became quickly bored with it as a steady diet. Here was a foretaste of Johnson's style in the White House.

In 1948 Lyndon Johnson realized his ambition to become a United States Senator. His eighty-seven vote margin out of the half million votes cast underlined the closeness of the race. Accusations were filed against him for buying the election, and in fact, these charges were upheld in the Texas courts. (They were overturned on a technicality by the U.S. Supreme Court.) But for Sam Johnson's boy, the ends justified the means. He entered the Senate like a big winner with no regrets or explanations.

Despite his outward confidence, Johnson remained the same driven man as before. He was unable to enjoy for more than a short time the fruits of his hard-earned success. He seemed never at peace. There were few free evenings at home; at work he was always in motion. "In a car, he gave driving instructions without letup to the person behind the wheel; when he drove, he shouted epithets at other drivers he believed were impeding his speeding progress."[21] Tense living had contributed to chronic kidney ailments and periodic outbreaks of painful skin rashes. Heart attacks, kidney and gallstone operations would plague him in years to come.

Johnson's debut in the Senate was accomplished by several significant refinements of his maturing style. As in the House, he sought control over his environment. Fast-talking the sergeant-at-arms, he swung a four-room office for himself, space that was normally reserved for his seniors. Subsequently, he wedged twenty employees in three of the rooms. Breaking another supposedly firm rule, he wangled four phones and put his employees to work on them immediately, calling the other ninety-five Senators for framed, autographed photographs to hang on his walls. Here was Sam Johnson reincarnate: concerned with appearances and ever-dedicated to projecting a powerful image. Here was a fundamental component of Johnson's style that would accompany him to the White House.

A second feature of Johnson's style became increasingly evident in the Senate. Johnson was a tyrant with subordinates. As in the House, the workload was geared to a fever pitch. Horace Busby, a fellow Texan who worked for Johnson on and off during his career, recalled "that working past midnight was not an unusual experience. At a staff meeting, Johnson told his employees that he expected them to answer six hundred and fifty letters a day, handle five hundred telephone calls, and charm about seventy visitors. Each employee was ordered to keep daily tabs on letters and phone calls answered."[22]

"For a time, Johnson ran his office around the clock on an assembly-line basis. He divided his staff so that at every hour during the twenty-four, typewriters would be pounding and the growing volume of mail answered. At some time during each shift he would come dashing through the office rooms calling out like a cheerleader, "C'mon, let's function . . . let's function."[23] Often it seemed that Johnson's drive for control resulted in over-control. Despite the frenzy, his team often seemed to accomplish less than those of other Senators. Said one experienced observer on Capitol Hill, "Johnson had an unfortunate tendency to waste talent, to assign highly priced and highly educated assistants to menial chores."[24] Nevertheless, Johnson chose to captain a bustling ship, firing broadsides when others might choose rifle shots. His approach to the Great Society and his response in Vietnam would follow this pattern.

In addition to being a stern taskmaster, Johnson was known to line up male employees, criticize their attire, and make suggestions. The girls could also expect his criticism when they were overweight or did not apply sufficient makeup.[25] Not unexpectedly, Johnson's staff remained a chronic problem to him. Turnover was extremely high. He retained lasting relationships with only two aides: Walter Jenkins and Bobby Baker. Both would be lost to him after he left the Senate: Jenkins because he was arrested for homosexual activities and Baker because he was imprisoned for influence peddling.

The third element of Johnson's style that emerged in the Senate was the extensive means he devised for extending influence. Johnson didn't just practice the art of persuasion, he made a science of it. He established an elaborate network of contacts, extending to Congressmen, their staffs, and sundry Capitol Hill employees. He was reputed to know more about what was going on in some offices than the Congressmen themselves. While his fellow Senators were discussing the issues of the day, Johnson was diagramming the Senate power structure. He dichotomized the chamber into "whales" and "minnows" and proceeded to make friends with the "whales." He wanted to know the personality of each of his colleagues—especially their weaknesses, their vulnerabilities, their pride and fears. According to one source, "he [became] a virtual encyclopedia of the fallibility of his fellow legislators."[26]

Men were his books; his knowledge about them became his instruments of control. He even took note of handshakes. "When you extend a handshake to a fellow," he once said, "you can tell from his pulse and evaluate him by the way his hand feels. If it is warm and if he has a firm grasp, then you know he is affectionate and that he is direct. And if he looks you in the eye, you usually know that he is dependable."[27] Senator Barry Goldwater used wrestling terminology to describe Johnson's way of greeting someone. He called it "the 'half Johnson' when he grabbed you by the arm; the 'full Johnson' when he hugged you by the waist and breathed into your mouth."[28]

Johnson's genius was not only in acquiring information but in being able to use it. It was his ability to *combine* a sophisticated intelligence system with persuasive abilities that gave his style real power. He became a master of looking inside other people's skin, seeing the world from their perspective, and persuading them that what he wanted was what they wanted.

Johnson's approach was varied. It could last ten minutes or four hours. It tended to envelop its target. To get what he wanted, he would use supplication, accusation, cajolery, exuberance, scorn, tears, complaint, and the hint of threat. "[His approach] ran the gamut of human emotions. Its velocity was breathtaking, and it was all in one direction. Interjections from the target were rare. Johnson moved in close, his face a scant millimeter from his target, his eyes widening and narrowing, his eyebrows rising and falling."[29] As one victim described it,

"Lyndon got me by the lapels and put his face on top of mine and he talked and talked and talked. I figured I was either getting drowned or joining."[30]

One key to Johnson's persuasiveness came from his ability to know, and his willingness to use, every inch of turf available in human communications. Unspoken rules in our culture prescribe appropriate speaking distances and the propriety of gestures and touch. Johnson violated these rules by pressing his nose to the victim's face, gripping his lapel, grasping his thigh. These encroachments had the effect of embarrassing and distracting the listener.

Within each of us are powerful, near-automatic responses which strive to preserve poise when we are embarrassed. These mechanisms were exploited by Johnson. Struggling to keep one's cool in the face of Johnson's assault was preoccupying in its own right. The simple mechanics of maintaining poise required attention—resisting expressions of panic, stilling a quiver in the lips or a blinking of the eyelid. These become self-conscious concerns when a person comes too close. Nose-to-nose in Johnson's enveloping presence, we find ourselves nodding affirmatively to an argument we have not heard. The nod isn't assent; it is made to buy a little more space and a little less pressure. But this, in turn, becomes his leverage point and a bargain is made before we can recover our composure. Lyndon Johnson's "treatment" is complete.

Johnson, like any good negotiator, understood the value of tension in forging agreements. He could hone the drama to a keen edge. And for many men, that was convincing enough. High drama is rare in most lives. Perhaps some dared not ruin such drama by refusing to cooperate.

A combination of circumstances catapulted Johnson into the majority leadership of the Senate in 1956. Despite his newfound power, he remained notably quiet in floor debate and assumed a low profile on most issues. Neither in the House nor in the Senate had his name been associated with major initiatives or significant bills. From his standpoint, involvement in any cause at its inception was like shooting craps; he disliked being drawn into circumstances without first knowing the odds. Perhaps this was another manifestation of his striving for control, for inexorably, Johnson gravitated toward safer battles on his own ground. It was in the confines of the cloakroom that he gained his reputation. There he could control the outcome.

As Majority Leader, Johnson employed a package of techniques in moving bills through the Senate. On any major piece of legislation, he rarely made a commitment as to what would pass. After making a near-mathematical determination of who was for and who against a bill, he began to formulate a winning compromise. At this point, he would start rounding up votes and move quickly toward passage with the minimum of debate.

Johnson carried this approach to the White House where it worked far less effectively. As Majority Leader, he had acted as a broker—working in secrecy and seeking the "compromise" package. In the Presidency, this same formula would not do. An American public, in search of leadership, regarded wheeling and dealing as below the Presidency. Aggravating his problems, long years in the legislative halls had distorted his sense of truth. In some ways, Congress has designed a system to deceive the public: There is an image to be presented back home. Johnson was a master of that image. But the spotlight on the White House was far more intense than the more permissive atmosphere of the cloakroom.

On November 23, 1963, after the tragedy in Dallas, Lyndon Johnson became President of the United States. In the turmoil immediately following Kennedy's assassination, it was difficult to discern how Johnson's approach to the White House would differ from his predecessor's. Gradually, one distinction became clear. Johnson sought to fashion his Presidency after the model of Franklin Roosevelt. He had long admired Roosevelt's ways. "Roosevelt was Johnson's idol," said one observer. "He studied with fascination how FDR played off subordinates, one against the other."[31]

At first glance, Johnson's aspirations to emulate Roosevelt seemed natural. Surely Johnson, the master negotiator, would excel in a bargaining system. But problems arose because Johnson lacked FDR's optimism and imperturbable sense of security. Such traits are necessary to ride out the tempests that the bargaining approach sets in motion.

There is an important difference between intervening in outside situations (as a neutral third party) and managing the day-to-day squabbles within one's own staff. Johnson thrived on playing the mediator in deadlocked disputes. Success in this role continued to bring him acclaim. During the national railroad strike of 1964, Johnson intervened with stunning success. But when dealing with problems within his own administrative family, his tolerance for conflict was very low. Whereas Roosevelt thrived on the pulls and tugs of competing positions, Johnson sought consistent advice and was uncomfortable amidst the play of ideas. Johnson not only disliked being exposed to conflicting *ideas* but generally sought to repress conflict among his staff. Interestingly, once while a Congressman, his staff's rivalry reached disruptive proportions; his subsequent wrath ensured that staff quarrels would never again be open affairs. Johnson's expectation, as a legislator, and later as President, continued to prescribe that grumbling about others be kept to oneself.

Johnson's behavior in the White House provides a fascinating insight into the ways in which a man's personality and management approach are interwoven. We see Lyndon Johnson at the outset of his Presidency, striving to adopt Roosevelt's style just as in earlier years he had adopted the techniques of his Congressional "Daddys." But fundamentally, FDR's style didn't suit him. Johnson could evaluate alternatives once they were presented to him, but he was not adept at creating his own or drawing ideas from a barrage of conflicting opinion.

Gradually, Johnson recognized his need for a system that distilled information down into a form that he could use. His earlier managerial approach from the Senate days was dusted off: emphasis was placed on papers arriving on time and reports being made, on making terse telephone calls and answering mail with increased efficiency. As the system evolved, it increasingly took on a *formalistic* character. Like Eisenhower and Truman, LBJ sought to preside at the apex of his information system. He manned the pyramid below with the largest White House staff in history: at the first level down were Johnson's ten or so Special Assistants; reporting to them were another thirty White House aides.[32] Johnson did not let his team function with anything like the open-door policy of Kennedy or of FDR, whose top aides could walk in at will. Marvin Watson, Johnson's Appointments Secretary, imposed a far more comprehensive grip on Johnson's calendar than O'Donnell had done with Kennedy's. Watson's surly gatekeeping brought him into serious conflict with Bill Moyers and McGeorge Bundy during the course of his service. This was exacerbated by LBJ's tendency to periodically require even his closest aides to go through Watson as a kind of purgative discipline. Said one close observer, "It is undeniable that Watson has exercised virtually unlimited authority over many outstanding people. . . . He is regarded by many as a kind of small-bore Joe McCarthy working within the White House."[33]

Consistent with a formalistic approach, Johnson came to want his written communications short and to the point. Subtlety eluded him; he did best with one-dimensional ideas. "He liked recommendations to be on memos rather than in person," recalled one aide, Lee C. White: "There were a whole series of them in which he checked the 'disapproved' box."[34] He insisted that the flood of briefing materials reaching him be boiled down. A paragraph, a page—he saw little need for routine reports to run longer. A fundamental handicap for Johnson was that he disliked reading. He admitted at one time that "he had not read six books through since college."[35] Unfortunately, a President has little recourse but to read, and in vast amounts, if he is to stay on top of his job. With all its drawbacks, written communication is vastly more efficient than verbal briefings for keeping the President up to date on most matters. Yet Johnson found his reading load one of the most unpleasant aspects of the Presidency—and the system had to accommodate to his preferences.

In many other respects, Johnson's drive for control remained much the same as it had in the Senate. At times he seemed preoccupied with the *appearances* of command. Historian Eric F. Goldman, Special Consultant to the President, recalls:

[For] long furious hours the President [devoted] himself . . . to every thing in the White House, minuscule as well as monumental in significance. Lyndon Johnson went over guest lists for social functions name by name; he checked the equipment for White House cars; he would go walking around the building poking into things. . . . Day and night, the President intervened in matters big and small that were supposedly in the hands of subordinates.[36]

The consequences of Johnson's intrusions into detail were mixed. At times his minute inquiries gave a healthy jolt to the system. More typically, they sent a shock wave through the hierarchy but little more. To some observers, these forays seemed wasteful expenditures of the President's time. Bill Moyers echoed this theme in an interview following his departure from Johnson's staff, "I think Presidents make a mistake," he said, "if they try to manage too comprehensively the intricate details of government. . . . And to some extent, LBJ was tempted in this direction. . . . He wanted to know as much as he could about what was going on . . . and he became so involved in the operations of [some things] that he usurped the managerial responsibilities of [his subordinates]."[37] The hitch, for Lyndon Johnson, was that he equated the exercise of management with the exercise of persuasion; he was managing for appearance' sake rather than for the decisions.

A central weakness of Johnson's system stemmed from his methods of managing men. The core of the problem was Johnson himself: his personality repeatedly overshadowed his management system. While Johnson gravitated toward a more-or-less orderly formalistic type managerial system, his personal style frequently disrupted his staff and the system he sought to institute.

Johnson's White House, like Roosevelt's, was one in which a subordinate's rewards were few and far between. The free and easy exchange and liberal praise of the Kennedy era were gone. Johnson insisted "on being credited with having spawned every idea which came out of his White House."[38] He disliked having his aides receive too much publicity and his punishment for such transgressions was prompt. When a series of stories appeared describing Jack Valenti as the closest aide to Johnson, Valenti suddenly found himself physically moved a notch away from his boss and required to go through Appointments Secretary Watson. This was known in Johnson staff parlance as "the freeze-out"—a term applied to LBJ's coldly distancing himself from a transgressor. The consequence of "the freeze-out" was that it constantly changed the pecking order; it also made it tempting to generate rumors that might chill a competitor's relations with the boss.

Johnson demanded loyalty. Nothing less than total loyalty would suffice, and his ability to keep tabs on the outside activities of his aides ensured that he got it. Once when considering an appointment, the question of what the President really meant by "loyalty" came up. Johnson rose to the occasion with a characteristically vivid reply. "I don't want loyalty, I want *loyalty*," he said. "I want him to kiss my ass in Macy's window at high noon and tell me it smells like roses. I want his pecker in my pocket."[39]

Johnson's loyalty downward hardly commended itself as compensation. His quickness to disassociate himself from Bobby Baker and Walter Jenkins—though wholly justifiable in political terms—was noted with interest by fellow subordinates.

Columnist Patrick Anderson has applied the term "Caligula's Court" to Johnson's unusual ways of managing his staff.[40] Staff turnover was high. Of the twelve top aides appointed after his election in 1964, only two remained when he left office four years later. Johnson's carbide-tipped personality simply ground away his advisers. First the Kennedy crew fled; then his own team turned over—George Reedy, Jack Valenti, Horace Busby, and Bill Moyers came and went. The staff that remained at the end had a different cast: they were Johnson's operatives; the original team had been more truly "advisers." A case in point is the contrast between Bill Moyers and Joe Califano. Moyers had worked for Johnson in the Senate and had the reputation of "going to the mat" with LBJ over important issues of disagreement. Moyers' gift in addition to his independence (which in itself was a rare attribute on Johnson's staff) was in his understanding of the bureaucracy. "It has a life of its own," he once said. "It can be a President's worst enemy unless he can find a means to stamp his own ideas and beliefs on it."[41] Moyers recognized that the bureaucracy was not run by Cabinet officials but by Assistant Secretaries and top level bureaucrats who make day-to-day decisions. His skill in dealing with these men paid dividends in implementing the Great Society programs. One career official who has dealt with Presidential assistants since the Eisenhower Administration says, "I never knew anyone else in the White House like Moyers. You find that most of the presidential expediters, men like Adams and O'Donnell, get in the habit of running over people. 'I'm the President's man,' they say. 'Do what I tell you.' Moyers was the very opposite of that. He was always receptive, he always made time to discuss an issue, and he wanted to involve himself in issues that other White House people weren't interested in."[42]

Moyers wanted Bundy's job when the latter resigned early in 1966, but Johnson gave it to Walt Rostow. Soon after, Moyers was shifted to become Johnson's Press Secretary, a post from which he would ultimately resign to return to private life. Moyers' relationship with Johnson was generally on the decline after Rostow's appointment. What prompted the change? Even Moyers himself seemed puzzled. Had he truly fallen from favor or had he merely borne the brunt of the periodic ritual of authority?

In contrast to Moyers, Califano was an impatient expediter of his boss's will. As Johnson became more unreachable during the war years, Cabinet members were increasingly told to "talk to Joe." This bred resentment and enemies. Some called Califano the "hatchet man." Yet from another point of view, Califano was well suited to Johnson's evolving system. As his White House became more like Eisenhower's, the "king" of the staff pyramid by necessity had to be more like Sherman Adams. On the surface, at least, there was an internal consistency; below the surface there was more turmoil than Eisenhower saw in a lifetime.

The heat in Johnson's system was of his own making. The West Wing pressure cooker built up steam by depriving aides of their private lives and by keeping them on call around the clock. When Jack Valenti took a late flight to New York City for a Broadway play and returned that same evening, Johnson coldly ignored him for a month. Long before, a friend had observed that, "Lyndon has a clock inside him with an alarm that tells him at least once an hour to chew somebody out."[43] One time Johnson's voice carried down the corridors of the White House as he bellowed, "I thought I told you, Jack, to fix this f—ing door-knob!"[44] When Budget Bureau Director Kermit Gordon took his first evening off after weeks of sixteen-hour days to go to a concert, Johnson by chance happened to try to phone him. The following morning when he came to a White House meeting, Johnson sprinkled him with sarcasm. "Well, playboy," he snarled, "did you have a good time?"[45] To McGeorge Bundy who innocently walked into the Cabinet room while Johnson was talking with Ambassador Henry Cabot

Lodge, he snapped, "Goddamit, Bundy! I've told you that when I want you, I'll call you."[46] Bundy departed like a rejected suitor.

For Lyndon Johnson, his staff was an intimate thing. It was truly a part of his family and he projected upon it many of the ambivalences from his past. His rage and subsequent efforts to repair damaged feelings seemed, at times, almost an enactment of childhood fantasies. Occasionally, his dependencies from that period were also visible. For example, one night after a series of long meetings, Johnson asked his aide Horace Busby to sit with him upstairs while he had his regular nightly massage —and then to stay with him until he fell asleep. There might be something he would want to say, and Busby would be there to receive it. After the lights went out, Busby waited in the dark for the President to doze off. Thinking after a half hour that he had fallen asleep, he tiptoed toward the door.

"Buz," the voice came from the darkness. "Buz, is that you?" Busby said yes, it was him.

"Buz, I'm not asleep yet." And Busby returned to his chair. More minutes passed in the early morning. Now certain that he was listening to the rhythmic breathing of deep sleep, again Busby gently moved out of his chair toward the door.

"Buz, are you still there?" This time, embarrassed at his second miscalculation, Busby said yes, he was still there and he was just moving over to the window to adjust the curtain. It was fully an hour later before Busby finally left the sleeping President to return to his own quarters.[47]

Johnson's manner injured his subordinates' pride and self-respect and aroused deep-felt anger. More than a few Johnson aides, once free of his grasp, struck back with critical memories. Reedy, Goodwin, Moyers are among these. Johnson expressed dismay at these "betrayals"; aides close to the President reported that he was frequently surprised and hurt.

Johnson likes to compare himself to Franklin Roosevelt, but as regards his staff, he compares rather poorly. Roosevelt attracted men who were prepared, literally, to die for him. Several did. Johnson did not inspire that degree of dedication. Walter Jenkins' resignation was imperative when he was arrested on a morals charge in October 1964. But Reedy, Moyers, Valenti, Busby, and Jacobsen all left the White House because they had decided there were better things to do than work for Lyndon Johnson, even if he was President of the United States.[48]

An important difference between the Kennedy and Johnson staff operations was in their dealings with the rest of the Federal Government. Where President Kennedy tended to use his staff against the bureaucracy, President Johnson put greater store in the wisdom and experience of his Cabinet officers and career government workers.

Johnson's distance from the bureaucracy insulated it from the vicissitudes of his temperament. Although his successes there were far from even, he had a significant advantage over Kennedy. As a long-time Congressman, he had learned the ropes of how to get things done through the agencies. Moreover, Johnson was, in a certain sense, an organization man. He scorned Kennedy's penchant for probing deeply into the bureaucracy and short-circuiting command. "I talk to Dean Rusk, not to some fifth-desk man down the line," he once said.[49]

Johnson was resourceful in managing the Executive bureaucracies. He worked through the system, yet was aggressive, and at times creative, in his approach. He used his White House staff extensively to prod the agencies and to follow up on their promised actions. In addition, he gave his Cabinet officers virtually unlimited authority to carry out Executive-branch reorganizations; this technique permitted him to shake up the system and to make it more responsive to his leadership. Johnson was aware that an organizational face-lift can affect the sentiments within. As he embarked on the novel programs of the Great Society, he was determined to have an independent agency run them. "The best way to kill a new idea is to put it in an old-line agency," he commented one day.[50] Here were glimpses of FDR. From this line of reasoning came the Office of Economic Opportunity (OEO). Yet unlike FDR, Johnson was not one to countenance widespread strife in his Executive family. When OEO came under vicious bureaucratic fire from Labor, Agriculture, and HEW (with each arguing that the new programs should be handled under its department), the President played the peacemaker. The Job Corps was retained within OEO along with the radical concepts for Community Action Programs; Neighborhood Youth Corps remained in Labor; Institutional Vocational Education stayed in HEW. For many, the result seemed the archetypal mishmash of a Washington compromise. Yet Johnson's willingness to horse trade gave him leverage. Each agency knew that the status quo was contingent on results; their claim to future funds and programs depended on performance.

Gradually, the distractions of the war diffused LBJ's direction of the Great Society. He saw fewer officials and was frequently out of touch with the domestic effort. Charges of inefficiency and lack of responsiveness were commonplace. Many of the novel programs were encountering snags and the General Accounting Office was uncovering waste, extravagance, and fraud. Accompanying these problems was a gradual demoralization of the domestic agencies. As the war progressed, budgets grew tighter. The President's public and Congressional support plummeted. On every front the Administration grew less willing to take risks. As if to compensate for the dissent, the White House insisted on an unnatural degree of interagency solidarity. Friction was thus eliminated by decree—and with it some of the creativity that interagency competition had sparked. One observer said:

Johnson never ordered that internal debate be halted. . . . Probably he was truly irritated at the suggestion that creativity had diminished. But because the Presidency is a very personal thing, LBJ's strong will permeated the government. The message which came through to all departments was that one man—the President, Lyndon Johnson—was to stand above all others on the landscape. He was to be the voice. Original thought—that which survived—was not to be aired until the President chose. Lassitude was inevitable under such a system.[51]

For Lyndon Johnson, the eighteen acres on Pennsylvania Avenue may have come to seem in many ways like an island in a foreign land. There remained, however, one bridge to familiar territory—the link between the Executive and Congress. Here the contrast of approaches between Kennedy and himself were encouragingly to his credit. Dignity and aloofness might have added to Kennedy's image as a national leader; but these attributes had worked to his disadvantage on the Hill. Kennedy may have dutifully followed the progress of his bills on the Hill, but fundamentally he was unwilling to get in and scrap, to beg and to threaten, to get his hands dirty.

It is doubtful, however, that national grief over Kennedy's death or growing public acceptance of the New Frontier measures—such as Medicare and Aid to Education—would have guaranteed passage automatically. Johnson got them through and much more. From the outset, he sought to gain the upper hand. His opening move as President was to demand that the Senate-House Conference Committee stay in session through Christmas if necessary until the Administration's bill authorizing a wheat sale to Russia had passed. In classic form, Johnson had staged a show of strength on a near-sure bet. But in the practice of power, symbolism means a lot. Congress awakened to the new year and the new master. The message was clear: the President is prepared to get tough. Over the succeeding years, until the attrition brought about by Vietnam destroyed his consensus, Lyndon Johnson proved deserving of his legend. Reasoning together in a nose-to-nose chat with a Senator in the Oval Office, rigging Congressional committees to get the Great Society legislation through, resorting to naked power on Medicare, calling in IOU's on the Voting Rights

Bill—this was Lyndon Johnson in full form. His style fit the task and he excelled. At the heart of his success was the close attention to people and particulars that had distinguished his tenure as Senate Majority Leader. Some nights he got but a few scattered hours' sleep, pacing the West Wing, calling up key Senators in the middle of the night, demanding last-minute body counts, shoring up slipping support with phone calls and bargains and hints of retaliation. As in the Senate days, "he seemed to know where every wire of power ran, whose influence was waxing and waning, the rules and habits of committees, what each had done three years before and wanted to do next year, and the skeletons and hopes in scores of closets."[52] And on a night off, it was still on his mind. FDR might chat with sophisticated friends, Truman might play poker and Ike his bridge, Kennedy might choose a lively party, but Lyndon Johnson liked to talk politics and his evening friends came from the Hill.

Ironically, the problems that came to haunt Lyndon Johnson derived in no small measure from his success. While he filled a fat logbook and realized the legislative framework of his dreams for a Great Society, the legislation did not take root in the country at large. He could not instill his aspirations in the people, he did not talk their language and while he felt secure in the legislative world, he lost touch in an important way with the nation. "I'm not sure whether I can lead this country and keep it together with my background," he once said.[53] Indeed, this was the central challenge of his Administration—and he could not overcome it.

Philip Geyelin, in his perceptive book of mid-1966, has said of President Johnson:

. . . by political background, by temperament, by personal preference he was the riverboat man . . . a swashbuckling master of the political midstream—but only in the crowded, well-traveled familiar inland waterways of domestic politics. He had no taste and scant preparation for the deep waters of foreign policy, for the sudden storms and unpredictable winds that can becalm or batter or blow off course the ocean-going man.

He was king of the river and a stranger to the open sea.[54]

Johnson stumbled through a series of crises in foreign policy. When bloody rioting over issues of sovereignty erupted in the Panama Canal Zone and demands were made that the U.S. end its sixty-two-year-old treaty arrangements for U.S. operation of the canal, Johnson reflexively adopted a hard line. While there were sound policy reasons why the U.S. might not want to relinquish its control of the canal, the U.S. position became overstated when Johnson's prestige became engaged. Many felt that the United States became needlessly involved in a hassle over language in framing a proposed mediation agenda. While the situation was to take an astonishing turn for the better before the year was out, the crisis did little for the Administration's standing in Latin America. "Criticism of [Johnson's] performance boiled down to the charge that he should have been bigger about it."[55] Was it really necessary for the United States to bully such a little country on minor points? From Johnson's standpoint, the answer was yes: "They were killing people," he told a reporter, "and some thought we should write a new treaty right off, or at least agree to do it. But you can't say, 'I'll give you a blank check' when there is a pistol pointed at your head."[56]

The Dominican intervention brought a variation on the same theme, but its consequences were far more portentous. When the Dominican Republic erupted in revolt in April 1965, the White House received a cable from the Ambassador in Santo Domingo, requesting that U.S. Marines be landed to save American lives. For Johnson and his advisers, there were two threats: first, danger to American lives, and second, the possibility of a Castro-type takeover. While the likelihood of either was uncertain, both were unacceptable. Thus the U.S. intervened.

Throughout the Dominican crisis, the President's moves were impelled by events; he was forced to act without his trusty consensus firmly in hand. The irony was that Johnson probably had it with him all the time. But when criticism appeared in the press, questioning the commitment of 31,000 Marines, Johnson could not, as Truman did, hold his peace. Instead, he lashed out at his critics in an intemperate display of ridicule and self-justification. He compared the circumstances there to the Alamo.[57] Before the week was through, he had added another imaginary scene, which he described to a news conference: "Some fifteen hundred innocent people were murdered and shot, and their heads cut off, and . . . as we talked to our ambassador to confirm the horror and tragedy and the unbelievable fact that they were firing on Americans and the American embassy, he was talking to us from under his desk while bullets were going through his windows, and had a thousand American men, women, and children assembled in the hotel who were pleading with their President for help to preserve their lives."[58] In fact, the Ambassador was stunned when he heard of Johnson's description and termed the story a fabrication when haled before the Senate Foreign Relations Committee. Before the episode would drift into oblivion, Johnson would issue several more clarifications—and contradictions. Johnson emerged from the episode with a tarnished image. His credibility gap was widened and his reputation was now that of a fast-shooting commander in chief who manufactured reasons to suit his actions. This would harm him in the major undertaking of his Administration—the waging of war in Vietnam.

Kennedy had periodically expressed nagging doubts about Vietnam. Was it worth doing? He had feared sending in combat troops—although the number of American advisers there had reached 16,900 by the time of his death. "But could it be done?" he asked repeatedly, "if the French couldn't do it with 300,000 men, how could we?"[59] In the last weeks of his life he talked with some aides, among them Kenny O'Donnell, about trying to keep the lid on until the 1964 election and then trying to negotiate his way out. He had spoken in a similar vein to Senator Mike Mansfield.[60] But while his doubts may have been growing, his actions and public pronouncements did not reflect this. Thus, he passed to his successor the momentum of American involvement, along with the brilliant, activist can-do Kennedy team, a team which under Kennedy had been tempered by his skepticism and knowledge of their foibles but which now found itself harnessed to a classic can-do President.

Johnson inherited the Kennedy people, but although they were the same men, they were used in a strikingly different way. Kennedy, ever alert to the dangers of distortion, deliberately drew upon the knowledge of outsiders; he read field reports himself and confronted his senior people with the opposing views of younger aides who were encouraged to challenge existing assumptions. Kennedy did not view dissent as a personal challenge. Even as a Presidential candidate, he had sat among his aides as they discussed the issues. All of them were equals. And with his sensitivity to personalities, he knew the players and their weaknesses: McNamara, a man of great loyalty, brilliance and force, but at times prone toward single-mindedness; Bundy, superb analyst, but at times arrogant and unwilling to admit a mistake; Rusk, a loyal, thoughtful man, but apt to conceal his inner doubts and go along with the majority.

Johnson's style was different, very different, and Vietnam would reveal its most serious shortcomings. "From the start, there was a different atmosphere," says one observer, "more constrained, less free and more fearful."[61] Kennedy liked the press and read avidly; Johnson viewed the press darkly, disliked reading, and followed only favorable commentators. Johnson distrusted younger men, feeling that they were too inexperienced. He would not reach down to them in the departments; thus he deprived himself of their questions, which he lacked the inclination to ask.

Johnson's style had a great impact in shaping Vietnam policy: on the one hand was his desire to call all the shots himself, his almost neurotic desire for secrecy, his tremendous intensity and drive for achievement. On the other hand an immensely complex and ambiguous war begged for careful analysis and a thorough identification of all the options. The deliberations on Vietnam would suffer from the discrepancy between the President's ways of doing things and the requirements of the situation. Policies would be set by a very few men, Kennedy's men, to be sure, but somehow different under new leadership. And while Johnson tended to deprecate his advisers privately, he tended to exaggerate their strengths publicly and was perhaps far more dependent upon them than Kennedy had been. To Johnson, Bundy was not just an instrument of analysis but a small-gauge Socrates; McNamara was not just a forceful manager with a steel-trap mind, but a man of broad judgment and wisdom; Rusk was likewise embraced as a wise, almost omniscient Secretary of State.

In the early months of 1964, a subtle change began to take place. The change was the blend of different styles and different circumstances. Vietnam gradually became a more sensitive, more delicate subject, and the principals became more guarded in discussing it. David Halberstam writes in *The Best and the Brightest* that Chester Cooper, a CIA analyst extremely knowledgeable about Indochina, found it more and more difficult to reach McGeorge Bundy. "As the questions became graver and the failures more apparent," Halberstam continues, "Cooper began to write memos to his boss expressing doubts about the situation in Vietnam. But he soon found that the subject was so delicate that it was better to write them by hand so that Bundy, reading them, would know not even a secretary had seen these words and these thoughts."[62] Here, perhaps, was a reflection of Johnson's stress on secrecy. In a similar vein, the private papers of McNamara's assistant, John McNaughton, contain memos to McNamara questioning troop and bombing commitments and supporting his arguments with statistics. The memos were so closely held that only McNamara and McNaughton had seen them. In all public documents, on the other hand, McNaughton had stood as the undoubting agent of statistics that supported the war, ostensibly devoid of blood and heart.[63]

An effective managerial system must remain open to outside information. Johnson's system failed this requirement not simply because his style was different from Kennedy's but because his own personal characteristics corrupted the system he devised. Kennedy's detachment permitted him to collect information from every quarter without prejudice to the purveyors of bad tidings. Johnson, in contrast, conceived of "team spirit" as a contagion of unanimity and showed a tendency to slap down those who sang out of tune. CIA Chief John McCone was the first to exit; although more hawkish than Johnson, McCone had insisted too often on telling the President the blunt truth. The Commandant of the Marine Corps, General Shoup, survived longer, but Shoup recalls that on one occasion when he delivered a pessimistic report to the NSC, Johnson, not liking what he heard, started to interrupt with, "Speak up, speak up." The General turned a steely gaze on Johnson and not raising his voice said, "Everyone in this room can hear me and so can you."[64] Yet in time, Johnson's pressures were felt and "the straight information" began to have a bend in it. A focal point was Bundy, whose day-to-day encounters with Johnson perhaps heightened his sensitivity to his boss's needs. First Harriman and Hilsman were squeezed out; Bundy no longer encouraged their access to the President or shared his doubts with them. Hilsman's presence had been crucial; because of his place within the pessimistic group, he linked the younger, less important analysts in the field with the top. Undersecretary of State George Ball found that memos to Bundy expressing doubts on the progress of the war weren't getting through to the President. Ultimately he found a channel through Bill Moyers, but that, too, was closed when Moyers left. Vice President Humphrey also felt the not-too-subtle pressures of censure in his last-ditch attempts to prevent the bombing of North Vietnam. Johnson received Humphrey's objections with particular coldness. "Then," according to Townsend Hoopes, former Undersecretary of the Air Force, "[Humphrey] was banished from the inner councils for some months thereafter, until he decided to 'get back on the team.' "[65]

Perhaps the most thorough analysis of the Johnson Administration's Vietnam War decisions is contained in the Department of Defense's study known as the Pentagon Papers. In restrained but unambiguous terms, the historians and political analysts who prepared this study call attention time and again to the poor quality of the decision-making procedures used by the policy makers who met regularly with President Johnson. They emphasize in particular the group's failure to canvass the full range of alternatives and their superficial assessment of the pros and cons of the optimistic military recommendations. Neil Sheehan in *The New York Times* book *The Pentagon Papers* adds, "The study indicates no effort on the part of the President and his most trusted advisers to reshape their policy along the lines of . . . [the] analysis."[66] A case in point is cited by political scientist Irving Janis who notes, "In the fall of 1964, . . . the high hopes of President Johnson and his principal advisers that Operation Rolling Thunder [massive bombing of the North] would break the will of North Vietnam were evidently not diminished by the fact that the entire intelligence community," according to the Department of Defense, "tended toward a pessimistic view."[67] We get still another example of the decision process following the North Vietnamese torpedo boat attack upon U.S. destroyers in the Tonkin Gulf. Throughout the morning, there were unclear and fragmentary reports of combat. From the start, Johnson made clear that there would be retaliation, bombing most likely. Here the contrast to Kennedy is most striking. The detached Kennedy might have collected facts with a disconcerting lack of emotion, then convened his team to contemplate the options; but Lyndon Johnson's ego was on the line. He did not solicit advice; he requested ratification. His comment after the first retaliatory strike on Hanoi is revealing: "I didn't just screw Ho Chi Min; I cut his pecker off."[68]

There are indications that Johnson did permit a few advisers to express doubts—but in such a way as to effectively neutralize them. When Bill Moyers became a dissenter, Ambassador Llewellyn Thompson tells us that when Moyers arrived at a meeting, the President greeted him with, "Well, here comes Mr. Stop-The-Bombing."[69] Similarly, Undersecretary of State George Ball, who became a critic of Johnson's policies, was cast in the role of "the in-house devil's advocate," a role which tended to nullify his influence on the President's policy-making team.

The neutralization of critics and the contracting circle of the "Tuesday lunch group" (as the Vietnam policy-making group was called) would become a deadly trap for Lyndon Johnson. "He and the men around him did not spend weeks of painful debate," says one observer, "measuring both our and the enemy's resources, deciding on the best way to commit American troups, how to get the most for our men. . . . There was in fact remarkably little discussion of strategy. It had begun as 'security,' had gone to 'enclave,' and then, without the enclave ever being tested, under pressure of events, they had gone to what would be 'search and destroy.' "[70]

The actors were basically the same but how different the process from the days of Kennedy. We see the cast of Johnson's personality—and the undertones of the formalistic approach of the Truman and Eisenhower days. Johnson's memoirs read like a script from the Korean Decisions of 1950, describing consensus and solidarity among advisers. Johnson emphasizes the unanimous agreement of the group in his descriptions of the meetings in which major escalations were recommended. "All my advisers agreed," writes Johnson, "that we should carry out this acceleration."[71] But Johnson, unlike Kennedy, had not learned from the Bay of Pigs that the question is not *whether* advisers agree but *how* that agreement is reached.

There were many Lyndon Johnsons; among them a Johnson when things were going well and a Johnson when things were going poorly. As circumstances deteriorated in Vietnam, flaws in his ways of soliciting information opened into chasms of misunderstanding. Increasingly he seemed less responsive, and to the men around him, less reasonable. There would be a steady exodus from the White House during 1966 and 1967 of many men, both hawks and doves, who had tried to reason with him and failed. First had been Bundy, then Moyers, the aide who had been closest to him, then came McNamara, "[Mc-Namara's] access was in direct proportion to his optimism," says one observer. "As he became more pessimistic, the President became reluctant to see him alone."[72]

With Bundy gone, the crucial link in Johnson's National Security policy machinery was Walt Rostow. Rostow briefed the President each morning, saw him several times a day, and selected the papers for his night reading. A former Administration officer has said:

Astride the main channel, Rostow could develop for the President all the options . . . or some; could pass along all the views expressed, or some; could send them forward without comment, or with his own recommendations. . . . The evidence leaves no doubt that he used his positional advantage to argue his own case—for a ground strategy of relentless pressure, for heavier bombing, even the invasion of North Vietnam—and that he was not as scrupulous as McGeorge Bundy about making certain that the President heard the full arguments on all sides of the issue. He shaped the evidence and maneuvered to set at discount with the President the views [of men like McNamara and Harriman] that were at odds with his own.[73]

Was Rostow conspiring to advance his own design? Or was he merely abiding by Johnson's wishes? A singular drawback of Johnson's operator-dominator personality was that he consumed his subordinates. In the process, and possibly in Rostow's case, he warped their independent judgment and integrity. It is hard to imagine that Johnson's displeasure with contradictory advice and his hunger for reaffirmation of his actions did not substantially influence—indeed, corrupt—his advisers. If the power of personality was not enough to distort the system, the demise of more independent aides such as Bundy and Moyers added credence to the norm of conformity. "Of course I tell the President, 'No,'" went the White House quip. "Just the other day President Johnson asked me if I had any complaints about the way he was running things."[74] When McNamara began to question the bombing, Johnson abused him with the analogy of a man trying to sell his house while one of his sons pointed out the leaks in the basement to prospective buyers. The analogy itself was richly revealing of Lyndon Johnson and ultimately came to reflect an operating philosophy.

In hindsight, it would seem that Vietnam had exploited Johnson's every weakness—his impatience, his intensity, his drive for consensus, his operator-dominator relations with aides, his intolerance of ambiguity, and above all, his pride. In the same way that the Cuban invasion had exposed Kennedy, Vietnam was Lyndon Johnson's Bay of Pigs—in slow motion.

Dean Acheson had once warned Johnson never to let his ego get between him and his office. Lyndon Johnson had let this happen and it toppled his Administration.

Many of Lyndon Johnson's crisis decisions would embody personal idiosyncrasies that no system could entirely eliminate. Johnson would consistently respond to foreign threats to his control and prestige with defiant, "Texas Ranger" tactics. Lyndon Johnson's White House, like Eisenhower's, contained a blend of "system" and "personality." The two men are of interest because both succumbed to the hazards of the formalistic approach to management; both relied on an elaborate chain of command which filtered information in the process of collecting it. From the standpoint of personality, the two Presidents could not have been less alike. Ike erred on the side of passivity, Johnson on the side of hyperactivity. Yet each in the end suffered from isolation from the "facts." For Lyndon Johnson, this problem arose because he hated bad news. A succession of setbacks—the Tet offensive in Vietnam, the *Pueblo* incident off North Korea, inflation, McCarthy's stunning success in the Democratic primary in New Hampshire—each took its toll in his ability to bear up under further adversity. As his term of office wore on, it became evident that a lifetime of learning was failing him. As a child, later as a Congressman, he had dealt with adversity by simply painting over it. With remarkable success, his mastery of hyperbole enabled him to transform unpleasant realities into new "realities" of his own choosing. But in the spotlight of the Presidency, he could no longer convince people that problems didn't exist. There were signs that the public did not want to be lured from reality. Half of the nation's population by 1966 had gone through high school and 10 percent through college. They were not only capable of understanding the issues of the day but demanded to know the facts. As the press sought to provide them, Johnson struggled mightily to preserve appearances: this was the formula that Sam Johnson had taught him as a boy. The result was the Credibility Gap.

Not since President Hoover had a twentieth-century President been so unable to establish a warm relationship with the citizens of the nation. In part, the problem was that Lyndon Johnson was out of step with his times. "An accidental President," Hugh Sidey has written. "A great man of immense girth, wandering as a stranger in the Pepsi Generation. Coarse, earthy —a brutal intrusion into the misty Kennedy renaissance that still clung to the land."[75] But the Kennedy footsteps that he was forced to follow left an imprint deeper than style alone. Kennedy had established a whole new standard of professionalism for the Presidency—and that standard included honesty.

When Lyndon Johnson braced the nation for a $100 billion budget in 1965 and then announced a figure $3.5 billion less, many felt deceived. Over the next four years, a flood of such deceptions simply abused the public confidence. Semantics for the warfare in Vietnam strained the credulity of TV viewers nightly. There was more: he denied that Richard Goodwin was his speech writer one week and publicly acclaimed his work the next; he denied Abe Fortas would be nominated to the Supreme Court, and he said that Bobby Baker was not his protégé but only a Senate employee. In the fall of 1965, when aluminum producers announced a price increase, the government suddenly announced it was dumping on the market some 200,000 tons of stockpiled aluminum, yet the White House denied any connection between its actions and the price increase which was soon rescinded. Johnson campaigned through the fall of 1964 attacking Goldwater's proposals to enlarge the American part in Vietnam as a "reckless action" and urging great restraint before bombing the North; two weeks after Inauguration he ordered sustained bombing of the North, denying that this was an "escalation of war" but only a "reprisal raid."

Tragically, Lyndon Johnson, a most sensitive man, found himself subjected to a more sustained public outcry than any President in recent times. Riots, demonstrations against the war, burnings in effigy, all deeply affected him. By November of 1967, the Gallup Poll revealed that Johnson's popularity was down to 38 percent and that if the Presidential election was held then he would lose to any of five Republicans. In this climate of despair, he startled the nation by refusing to run again.

Accompanying this deterioration of Lyndon Johnson's public fortunes was an increase in his personal isolation. Attacks from critics in the Congress, in the press, and on the campuses stung him. "I'm the only President you've got," he complained. "Why do you want to destroy me?"[76] Close friends urged him to look on dissent as a necessary part of political life. But as had been true throughout his life, any hint of inadequacy drove him to try to convince every doubter. When that failed, perhaps as a mechanism of self-preservation, Lyndon Johnson began to erect a screen. At the beginning of his Presidency, he had sought to use his Cabinet and therefore scheduled regular meetings with elaborate agendas; later in his term, those sessions turned into rambling monologs with Johnson talking out his worries and his hopes. Johnson had always been given to thinking out loud, but increasingly he seemed to be doing it at the expense of listening. By 1967 his circle of top advisers shrank to five: Rusk, McNamara, Clark Clifford, then a Washington attorney, Abe Fortas, and John Gardner, HEW Secretary. And then with the departure of McNamara and Gardner, there were only three. Three might be enough if discussion was rigorous and the dis-agreements provoking. But even within his inner circle, John-son's demands for consensus quilted his advisers into patterns of static harmony. Bill Moyers said:

The men who handled National Security Affairs were too fond of each other. Great decisions were often made in the warm camara-derie of a small board of directors deciding what the club dues are going to be for the members next year. The reason why this was a handicap is simply that when you're debating fundamental policies, the consequences of which are profound, you should press your de-bating opponents to the very limit of their reasoning faculties.⁷⁷

Johnson's hunger for consensus was operative in domestic affairs as well. An example of this is the Administration's han-dling of the budget in 1966. Summoning in his "troika" (the Secretary of the Treasury, the Budget Director, and the Chair-man of the Council of Economic Advisers), he solicited their advice, but it soon became clear that he already had his posi-tion. Soothing CEA Chairman Walter Heller's doubts, skillfully parrying the more detailed questions from his Budget Director, he swiftly moved the discussion toward closure. As the meeting ended, Johnson shook everyone's hand as they filed out. One of the economic advisers present summed up Johnson's per-formance. "He pulled all of us to his way of thinking and left not the slightest doubt which way he was going."⁷⁸ In fact,

Johnson had summoned the "troika" not to get its advice but to influence it.

In matters of war and peace, Johnson cast a scattered image. He pursued a war he desperately wanted no part of, he manufactured "guns" and sought "butter," he practiced containment but preached the elimination of poverty. Johnson lacked Truman's practical horse sense, Eisenhower's experienced caution, Kennedy's cool grasp of reality. More basically, he lacked a clear sense of himself that might have shown him the way through this difficult period. Lacking his own sense of purpose, he sought to derive it from others. Until the end, he kept searching for the magic, unifying concept that would pull the nation together.

"Agreement can always be reached by increasing the generality of the conclusion," Dean Acheson said once. "But when this is done, only the illusion of policy is created. The President gives his blessing to platitude."[79] Herein lay Lyndon Johnson's problem. A lifetime of experience had made him the master of consensus; as President he became the prisoner of dissent. More importantly, his personal history somehow prevented him from growing in office. In virtually every respect, his practices in the Presidency were repetitions of his past. This was the real tragedy for Lyndon Johnson—and for the nation.

CHAPTER SEVEN

NIXON'S COURTSHIP WITH CRISIS

On April 30, 1973, President Richard Nixon appeared visibly shaken before television cameras. Acknowledging that his staff's involvement in the Watergate break-in and cover-up was far more extensive than he had realized, he announced that he was accepting the resignations of H. R. Haldeman and John Ehrlichman, his two principal aides, along with John Dean, Counsel to the President. Within two weeks of this announcement, seventeen of Nixon's associates and employees had resigned or were under investigation by the Department of Justice, the FBI, a Federal grand jury, or the U.S. Senate.[1] Nixon himself had issued still another statement, a 4,000-word defense which conceded that there had been "wide ranging efforts [by his staff] to conceal the . . . involvement of members of the Administration" and ". . . that to the extent [he, the President] had contributed to the climate in which they took place . . . [he] should have been more vigilant."[2] This was not to be the final act in the unfolding drama of the Watergate. But it captured the essence of an extraordinary episode in American history. From the standpoint of this study of Presidential management, it dramatized the manner in which a President's system of management not only shapes events but entraps participants. For regardless of the President's foreknowledge of the illegal acts, it was clear that his *formalistic* system had succeeded in isolating him—either from the transgressions of his subordinates (if he truly did not sponsor their activities) or from a realistic appraisal of the marginal benefits of such acts and possible grave consequences (if he did). The episode revealed the man—in his anguish, his anger, his aloneness. And perhaps late one night, pacing the empty corridors of the Executive mansion, he, like many Americans, searched for a clear understanding of how it all began. In the question resides the puzzle of Richard Nixon.

Richard Nixon, the second of five brothers, was born in 1913. Two of his brothers would die by his fourteenth birthday. Hardship left a mark on his early life. His mother, Hanna, came from a Quaker family of standing within the community; in the eyes of many she married below her place in becoming the wife of Frank Nixon, a local trolleyman. Throughout Nixon's early years, Frank moved through a succession of business ventures, never finding success. Ultimately, the family resigned itself to the subsistence earnings from their gas station and small grocery store.

Frank was something of a blowhard, with a nasty temper and a mercurial disposition. When Hanna visited friends, Frank sat outside in his car and honked the horn. At the store, Hanna dealt with the customers while Frank grumbled behind the scenes, lifting, packing, and butchering. Hanna and Frank remained partners in a marriage that was cordial but never close. In contrast to Frank, Hanna was known in the community for her kindness. She seemed ever conscious of the needs of others.

In Nixon's youth, a man-sized burden of hard work was imposed on him. His chores occupied much of the days and early evenings when he was not in school; neighbors recall him doing his homework from ten to twelve at night, even in junior high school. Each morning he would arise at 4:30, drive thirty miles to Los Angeles to pick up groceries, then return to Yorba Linda and unpack them at the store.

But perhaps the larger burden came from his unfulfilled yearning for love and support. There was never a strong bond of affection between Frank Nixon and his sons. Periodic whippings, a tendency to ridicule, and stern admonitions were almost the sum of his paternal repertoire. Young Richard learned to abide by his rules and avoid confrontations. In his brother Donald's words, "Dick was . . . the peacemaker. When we had fights he would step in and talk us out of it." This tendency to avoid conflict would carry into his Presidency. Associated with this trait was a tendency to conceal anger. "He saved things up, though," his brother, Don, continues. "Once I did something that finally made him angry, and he didn't just criticize me for that. He went back *two years,* telling me all the things I had done wrong. It really made me think, I'll tell you."[3]

Richard Nixon's principal bond was with his mother. According to Donald, "Dick had more of mother's traits than the rest of us; he was [her] standby at the store."[4] The two were viewed as more sympathetic and understanding. When a neighborhood woman was observed shoplifting, Frank and the other male members of the family wanted to call the police. Richard and Hanna urged an alternative solution and they prevailed. Hanna took the woman aside for a long talk, which put an end to the problem. Yet despite these kindred qualities, the relationship was complicated by Hanna's frequent absences. During Richard's infancy, his father's business setbacks forced his mother to work. Young Nixon was left in the care of a neighbor who "practically raised him," according to one source.[5] At the age of six he was deemed old enough to work too. And in time there were further separations from his family. It is known, for example, that he was sent off to live with relatives in northern California for four months when he was ten; when he was twelve, his mother departed for Arizona for two years in order to care for her oldest son, Harold, who was ravaged by tuberculosis.[6] Under these circumstances, perhaps the young boy developed a sense of being abandoned—possibly even a deep shame for not being worthy of love. The following story, written at the age of ten and sent as a letter to his mother, is interesting in this respect.

My Dear Master:

The two boys that you left me with are very bad to me. Their dog, Jim, is very old and he will never talk or play with me.

On Saturday the boys went hunting. Jim and myself went with them. While going through the woods one of the boys tripped and fell on me. I lost my temper and bit him. He kicked me in the side and we started on. While we were walking I saw a black round thing in a tree. I hit it with my paw. A swarm of black things came out of it. I felt pain all over. I started to run and as both of my eyes were swelled shut, I fell into a pond. When I got home I was very sore. I wish you would come home right now.

Your good dog,

Richard[7]

Whatever the deeper meanings, the tale conveys hurt and makes a cry for help.[8] Evidently, his pleas went largely unanswered. Gradually, Richard Nixon came to rely on himself, denying his needs for affection and disciplining his mind and body to a single-minded focus on his future.

As Richard Nixon approached adulthood an important personal transformation occurred. Based on information in Richard Nixon's writings and recollections, it would appear that he began to stress certain values—hard work, self-discipline, coolness under pressure. Other aspects of his personality—his sympathy for others, his sensitivity and vulnerability to hurt—disappeared or are reserved exclusively for his private life beyond the public view. He lived out these values with fierce conviction. At Whittier College, Nixon became known for his intensity and self-discipline. At Duke Law School, according to his roommate, "he never expected anything good to happen to him, or anyone close to him, unless it were earned."[9] Nixon's values and beliefs about himself come through most clearly in his autobiographical account *Six Crises*. Reflecting on his experiences as a Congressman, he states, "I had learned from the Hiss case that what determines success or failure in handling a crisis is the ability to keep coldly objective when emotions are running high. I found myself almost automatically thinking and making decisions quickly, rationally, and unemotionally."[10] Here is the public Richard Nixon: the coolly rational man.

In the crucial decisions leading to his actions against Alger Hiss, and again in the crisis in 1952 over his political finances, which led to the famous "Checkers" speech, Nixon describes himself as a man who gathers the facts, then retires alone to weigh the options and decide. Recalling the agonizing deliberations leading to his decision to stake his career on the "Checkers" speech, he writes:

After the [aides] had left the room, I sat alone for another two hours and reviewed the entire situation. I realized that although others could help direct my thinking, the final decision in a crisis of this magnitude must not represent the lowest common denominator of a collective judgment; it must be made alone by the individual primarily involved.[11]

Continuing his account of the "Checkers" speech, Nixon recalls his reactions once he had decided to give the speech on nation-wide television:

A new tension was now building up—the tension that precedes battle when all plans have been drawn and one stands poised for action. This speech was to be the most important of my life. I felt now that it was my battle alone. I had been deserted by so many I had thought were friends but who panicked in battle when the first shots were fired.[12]

A poignant aspect of Nixon's recollections is the man's sense of aloneness. It is of interest that he felt this during the Fund Crisis since, as an experienced politician, he might have read these events in a different way. It is true that Eisenhower adopted a neutral stance during the episode. Yet at the same time, Nixon's staff and supporters remained ardently loyal. On the West Coast where he was campaigning at the time, crowds were large and sympathetic. Key Republican party members— Karl Mundt, the Republican National Committee Chairman, Robert Taft and William Knowland—had all come out in his support. Even Oregon's liberal Governor Douglas McKay endorsed Nixon warmly with the knowledge that in doing so he risked losing his own election. (Harold Stassen and Thomas E. Dewey, who were to come out against Nixon later, had not yet made their positions known.) But trust the teller, not the tale; the perception of aloneness remains a Nixon trademark.

Throughout *Six Crises* Nixon talks repeatedly about the great tension and soul-searching which preceded each of his decisions to face a crisis. The decision made, Nixon describes periods of great physical denial where sleeping and eating were discontinued almost as a discipline to focus his mind on the task at hand. After these periods, he describes a time of letdown and depression. There would seem to be a pattern in all this, of a man whose greatest sense of himself and his powers occurs, as it were, when his back is against the wall. It is then, in defiance of overwhelming odds, in the face of abandonment and ruin, that he seems most capable of mustering his resources and striking back. This pattern may, of course, be erroneously perceived, or it may be nothing more than the coincidental imprint of destiny on a man's life. But it is at least possible that such a pattern becomes its own prophecy. It is possible that a man, even a President, could perceive circumstances to create the tone of crisis and isolation in order to trigger the remarkable process that permits him to rise to the occasion. It is of no minor interest that Richard Nixon has described these decision episodes as "exquisite agony."[13]

We have traced one thread of the Nixon personality—the disciplined, self-controlled professional. But as the prevailing view has it, there are two Richard Nixons: one is the stiff, self-controlled person we have described thus far; the other is characterized as furtive and angry, plotting quietly in the background, lashing out at Congress, the press, and the bureaucracy. These two impressions have wide currency—and indeed, with some basis. But they are only facets of what is perhaps the most perplexing of recent Presidents. What lurks beneath? The answer lies in developing a broader understanding of the man.

The biggest obstacle to fitting together the puzzle of Richard Nixon is that the key pieces are hard to come by. Personal information on his predecessors is relatively available, but this is not the case with Nixon. Part of the reason, of course, is that he is still a sitting President; the biographies and inside stories will presumably be written when his Administration ends. But equally important is Nixon's immense sense of privacy. Details of his childhood and his life style in the White House are sketchy and he intends it that way. Yet while this is a problem, it is also a clue. The key to understanding this President lies in recognizing that those aspects of his life that we have been allowed to glimpse are *only aspects,* not the whole.

What of the angry Nixon? There has always been a Nixon lashing out—against Congressional opponents, Alger Hiss, and the Communists. When as Vice President he was visiting South America, he experienced great hostility. Nixon has written that as the rocks flew, he "could not resist the temptation to get in one good lick,"[14] and experienced "an almost uncontrollable urge to tear the face in front of [him] to pieces."[15] In Peru, when a rioter spat on him, he says he "at least [had] the satisfaction of planting a healthy kick on the shins. Nothing I did all day made me feel better," he adds.[16]

Richard Nixon's bitter rejoinder to the press following his defeat in the California gubernatorial race in 1962 was for many the long-awaited slip, a glimpse at the "real Nixon." His intemperate remarks about the accused murderer Charles Manson, his outbursts after Supreme Court nominees Haynsworth and Carswell were rejected, and his pronouncements following the Kent State shootings were viewed as more of the same.

Following his 1972 landslide, he lashed out against the bureaucracy and spoke about "whipping them into shape." After a sequence of disclosures in the press forced his admission of White House involvement in the Watergate, he spent a good part of a Cabinet meeting assailing the "partisan" attacks of the press and Congress. "Their target was not Haldeman or Ehrlichman," he said. "I know well who their target is."[17] There is no doubt that these incidents provide important insight into the Nixon character. But the key question remains whether anger is at the core of the Nixon personality. There are things which the anger theory cannot easily explain. Hindsight suggests, for example, that the invasion of Cambodia in 1970 was really not as impulsive an act as many critics at the time claimed. The Christmas bombing of Hanoi in 1972 following the breakdown of the peace negotiations with North Vietnam, likewise, appears to have been more a cold and calculated move to force the North to accept the peace agreement than a Presidential temper tantrum. In 1969 when the North Koreans shot down an unarmed U.S. reconnaissance plane, "the President's first impulse," according to *The New York Times,* "was military retaliation."[18] He selected targets for air strikes and prepared a speech to explain the bombing to the American people. Then, according to the *Times'* report, the decision was reconsidered. The President concluded that while he wanted to demonstrate toughness, he did not want another Gulf of Tonkin incident. Thus Nixon stepped back from the brink. He and his system had resisted the first angry reaction.

The Korean incident, while frightening for what might have occurred, demonstrated that reason could prevail over passion. And while much has been said of Nixon's anger, the Administration's performance reveals a significant number of instances in which this has been the case. On a number of occasions following setbacks that were known to have made the President angry, Nixon appears to have taken his lumps and has endeavored to regain the Administration's composure. After Carswell's defeat, he swallowed his pride, castigated Congress, and nominated Harry Blackmun. Following his harsh words after the Kent State shootings, he ordered a full investigation of the incident, and received six Kent State students and eight university presidents. In the backlash of the Cambodia invasion, he back-pedaled, assuring Congress that the U.S. would be out in three to seven weeks and that he would not order troops in deeper than twenty miles without Congressional approval. In 1973, when Congress sought a showdown to end all bombing of Cambodia, the President talked tough, but readily accepted a compromise. After Special Prosecutor Archibald Cox's firing and the startling public outcry, he surprised even his own lawyers by reversing his stand and delivering the Watergate tapes to District Court Judge John Sirica. These incidents might well be viewed as acts of political calculation, but they hardly seem the intemperate by-products of outrage and petulance.

Perhaps the greatest difficulty with the anger theory is that there are few indications of Nixon working his anger out on his staff. Surely, given the pressures of the Presidency, one would expect such anger to surface from time to time. Even if it were not reported, there would have been signs of staff unrest and turnover. This has not been the case prior to Watergate. Moreover, it is of note that even Secretary of the Interior Walter Hickel, after his bitter resignation, directed his invective at John Ehrlichman and Bob Haldeman, not the President.

Perhaps at heart Nixon remains the sensitive, vulnerable figure glimpsed in childhood. Early life taught him to conceal the ways in which he is vulnerable; political life reinforced that learning. The visible aspects of the man—his self-containment and periodic outbursts—are more revealing of his defenses than they are of his inner self. Self-containment is the shield; anger is the outlet.

Given the dimensions of Nixon's self-control, it is not surprising that frustration percolates beneath the surface. Nixon's brand of self-control covers the full range of professional con-

duct. His constant theme is the stress on hard work and coolness. "I have a reputation for being the coolest person in the
room," he states. "In a way, I am. I have trained myself to be
that. I never allow myself to get emotional."[19] He believes a
leader must set the upbeat: "I always have to be up—or at
least appear that way."[20] But perhaps the most remarkable
aspect of his self-control is the degree to which it is imposed on
his physical being. Says one aide, "The President gets irregular
but terrible attacks of hay fever, but his doctor says he has no
allergies, definitely no hay fever. [The reason is] he doesn't tell
the doctor; he disguises it. I've been with him in meetings
when he looked perfectly fine. Then as soon as the other people
left, he was sneezing and his eyes were watering."[21] In the
same vein, he concealed from his personal physician the symp-
toms of viral pneumonia which eventually hospitalized him for
a week. "I suspect it did not come on suddenly," his physician
told reporters. "I suspect he felt tired and didn't want to say
anything about it."[22]

Rare indeed are the glimpses of the vulnerable Nixon, despite the fact that at times he almost confessed his weaknesses.
Shortly after reelection he told one reporter, "After [all] the
devastating attacks on TV, in much of the media, in editorials
and columns you'd think I'd be elated then. But it has always
been my experience that it doesn't really come to that. You're
so drained emotionally at the end, you can't feel much."[23] In a
subsequent interview he said, "I could go up the wall watching
TV commentators. I don't. I never watch TV commentators or
the news shows when they are about me. That's because I don't
want decisions influenced by personal emotional reactions."[24]

In pursuit of the inner Nixon one finally asks the people who
work closest to him. "He is privately a man of warmth and
kindness," they say. They enumerate acts of surprising thought-
fulness, surprising not because of their magnitude but because
the President took the time for them: refusing to go to any
more football games because "twenty people have to be dis-

placed"; sending an encouraging letter to the ill mother of an assistant; making a point of meeting an aide's family and saying to him, "They're nice"; making a plane available to Margaret Truman Daniels within half an hour of hearing of Harry Truman's illness; inviting one of the White House elevator operators to Key Biscayne with him when he learned the man likes to fish; writing a three-page letter of advice to the son of an assistant when he learned that the boy was entering law school.[25] These were private acts—intended for the recipient, not the press. This is the private Richard Nixon. There is apparently an intellectual side of the man, too. "If I had my druthers," he said in 1966, "I'd write two or three books a year, go to one of the fine schools—Oxford, for instance—just teach, read, and write. I'd like to do that better than what I'm doing now."[26] "What is the most different [between the public and the private man]," said one aide, "is that in private he is unafraid to let his intellectual sophistication come through. In public, in his speeches, he thinks the best way to reach people is through the lowest common denominator."[27]

But such glimpses into the inner man are rare indeed. The hallmark of the Administration is that even the most innocuous details about the leader are withheld—attributed to the boss's uncommon sense of privacy. "Does the President wear glasses at all for reading?" "Now and then," said an authoritative source, "but don't quote me." "Does he catnap at all?" "Yes," said another man, "but get it from somebody else." An assistant who should know said, "Election night the President was in agony. A tooth had broken off and medication didn't help the pain. But don't quote me."[28] Privacy reigns.

Our portrait of the Presidential character has identified several important characteristics: first, his thin-skinned sensitivity and vulnerability; second, a determination to conceal this inner self through self-control and by distancing himself from others; third, a belief that success stems from hard work and attention to detail, and, finally, periodic outbursts of anger which appear the safety valve for all that goes on within. Inevitably, these aspects of the man came to be reflected in his management system. His personal traits militated against the use of a competitive system such as FDR's; likewise, his immense sense of privacy and tendency to mask feelings were ill-suited to the collegial teamwork that characterized Kennedy's years. Long before election day, the dictates of character had in large measure ordained that Richard Nixon's style would be *formalistic*. And while it is an overstatement to suggest that an incident such as the Watergate was predetermined, there is little doubt that its likelihood was increased by the extraordinary extent to which Richard Nixon's idiosyncrasies come to be reflected and magnified in his managerial system.

Consider its major ingredients. First and foremost, Richard Nixon, the private man with a preference for working alone, wanted machinery to staff out the options but provide plenty of time for reflection. This entailed a staff arrangement somewhat like Eisenhower's in form but significantly different in function. Nixon, like Eisenhower, used an extensive staff system. Both Presidents wanted aides to research issues and present their analyses on paper. But here the similarities ended. For Eisenhower channeled the staff work to committees which, in turn, recommended a course of action to the President. Nixon, on the other hand, sought to avoid the cumbersome committees who did not fit his decision-making style. Nixon wanted his aides to present *him* with the options; he would do the choosing.

Nixon had learned from experience that it was essential to delegate—and in this respect his approach corresponded rather closely to Eisenhower's. Up until the 1968 campaign, Nixon's loner instincts made it difficult for him to trust and delegate to others. Murray Chotiner describes him in 1960 as "the hardest candidate of all to manage" because "he insisted on perfection and on trying to do everything himself."[29] John Ehrlichman confirms this viewpoint:

He was uptight in the campaigns of '60 and '62. He was unable to delegate authority. He didn't feel he could rely on anybody else fully to take some responsibility for his political future. But by the '68 campaign, he had come to see that he couldn't hold all the strings in his hands, that that was self-defeating.[30]

Gradually Nixon came to recognize that his system must satisfy two requirements: first, it must provide thorough staff work and, secondly, it must shelter him sufficiently to permit his habitual pattern of working and thinking alone. In essence, Nixon wanted a formalistic system that neither swamped him in detail nor isolated him too much from the action.

A second major determinant of Nixon's system was his choice of aides. In fact, his appointments surprised many. H. R. (Bob) Haldeman, an advertising executive, and John D. Ehrlichman, a Seattle zoning lawyer, were suddenly catapulted to the lofty command posts in the West Wing. They fit no pattern, resembling neither the political cronies of the Truman era nor the superstars of the Kennedy or Roosevelt administrations. Haldeman and Ehrlichman were advance men; slots most Presidential campaigners relegate to unimaginative newcomers. Such was not the case with Candidate Nixon. With the election won, he did not recruit his White House staff from the usual talent sources of speech writers or idea men. Instead, Nixon sought his facts-oriented campaign schedulers. The election won, politicians and issues men awoke to discover the coordinators and technicians in control.[31] The President, with his penchant for order, favored men who offered order.

A third important ingredient of the Nixon system is loyalty. Nixon, the vulnerable, private man, wanted loyalty of a very special kind: a loyalty different from John Kennedy's code of mutual support or Lyndon Johnson's dictated subservience— for in these former Administrations, loyalty deterred few from "telling all" after they left the President's service. In contrast, loyalty Nixon-style involves a code of silence—a code which will stand its severest test not from the usual temptation to indulge in flights of autobiography, but under the cross-examination of Watergate prosecutors. The resilience of Nixon loyalty is noteworthy, for the President has evidently bound men to him in ways that baffle onlookers. In part such loyalty is enhanced by selecting unknown men whose only reason for being is by the President's grace alone. Other Presidents have chosen similarly. But this President's ability to attract and retain men of outside stature such as Henry Kissinger, Roy Ash, and George Shultz causes us to look for supplementary explanations. It seems clear that Nixon's close associates respect him; his personal sensitivity and intelligence are said to be quite engaging at close range. But, in addition, the President undoubtedly derives cohesive power from his tendency to view events in terms of battling insurmountable odds and against outside enemies. Such a division of the world obfuscates, but also motivates. Unquestionably, the cohesiveness of Nixon's staff results in part from this shared sense of banding together to help the boss fight a hostile environment. And perhaps it is here that we capture a valuable insight, not only into one source of his capacity to inspire loyalty, but into one of the motivational antecedents of the Watergate.

Loyalty distorts as well as binds. Consider, for example, the prevailing Nixonian outlook on Washington social life. One aide remarks:

I read the local society pages, as one does to keep up with what's going on in Washington, and many of the dashing figures I read about there aren't worth ten cents over here in the Executive branch. They like that car with the light in the back window and the telephone, but some of these heroes of the society page are almost disaster areas for doing the job the President wants them to do. They really aren't "beautiful people." They're just being used by Washington hostesses and they aren't astute enough to know it.[32]

There are, in fact, considerable sanctions in the Nixon White House against such "socializing." Criticizing Haldeman's role as Social Commissar, one nettled aide states, "The worst crime he can think of is cosmopolitanism."[33] Haldeman was, in fact, widely thought to have helped shunt both Secretary of Commerce Peter Peterson and CIA Director Richard Helms to lesser jobs for having mixed with Democrats on the Washington social circuit. "Though Haldeman denied it," says another source, "even Henry Kissinger is thought to have offended him by indulging in the swinging life."[34] "You don't party in this crowd," summarizes another aide. "It's not by accident that our morning staff meetings are scheduled for 7:30 A.M.; it keeps us home at night and that's the way the bosses want it."[35]

There is, of course, nothing particularly damning about a grain of negativism or avoidance of the Washington social scene. But these facets of Nixon staff life are nonetheless noteworthy, not because they are causal but because they are *contributive*—first, to the type of tightlipped loyalty the President demands, and secondly, to the conception that what lies outside the President's sphere is essentially unfriendly or untrustworthy. This tendency contains an inherent danger, for leadership predicated upon mistrust and fear can not only harbor these qualities but itself come to emulate them.

A fourth element of the Nixon style concerns his handling of conflict. As we have seen with other Presidents, the management of conflict importantly determines the shape of the Chief Executive's staff machinery. Nixon is no exception, and interestingly, he is an extreme conflict avoider. In the words of one aide, "The President does his deciding on paper, in large measure, I think, because he hates to have to make tough choices in front of people and disappoint somebody. This way, decisions just sort of flow out of the Oval Office without the appearance of him having openly taken one man's side or the other."[36] Says another White House assistant:

The President does not like to sit there looking at people and bear bad tidings. I remember our first meeting right after the [1972] election—he told us we all had done a great job and he was proud as could be that we had been with him. Then, just as we were feeling fine, he turned the meeting over to [Haldeman] and left. The first thing Haldeman did was ask us all for our resignations. You could feel the jaws dropping. Haldeman became the heavy but everybody should have known it was the President's doing. Bob was just dropping the blade.[37]

Repeatedly, when the President is confronted with the proponents of opposing arguments, he turns fuzzy. When his White House staff and his first Secretary of the Treasury, David Kennedy, were at loggerheads over whether or not to cut the oil depletion allowance, the President held a "final" meeting with the adversaries but balked at making the decision.[38] When the Ash Council came forward with its controversial recommendations reorganizing the Bureau of the Budget and the White House domestic activities (and encountered opposition from then Budget Director Robert Mayo and White House domestic staff chief John Ehrlichman), the President scheduled a meeting to "settle it"; his response was so inconclusive it left all uncertain as to how to proceed.[39] The examples are endless.

The President's structuring of his staff to avoid conflict evolved gradually. Many will recall that first-term candidate Nixon ran for the Presidency promising to have a "small staff" and an "open" Administration with a strong Cabinet of "independent" thinkers.[40] His initial appointments seemed consistent with these promises. While his Cabinet members needed to be introduced to the unknowing public for their "extra dimensions," Nixon selected such independent figures as George Romney, Walter Hickel, and John Volpe. In the White House, Nixon appeared also to want diverse and independent viewpoints. Daniel Patrick Moynihan was recruited from the liberal establishment. Arthur Burns was included as a representative of the conservative right. Ehrlichman, appointed initially as Counsel to the President, was given equal stature with Moynihan and Burns in an effort to recognize the middle ground. It was a curious mixture. Nixon's day-to-day routine clearly signaled his preference for an orderly decision process, yet his choice of "counselors" brought divergent viewpoints into the fold, and with them, potential for conflict.

The result? The President got what he asked for and it was not his cup of tea. The conflict was sharp and the bargaining interminable. Nixon, the loner who preferred to make decisions in privacy, was ill-suited to the system he had devised. *Newsweek* recounts:

When [the President] looked at his White House staff three months after inauguration, his domestic policy system was in chaos. The chief White House aides—Moynihan, Ehrlichman and Burns—were spinning in overlapping orbits. The elaborate inter-agency committee system showed little promise of straightening things out. As the burden of paper work grew, the process of decision slowed to a crawl. "We were long on advocates and short on brokers," Ehrlichman commented. "The President himself was often left as the [final arbitrator]."[41]

In short, the system of conflicting viewpoints was intrusive; the President disliked being drawn into the squabbles of his staff. His solution was to establish a buffer to spare himself from the arbitrator's role. Ehrlichman was appointed as chief of the domestic staff, with powers equivalent to those of Kissinger's, to screen and coordinate domestic policy. Ehrlichman was a natural choice. He was nonideological and mid-spectrum in the disputes between Burns and Moynihan. It has been said that Ehrlichman "displayed the qualities the President regarded most highly: diligence, caution, an open mind, and absence of distracting personal flair, and above all, orderliness and efficiency."[42]

Ehrlichman was asked to clean up the mess. And the first casualty of the new arrangement was the adversary system that Ehrlichman had been designated to supervise. Burns was moved out to become Chairman of the Federal Reserve Board. Moynihan was promoted to an advisory position, stripped of his staff, and relieved of his chairmanship of the Urban Affairs

Council. The new system succeeded in insulating Nixon from staff conflict. Its price was increasing the distance between the President and "the action." In hindsight, the distance grew too great. The aftermath, including such incidents as the Watergate break-in, questionable uses of campaign funds, and conflicts of interests involving Cabinet members and other high officials of government reiterates an important lesson of the Truman and Eisenhower Presidencies: an information system must not only pass information upward but permit the manager to monitor mischief *downward.*

Nixon's reward system is a fifth element of his managerial approach. As we have seen in former Administrations, the nature of the reward system plays an important role in determining how smoothly the President's machinery functions. Nixon's rewards have generally been conspicuous for their consistency. First, only a handful of top aides talk to the President, and everyone else talks to them. Access is thus regulated by daily routine, not by the vicissitudes of Presidential favor, and is thus largely eliminated as a bargainable commodity and source of strife.

It is noteworthy that at the end of his first term, Nixon had by far the largest White House staff in history. Yet neither the showdowns over economic policy nor other ebbs and flows of White House life seemed to disrupt the prevailing amicability. "The staff is very noncompetitive," observed an aide.[43] After attending months of regular morning staff meetings, another commented that "the inevitable rivalries, the rise and decline of this or that individual in the President's favor are never evident."[44] Even the massive shakeup in the wake of the Watergate resignations has not precipitated the kind of power-grabbing melee that one might have expected. It should be added that in addition to the President's great consistency in managing his accessibility, his sentiments about interpersonal conflict are well known—and respected. Aides who defy the norms are punished by the simple expedient of exclusion. The departure of Moynihan and Burns carried a message that few have chosen to ignore. Thus, in summary, the reward system works effectively to keep the staff working together. This is an important requirement for the functioning of the formalistic approach.

The Nixon staff system that had begun to take shape by the end of his first term exhibited a great deal of outward order and precision. Its manner of operating had been importantly shaped by the several factors we have discussed. Careful staff work and conservation of the President's time were deemed paramount. Every paper was required to "track" properly and options were expected to be objectively presented and complete. The President's day, organized into half-hour segments, provided time to read, discuss, and above all, lots of time to think and decide. (A separate office is maintained in the Executive Office Building for this purpose.) Any matter, be it a legislative proposal or an important letter, was meticulously staffed out before it went on the President's desk. Each request for an appointment was put through a fine-mesh screen. The staff prepared a "script" about each visitor to the Oval Office that told who he was and the nature of his business. It even provided suggested subjects for small talk and indicated how long the audience was to last. "We don't run a revolving-door policy on appointments here," said one of the Presidential gatekeepers.[45] "We don't worry about isolation from people, but from ideas. And the best of these, we have found, come in on paper, not through conversation."[46] Nixon disliked "the laying on of tongues," as White House locution had it, "and much preferred spending three minutes reading a memo to hearing someone out in person for a quarter of an hour."[47] The President, not a man for large meetings, frequently went for months without convening the Cabinet or calling a session of the National Security Council.

Prior to the loss of many of his staff resulting from the Watergate and related matters, Nixon's system was arrayed into a highly formalistic hierarchy: information was passed up for

decision and the President's choices passed down for implementation. At the top of the staff pyramid was Haldeman—his
diligence and attention to detail harmonizing with the President's own tastes for order. Haldeman was the metronome in
the system—the pacer of the workload—synchronized to the
President's preferences. "He's the perfect alter ego," said one
long-time associate. "It's almost as if [he] ceased to exist when
Nixon took office."[48] Within the White House sphere, Haldeman was unquestionably the most powerful man next to the
President. Reporting to him, formally, were various echelons of
advisers and staffs, and informally, virtually anyone wishing
contact with the President—Congressmen, governors, mayors,
Cabinet members—there were few exceptions. "A 'private'
meeting with the President," says one occasional visitor, "meant
that Haldeman [would] be there with his pad taking notes."[49]
Yet interestingly, even Haldeman's lofty position did not en-
title him to many exceptions from the President's ironclad requirement for privacy. "I guess I haven't gone into [the President's] office on my own initiative ten times in the last four
years," Haldeman said in March of 1973.[50] These statements, if
we accept them at face value, suggest the lengths to which
Richard Nixon's formalism was carried.

The pre-Watergate days saw not only structured reporting
relationships but structured routine. The White House staff
met daily at 7:30 to identify problems and priorities for the
day; at 8:30 A.M., the top advisers (namely Haldeman, Ehrlichman, Secretary of the Treasury George Shultz, and Office of
Management and Budget Director Roy Ash) convened to further sift out the matters of importance to the President.[51] Then,
at precisely nine o'clock, the President would buzz for Haldeman to bring in a report on his staff meetings and the folders
containing material that the President must sign, take action on,
or read that day. A half hour later, Henry Kissinger, typically
carrying a thick briefing book, would arrive to give the President a report on foreign policy development. The schedule was

followed punctually. This was Richard Nixon in action. "Once a reporter wanted to get some shots," an aide recounts, "of the President striding up and down, gesturing with his arms, and so on. I said, 'It just doesn't happen. This is not that kind of President. I have never seen him do those things.' As a matter of fact, he conducts most of his business sitting down. He comes in in the morning and sits down in that chair, and that's where he stays all during his working day."[52]

How, one might ask, given the layering of staffs and narrow reporting hierarchy, did the President stay in touch? The response, as provided by one White House assistant, is richly revealing. At quarter to eight every morning, before he left his residence, the President received a blue-covered notebook with the title "The President's Daily News Briefing" embossed in gold. The news-briefing notebook summarized, in up to thirty single-spaced pages, news items and editorials from fifty-two newspapers, along with a digest of the previous evening's network news programs. Here, according to the aide, was the heart of the President's control system. "The President's news summary," he continued, "is one of the

principal ways through which he spots problems and keeps tabs on the adequacy of our performance. It's a very important document—he doesn't trust one newspaper or one TV network (and for that reason doesn't read newspapers or watch television). He relies instead on the composite picture he receives in the news summary which is put together by a member of Haldeman's staff between twelve midnight and 5:00 A.M. every day. The President reads the summary carefully, scribbles comments and questions in the margins indicating things he wants done. His annotated copy is then recopied and circulated for action."[53]

In the aide's view, the summary was unimpeachably objective: "I have such faith in it," he added, "I've stored my television set in the basement to give us more room in the living room. My wife reads the *Washington Post* but I rarely have time to."[54]

Here, with unusual candor, was a description of the system

through which the President purportedly kept abreast of his Administration's malfunctions. The linchpin was the objectivity of the news summary and a glimpse of one such news summary is revealing. On March 28, 1973, lead stories were focusing on Watergate burglar James W. McCord, Jr.'s disclosures that he was prepared to tell the truth about the burglary and would implicate Attorney General John Mitchell and top members of the White House staff. The President's news summary for that day, twenty-six pages in length, devoted a page and one-quarter to McCord's statements and the entire Watergate matter. This brief six-paragraph summary, which began on page 12, opened with the sentence, "McCord spent the day running errands and ducking questions as he refused to comment till he sees Sirica or the Ervin Committee."[55] The lead sentence of the next paragraph began, "Watergate trial prosecutors questioned validity of McCord's implicating Dean and Magruder since he had waited so long . . ."[56] The thrust of the summary was to underplay the attention given to McCord's admissions by the press, impugn his credibility, and underrate the seriousness of his allegations. Yet this was the President's link to the outside world during those crucial days when the Watergate cover-up was revealed. Clearly, warp in so vital a channel of information could seriously distort the decision-making process. If the President was unaware of the cover-up, the information system perpetuated his unawareness. If he did know about the cover-up, his system shielded him from the harsh reality of public exposure.

Isolation of the top decision maker is a risk inherent in the formalistic approach. The dilemma for Richard Nixon is that the very precision of his machinery has increased these risks. "Ehrlichman, Kissinger, and I do our best," Haldeman observed, "to make sure that all points of view are placed before the President. But we *do* act as a screen, because there is a real danger of some advocate of an idea rushing in to the President and actually managing to convince [him] in a burst of emotion or argument."[57]

The vital flaw in all of this is that even if such a system reliably presents the President with the "facts," it tends to screen out the public sentiment associated with those facts. To his detriment, Nixon's formalistic approach has led him time and again to decide in the vacuum of "rationality," only to leave him stranded amidst a public reaction that his method of decision-making either neglected or vastly underestimated.

The formalistic approach legitimizes a barrier between the President and the world outside the White House. This was evident in the first term when Cabinet members, contrary to the "open" membership promised them, found the President a difficult man to see. A Cabinet official who managed to swim through the tight net around the President to plead for a project often found himself ushered into the Oval Office by Ehrlichman or Haldeman. The aides opened the interview by explaining to the President that the official's problem had many sides to it, which were in the process of being staffed out, and the matter was not yet ready for a decision. "Intimidated by the staff's interceding," says one source, "the official would often 'fold his tent and steal away' without taking anymore of the President's time." Alternatively, a Congressman returning from the well-worn path to South Vietnam might gain an audience with Mr. Nixon. But, to save the President's time, Kissinger might quickly summarize his report, and leave the legislator time to relate only one key finding of his trip. This procedure leaves many of the President's visitors resentful—not of him, but of his staff. (But his aides know that when Nixon grows overtly polite and moves restlessly in his chair, it is time to ease the visitor out.)[58]

The Walter Hickel incident was a rather classic by-product of this approach. Numerous sources confirm that Hickel had been frustrated in his attempts to see the President. He held

Ehrlichman responsible and was further aggravated by press leaks—traced to sources in the White House—which rumored his impending resignation. When a Hickel aide leaked a letter to the press that had been written to the President, Nixon and his staff reacted angrily. Substantively, the letter was uncomplimentary; it criticized the Administration's handling of the Kent State situation. Press reports speculated anew that Hickel's resignation was imminent.

Hickel did not resign immediately, but further deterioration of his relations with the White House took its inevitable toll. The President, characteristically disliking such messy matters, asked John Mitchell to talk Hickel into leaving. But Hickel spurned the Attorney General's counsel, saying, in effect, the President had hired him and that the President should fire him. Several days later, Hickel was summoned to the Oval Office. Columnists Evans and Novak provide this account:

> With Ehrlichman at his side, Nixon now was forced to engage in the face-to-face confrontation he deplored. . . . [H]e began with a courteous statement about how well Hickel had performed his tasks at Interior after a difficult beginning. The conversation continued in sidewise fashion until Hickel asked the President to come to the point. He did, talking about a lack of mutual confidence. Finally, he asked for Hickel's resignation. . . .[59]

The incident captured several aspects of the Nixon style. First, his requirements for loyalty (which Hickel's leaked letter had violated); second, the President's tendency to avoid interpersonal conflict (despite the fact, according to one account that he had said beforehand, "I want to get the bastard");[60] and thirdly, the President's discomforture with having to deal with a messy problem on a person-to-person basis.

Several incidents during Nixon's first term revealed his system's occasional tendency to develop a distorted picture of the outside world. The Haynsworth-Carswell episode is illustrative, first, of the tendency of the formalistic approach to generate solutions that are politically unacceptable, and secondly, that such out-of-touchness becomes compounded when a President draws a defensive perimeter around the Executive office when his actions come under attack. The selection process that resulted in the nomination of first Haynsworth and then Carswell bore this stamp. The Attorney General was asked to winnow out an acceptable nominee—the President wanted a Southerner who was already serving on the Federal bench, a strict constructionist, and a Republican under sixty years of age. "Nixon insisted that the man be someone he did not know personally," says one source, "and that he would not get to know him personally before confirmation. That way," it was reasoned, "the choice would be entirely objective and the new Justice would not in any way be obligated to the President."[61] It was all classically Nixonian (and reminiscent of the way Eisenhower had chosen his Cabinet). It was systematic and abstract, and it underscored the President's desire to deal with personalities at arm's length. Clement F. Haynsworth, Jr., Chief Judge of the Fourth Circuit Court of Appeals, met the specifications. However, depersonalizing the selection process had certain drawbacks, among them, a tendency to become preoccupied with the "criteria" and overlook the character and personal aspects of the candidate to be selected. These weaknesses were exposed at the Senate confirmation hearings; first around an alleged conflict of interest (Haynsworth had presided during the litigation of a case involving a firm in which he held stock); and, second, around Judge Haynsworth's repeated votes against desegregation.

The stage was now set for systems failure number two—fundamentally a failure of judgment. The Administration pushed. The Senate balked. And communications with the White House, meager from the start, began to break down. First, the President became furious at this affront to his prerogatives. Next he refused to withdraw the nomination, and labeled the criticism of Haynsworth "malicious character assassination."[62] Following Haynsworth's defeat, White House aides were

amazed at the emotion that Haynsworth's rejection aroused in the President. In the privacy of the White House, Nixon inveighed against the liberal press which had built the opposition to Haynsworth, against organized labor for its vendetta against the judge, and most of all against all those Republican senators who had betrayed their President.[63]

The President's anger and determination to "fight it out" now escalated the affair from miscalculation to more embarrassing proportions of bad judgment. When G. Harrold Carswell became his second nominee, the die was cast for a major confrontation with the Senate. Carswell, too, was rejected, on the fairly convincing grounds of demonstrated mediocrity. Diminution of the President's stature was the cost.

Tracing the antecedents of the Watergate has been useful insofar as it illustrates several of the significant drawbacks of the formalistic approach. On the positive side the Nixon approach has handled some situations exceedingly well. The significance of the U.S. rapprochement with China and the formal ending of hostilities in Vietnam will require decades to evaluate accurately. But there is little doubt that the staffwork that produced these achievements represents Nixon's formalized system at its best. Like John Kennedy, Richard Nixon has devoted a great deal of his personal energies to foreign affairs and, as we have seen in other Administrations, such investments of the President's time and attention augur well for performance. Like Kennedy, Nixon has been determined to "call the shots." The big difference between the two lies in Nixon's extensive use of the National Security Council staff. As Nixon saw it, the NSC has never really achieved its full potential under his predecessors. As a manageable body headquartered in the White House basement, it appeared to him to be just the right vehicle for bringing foreign policy under a tighter Presidential rein. To that end, he invested Kissinger with more responsibility than any other NSC assistant since the system was established by Harry Truman in 1947. Deliberately reducing the role of the Secretary of State, Nixon put Kissinger in charge of the NSC's Senior Review Group which presides over interdepartmental bodies. Acting as a clearinghouse, Kissinger and his aides sifted the analyses from these groups to provide policy options for the President.[64] Kissinger utilized NSSMs (National Security Study Memoranda) as aggressive initiating devices, enabling the NSC staff to force issues that might otherwise be buried or neglected by the agencies. In the first hundred days, Kissinger and his staff churned out fifty-five NSSMs. (Of NSSM-1, an analysis of the situation in Vietnam, Kissinger recalls, "We found out how ignorant we were.")[65] Since then, more than two hundred NSSMs have been written. Like the professor he is, Kissinger often grades the NSSMs and tosses them back to their authors for more rigorous thought. "I'm like a maniac sometimes," he admitted. "[But] people know what I expect of them, and if they can't take the pace, it's best that they leave."[66] In fact, a number have left. Part of the reason behind their departure was Kissinger's killing work pace. But a larger reason was that the Nixon reward system offered little inducement to the exceptionally bright aide who aspired to Presidential attention. One observer comments that among the host of reasons for the exodus from NSC's ranks was a common one: "[Aides] were denied access to Nixon; they could not aspire to become Kaysens, Komers or Bators, men whose personal relationships with Kennedy and Johnson gave them leverage."[67]

Prior to becoming Secretary of State himself, Henry Kissinger, with his fifty-two professionals, built above the State Department duplicating its critical functions—planning and policy formulation areas. The elevation of the action to the NSC level greatly strengthens the President's control over the search for and evaluation of the options. It might also be noted that this system also comes strikingly close to Kennedy's dream, stated facetiously, of "establishing a secret office of thirty people or so to run foreign policy while maintaining the State Department as a facade in which people might contentedly carry papers from bureau to bureau."[68]

Along with its strengths, there were drawbacks to the Nixon-Kissinger system. First of all, any system which excludes the bureaucracy in formulating policy may not be able to count on the agencies to implement it. Secondly, Nixon's distaste for interpersonal conflict might easily have provided an incentive for Kissinger to conceal some of the policy differences that might arise between his staff and the State Department. Had Kissinger fallen into Walt Rostow's habit of screening out differing points of view, our lesson from previous Administrations suggests that this would lessen the quality of analysis and limit the alternatives identified. Thus far, the NSC system appears to have avoided this pitfall. It is known, for example, that vigorous discussion occurred on several occasions. Preceding the invasion of Cambodia, Kissinger is reported to have held a stormy session with five staffers who argued heatedly against the assault. During the Bangladesh crisis, according to confidential minutes disclosed by columnist Jack Anderson, advisers from the State Department fought Kissinger tooth and nail. They argued for the support of India despite the President's desire to favor Pakistan. In each instance, the President did what he had planned to do, but more for reasons of his own convictions than for the want of other alternatives.

An important facet of the formalistic approach, as noted earlier, is its capacities for thorough staffwork and stress on the merits of a problem. While these attributes are most prominent in the Administration's handling of foreign policy matters, they are periodically visible elsewhere. A case in point occurred in connection with the important decisions that led to the President's shift from voluntary controls to Phase I's involuntary wage and price controls. Most sources agree that the President and his principal advisers had been deeply dedicated to a reliance on free market forces. Yet there was no hiding from the Bureau of Labor Statistics' monthly indices that gave evidence of marching inflation. Nixon sought out his new Secretary of the Treasury John Connally, and the two began conferring on the economic situation for two and three hours at a time. Keeping their plans secret for fear rumors might further disrupt the economy, they began to sketch out the options open to the President. Publicly, they both sounded adamant against controls. But when inflation continued and the attack on the dollar reached near-crisis proportions in Europe, Nixon called all of his top advisers to a climactic conference at Camp David. Although, in characteristic fashion, the President let Connally do the talking and he the mediating, it was a no-holds-barred session. A drastic shift in policy was hammered out. "It was tough. A damn tough re-evaluation and re-analysis," Connally said afterward.[69] "It was," said Nixon, "a weekend that would long be remembered."[70]

The incident is significant in several respects. First, it demonstrated the capacity of the Nixon system to set ideology aside and concentrate on the substance of an issue. This is a strength of the formalistic approach. Second, as in foreign policy matters, the President injected himself deeply into the issues, and his personal involvement made a difference. But thirdly, and most importantly, the incident represented an exception to the President's normal way of doing business. He did not rely on his advisers to present him with the set of options they had defined. Instead, snatching a chapter from Franklin Roosevelt, we find the President working covertly with one adviser and pitting his views against the others. During one shining managerial moment, at the inception of Phase I, we saw the synthesis of the competitive and formalistic approaches. And it worked. The competitive approach with its power to develop new options and the formalistic approach with its capacity for thorough analysis were fused. The decision profited from it.

While Richard Nixon has rarely cast the image of FDR, he has exhibited the capacity to overrule his advisers on numerous and significant occasions. While dependent upon a multilayered staff, he is not, like Eisenhower, nearly so dependent upon their judgments. For example, he signed the Voting Rights Act of 1970, granting the vote to eighteen-year-olds over ardent protests of the President's top political adviser at the time, Attorney General John Mitchell, and the entire White House Congressional liaison staff. He went against the wishes of the majority of his Cabinet concerning both welfare reform and the reorganization of his Executive office. Against the strong advice of former Secretary of Defense Melvin Laird and Henry Kissinger, Nixon told the public that "the headquarters for the entire Communist military operation in South Vietnam" would be attacked in Cambodia.[71] In a similar vein, he pursued his own predilections in the Bangladesh crisis, supporting Pakistan and overruling contrary recommendations from the Department of State and Kissinger. He ordered the Christmas bombing of Hanoi over the objections of the Joint Chiefs of Staff.[72] These actions, whether or not we regard them as sound, provide a check on the formalistic system by reminding the staff that the President can think for himself. It keeps the staff on their toes, and adds an incentive to ensure all alternatives are identified.

A second fail-safe of the Nixon system stems from the President's tendency to look for what will go wrong. "He is not one to make assumptions based on optimism," John Ehrlichman has said.[73] Given the multiple layering of his formalistic system, and the corresponding increase in the likelihood that the more people involved in the communication system the greater the chance of miscommunication and error, a little healthy skepticism seems called for. Unfortunately, most of Nixon's skepticism centers on what can go wrong outside of his system—what his opponents might do and so forth. His biggest blind spot has been attending to what can go wrong from within.

Reviewing the Administration's performance, we find strengths and weaknesses of astonishing extremes. The Administration's achievements on the foreign policy front may one day be regarded as masterful episodes in U.S. diplomacy. In our examination of why the Administration has performed well in this area and less impressively elsewhere, there are indications that foreign policy problems dovetail nicely with the strengths of the formalistic approach. Diplomacy focuses on foreign governments which can be regarded more or less as unitary entities, about which intelligence can be gathered, options weighed, and with whom agreements may be negotiated. Such problems lend themselves to a sequence of carefully reasoned moves as in a game of chess. This mode of problem solving is far different from that which is often called for in the domestic arena where confusing cross-currents of public opinion and Congressional influence must be grasped and nurtured in a fast-flowing stream of events.

Like other Presidents we have studied, Richard Nixon's style is interwoven with the managerial machinery he has created. And perhaps more than most, he sees himself as the "head of an administration," as a G.S. 100 who sets policies, but above all, administers a decision-making process. To some extent, he has remained "the underdog fighting against" rather than "the statesman building amongst." To the extent this is true, he may have exaggerated the obstacles to leadership—and in the process, made them more real. Richard Nixon, like all men, is bound by his personality and his past; his idiosyncrasies have left their stamp upon his Presidency.

CHAPTER EIGHT

CONCLUSION

Every fourth year, Americans engage in a peculiar form of madness. Beginning in the early spring of election years, would-be Presidential candidates trace a path from New Hampshire west to Wisconsin. The madness begins within the ranks of the candidate's supporters, for if he is to brave the primary process, he must build a loyal following. He courts their support by reaffirming his commitment to their concerns and aspirations. In exchange, they make great sacrifices, enduring the hazards of weather, hecklers, and the press, catching bad meals on the run, sleeping infrequently—all in hopes of building a wave of victories that will carry their candidate to the White House.

The madness gathers momentum in the primaries and gradually the public at large becomes involved. Typically, party interest reaches its climax in time for the national convention. There the leading candidate discovers that despite his success in the primaries, he is not guaranteed the nomination. Now he encounters a whole new set of obstacles and must engage in a crasser form of politics: he must corral delegates, horse trade favors in return for their votes, wield power to intimidate dissidents, and execute deft compromises to build the winning coalition.

If the candidate wins his party's nomination, a quadrennial

drama unfolds—its predictability in no way dulling the public's appetite for the plot. First, the candidate begins to distance himself from his original following in search of the political middle ground. His original supporters become as disenchanted as he is preoccupied with walking this political tightrope. The drama is televised before ninety million Americans who watch nightly for a slip, a contradiction, a foolish mistake. Public fascination will pursue him unmercifully—observing his habits, his quirks, his family life, his staff. Frank Mankiewicz, George McGovern's campaign manager, has said:

[Such intimate attention to campaign details] has had a pernicious influence . . . and has changed the whole style and substance of American [campaigns]. . . . All this inside stuff, because of [its appeal, causes] a lot of reporters, particularly the commentators, [to become] obsessed with reporting inside stuff and ignore the things the public is interested in. Almost from the beginning of [the McGovern] campaign, there [was] far more attention devoted to polls and fund-raising and staffing . . . than to what the candidate [was] actually doing and saying.[1]

Ostensibly, Mankiewicz's complaint seems reasonable. Campaigns *ought* to be on the issues. In fact, the public usually participates in heated debate over the positions of the candidates. But curiously, this occurs despite the citizens' foreknowledge that the candidate, once elected, is not likely to deliver on the promises he makes.

We may ask what lies at the root of this process, seemingly so rife with contradiction: candidates risking primaries that do not secure the hoped-for outcome at the convention, debate over convention platforms that are ignored once the convention is over, emotionalism over issues that no one expects much action on, candidates stressing their positions while commentators focus on the process of the campaign itself. But before we dismiss Americans as entirely crazy, we should note that the wear and tear of campaigns and the exposure to the grueling public spotlight have a way of unmasking a man. How the public sees a candidate's personal qualities may play a large part in winning or losing elections. Was Eisenhower elected on his politics or on the basis of his image as a sincere statesman and leader? Did John Kennedy defeat Richard Nixon on the *issues*, or did the Nixon-Kennedy debates simply convince many Americans that Kennedy was more real and sincere? Was McGovern really defeated by his controversial positions or by his fumbles early in the campaign over the Eagleton matter and his economic policies that cast doubt on his ability to choose and manage men?

Americans have a keen sense of what they seek in a President. A prime function of the campaign may well be to expose the man as much as his positions. Insofar as this is true, our efforts to come to grips with candidates as human beings have suffered from not making our inquiry explicit. To be sure, we can learn much about a candidate from the campaign. In many respects, the campaign is a kind of Presidential pentathlon. The candidate must reveal charismatic qualities to attract a following, he must organize and administer a large and complex organization, he must maintain financial solvency, he must bargain effectively on the convention floor, and he must periodically rise above it all as a statesman. But far more information on these attributes is at hand than that which surfaces by happenstance during the campaign itself. The preceding chapters suggest that much of what a President *will be* is strongly indicated by what he *has been*. Truman's reliance on his staff, his drive to "do right"—even his stubbornness—were visible in his handling of the wartime investigations of the Truman Committee. Eisenhower, the conciliating Supreme Commander in Europe who relied on his army staff, served in a similar fashion in the White House. Nixon, working in secrecy and in solitude on the Hiss case, behaved in much the same manner as President; his tightly organized campaign machinery—complete with Haldeman on the top of the pyramid—was a near-perfect prototype of what he later installed in the White House.

It is not sufficient to argue that the past determines the present. The toughest question remains "How?" What the previous chapters suggest is that we can, in fact, go considerably beyond the conventional wisdom in answering this question, not only in predicting the personal traits which a candidate will carry with him into the White House, but how these together with his prior administrative experience will shape the way in which he organizes his staff. Given his management approach, we can predict how his system will function and what its strengths and weaknesses are likely to be.

It has been useful to think in terms of three approaches to management—formalistic, competitive, and collegial. Clearly, these labels oversimplify. But our intent has not been to confine complex behavior to simple boxes; rather it has been to describe these three patterns of management and to demonstrate their usefulness. To the extent that a manager adopts one of these patterns, he will incur costs and reap benefits predictably associated with it.

Three of the six presidents discussed utilized the formalistic approach. (Lyndon Johnson is a possible fourth and will be discussed separately.) We have been able to find some interesting similarities among them. Truman, Eisenhower, and Nixon shared a common emphasis on structure. The Truman Presidency saw the creation of such entities as the National Security Council and the Council of Economic Advisors; Eisenhower embellished these institutions with interlocking subordinate staffs; Nixon built the same institutions into his decision-making machinery, adding the largest NSC staff in history and an entirely new entity, the Domestic Policy Council. In each administration the President publicly emphasized his desire to make the "best" decision. Each employed his staff to preserve his time for the "big decisions."

Perhaps the most remarkable similarity among these three Presidents' administrations is the extent to which each fell victim to the same shortcomings. For example, all were embarrassed by scandals. A number of Truman's staff were convicted;

Eisenhower lost Talbott and Sherman Adams and was humiliated by the Dixon-Yates affair; Nixon has had to answer to perhaps the most far-reaching scandal in the nation's history, involving a long parade of horrors beginning with ITT and the Watergate. Each at one time or another made suboptimal decisions when their staff machinery insulated them too much: Truman in deciding to invade North Korea, Eisenhower in his handling of the Suez crisis and Little Rock, and Nixon in responding to the Haynsworth defeat and the Watergate break-in. They also shared in common the problem of having their intentions thwarted by covert bargaining among their advisers. Eisenhower's Cabinet members negotiated interagency compromises "out of court"; Clark Clifford has described his quiet struggle against Steelman "for Truman's mind"; and the inner workings of Nixon's domestic staff attest to similar difficulties. One point repeatedly reinforced by these observations is that the later a President interjects himself into the decision process, the more he limits the breadth of information available to him. The President's options are correspondingly reduced.

As we have seen, there is no effective substitute for the President's involvement. Eisenhower's system worked best when he was personally involved and committed—as in "The Chances for Peace" speech and the "Open Skies" proposal. Nixon's finest hours have occurred on the foreign policy front, where Kissinger's smooth-running policy analysis machinery has been accompanied by the President's own close attention and scrutiny.

In further comparing the Presidents who have used the formalistic approach, we can also note similarities in their personalities. First, each tended to be somewhat uncomfortable in managing people. Truman's shyness and sense of inadequacy led him into a "deference trap" with strong-minded subordinates such as Henry Wallace, Jimmy Byrnes, and Douglas MacArthur. Eisenhower steadfastly sought to keep "personalities" out of decisions and even refused to take part in selecting his

Cabinet. Nixon has likewise received wide attention for "depersonalizing" the Presidency. A second personal characteristic of these Presidents, perhaps less true of Truman, was their common belief that a well-designed management system should guard against, or at least compensate for, the human factor. Each wanted to hedge against human error—which is reasonable enough—but Eisenhower and Nixon, in particular, sought to *eradicate* it through "systematization" rather than recognize and allow for it on an individual-by-individual basis. A third similarity was the remarkable degree to which each tended to avoid interpersonal conflict. Each used his staff to screen out unpleasant encounters.

Lyndon Johnson remains an intriguing exception to many of our generalizations about management style. While LBJ tended toward the formalistic approach, his personality simply overshadowed it. This is not to say that he did not share characteristics with the other Presidents who chose this approach. He exhibited a preference for a structured decision process, he preferred to evaluate alternatives rather than participate in creating them, and like Eisenhower and Nixon, he was unhappy when conflict erupted within his own administrative family. But here the similarities end. Johnson's personality shaped a system that was, above all, idiosyncratic. His reward system, in particular, was not in the remotest sense geared to keeping his Administration running smoothly. Instead, his ways of rewarding and punishing aides seem to have been conditioned almost entirely by personal needs; that his impact was disruptive appears to have been secondary to his requirement for the exercise of control. This corrupted his system, resulted in the resignation of many talented subordinates, and caused many who remained to abdicate to his whims at the expense of honest counsel.

It is fascinating to note that while the Presidents using the formalistic approach had similar shortcomings, these same problems were almost entirely absent in the Roosevelt and Kennedy

Presidencies. Roosevelt's competitive system and Kennedy's collegial approach were strongest where the formalistic approach was weakest. There were few scandals and little of the behind-the-scenes shenanigans among aides that the President knew nothing about. Both FDR and JFK had a higher tolerance of interpersonal conflict. Both immersed themselves in the information process and derived satisfaction from reaching down and *shaping* the options—not just selecting from among those presented to them. The price they paid was that the personal demands on their time and attention were enormous. And because they were so intimately a part of the system, their Administrations tended to fail when they failed. Roosevelt's approach, in particular, was greatly dependent on his ability to forge workable solutions. His approach generated creative ideas, but the overlapping delegations of authority and conflicting personalities required his constant attention. During the war years, he could not do this, and consequently his chaotic system spawned inefficiency.

Kennedy's collegial approach did not demand as much Presidential centrality. Relationships were more cordial, delegations less conflicting, and the team shared collective responsibility. But the driving force behind the process was Kennedy's own commitment to identifying "all alternatives." When he performed this policing function, his system worked admirably; when he did not, teamwork tended toward myopic unanimity and mutual support. (This tendency became pronounced when Lyndon Johnson inherited Kennedy's team of advisers.) But even under Kennedy's stewardship, the decision-making process leading to the Bay of Pigs gives testimony to the vulnerability of his approach. In contrast to Eisenhower, Kennedy had created no self-sustaining system; when Kennedy faltered, so did his system. When his personal resources became overcommitted, when he ceased to badger his aides to ensure that all alternatives got a full hearing, his Administration stumbled. Thus we note an important trade-off between the various approaches. More fluid systems are more responsive, but they are also more dependent on the decision maker. The price of this dependence is exacted in the drain upon the decision maker's personal resources; his capacities determine his system's capacities. Those who use the competitive or collegial approaches must avoid becoming overextended. They must allocate their energies carefully.

Kennedy's system worked best within the closed environment of the White House. When functioning smoothly, it probably did a better job than either the formalistic or competitive modes. Kennedy's teamwork generated creative alternatives and staffed them out. It was more responsive than the formalistic approach, and it enlisted the President earlier in the decision process and consequently gave him more influence in shaping the options. Like the competitive approach, Kennedy's collegial system did not ignore conflict, but unlike Roosevelt, Kennedy was able to tap this energy and use it for solving the problem while avoiding wasteful friction and interpersonal strife.

In discussing the pros and cons of the three managerial approaches, we are implicitly stating criteria against which a decision-making process can be judged. One criterion is the degree to which the decision-making machinery screens and distorts information; a second is the extent to which the decision maker is exposed to both substantive and interpersonal conflict; a third is the overall responsiveness of the decision process; and a fourth is the thoroughness with which alternatives are staffed out and decisions are weighed. With these four criteria in mind, the following table gives the costs and benefits of the three managerial patterns discussed.

Listing the costs of each of the managerial approaches raises the question, "How can a decision maker possibly offset them?" Personality permitting, a President might seek ways to hedge against his system's shortcomings. For example, a President who adopts the formalistic approach might choose to establish

	BENEFITS	COSTS
Formalistic Approach	Orderly decision process enforces more thorough analysis. Conserves the decision maker's time and attention for the big decisions. Emphasizes the optimal.	The hierarchy which screens information may also distort it. Tendency of the screening process to wash out or distort political pressures and public sentiments. Tendency to respond slowly or inappropriately in crisis.
Competitive Approach	Places the decision maker in the mainstream of the information network. Tends to generate solutions that are politically feasible and bureaucratically doable. Generates creative ideas, partially as a result of the "stimulus" of competition, but also because this unstructured kind of information network is more open to ideas from the outside.	Places large demands on decision maker's time and attention. Exposes decision maker to partial or biased information. Decision process may overly sacrifice optimality for doability. Tendency to aggravate staff competition with the risk that aides may pursue their own interests at the expense of the decision maker. Wear and tear on aides fosters attrition and high turnover.
Collegial Approach	Seeks to achieve both optimality and doability. Involves the decision maker in the information network but somewhat eases the demands upon him by stressing teamwork over competition.	Places substantial demands on the decision maker's time and attention. Requires unusual interpersonal skills in dealing with subordinates, mediating differences, and maintaining teamwork among colleagues.

more fluid decisional machinery or reach further down the information channels when facing a decision of particular importance to his Administration. A Chief Executive who adopts the competitive style might commission formal study groups to ensure careful staff work on complex policy questions and thereby augment his ad hoc decision process. (Interestingly, Roosevelt adopted this expedient in establishing the Brownlow Commission to study and recommend ways to modernize his Executive Office.) A President who chooses the collegial approach might utilize a more formalistic structure for routine matters in order to concentrate his energies on the more sensitive policy areas.

However an Executive chooses to manage, his managerial approach sets a process in motion that not only "makes decisions" but also affects (a) the quality of those decisions and (b) how the decisions are implemented. We have noted strikingly dissimilar results as different Presidents with differing styles have dealt with the bureaucracy and Congress. FDR encountered many obstacles in using the competitive approach to coordinate his wartime agencies. Kennedy seemed also to be employing a competitive pattern in his dealings with the Department of State; his success, like Roosevelt's, was questionable. In contrast, Truman, Eisenhower, Johnson, and Nixon, utilizing the formalistic approach, achieved at least a semblance of control. It can be argued, of course, that the bureaucracy remained unmanageable and that the formalistic hierarchy simply concealed this fact. It would seem, however, that Johnson, using formalistic means, squeezed some measure of performance from the agencies. In the same vein, Kennedy, adopting a formalistic approach in delegating the management of the Department of Defense to McNamara, seems to have been well rewarded.

If the elaborate formalistic machinery is well suited to monitoring the bureaucracy, it seems equally clear that it is ill-suited to dealing with Congress. Whereas Roosevelt's and Johnson's competitive tactics were successful on the Hill, the formalistic techniques of Eisenhower, Truman, and Nixon were demonstrably ineffective. The competitive approach embraces conflict, acknowledges the importance of interpersonal confrontation, gives salience to bargaining, and employs secrecy and the hint of patronage to achieve its effects. In these respects, this approach appears ideally suited to the Congressional milieu. Insofar as Congress is concerned, there appears to be no substitute for bargaining. Kennedy's teamwork fell flat when applied to Congress. Fundamentally, his approach depended upon collective effort and shared purposes; these values seemed misplaced in the highly pluralistic and contentious setting under the Capitol dome.

These observations suggest that each of the patterns of management has its place in the various facets of the Presidency. Clearly, it would be the rare President who could use all three effectively. But to the extent that awareness of these requirements brings us closer to meeting them, we have come a considerable distance.

NOTES

PREFACE

1. Graham T. Allison, *Essence of Decision* (Boston: Little, Brown, 1971), pp. 124–125.
2. Remarks by Richard E. Paget, President, Cresap, McCormick and Paget, Washington, D.C., November 18, 1969; also see Thomas E. Cronin, "The Presidency as a Domestic Policy Executive." Unpublished paper for the Center for the Study of Democratic Institutions, December 29, 1971, p. 8.
3. Harold Seidman, *Politics, Position, and Power* (New York: Oxford University Press, 1970), p. 86.
4. For an excellent discussion of Executive-Cabinet relations, see Richard F. Fenno, Jr., "The President's Cabinet," in Aaron Wildavsky, ed., *The Presidency* (Boston: Little, Brown, 1969), p. 507.
5. Ibid., p. 506.
6. Ibid., pp. 506–507.
7. Thomas E. Cronin, "White House–Departmental Relations," op. cit., p. 584.
8. Ibid., pp. 583–584.
9. Ibid., p. 586.
10. Ibid., pp. 586, 588.
11. Richard E. Neustadt, *Presidential Power* (New York: Wiley, 1960).

ONE: PRESIDENTIAL STYLE

1. James D. Barber, *The Presidential Character* (Englewood Cliffs, N.J.: Prentice-Hall, 1972).
2. For example, see Juan Cameron, "Richard Nixon's Very Personal White House," *Fortune*, July 1970, pp. 104–108.

3. Alfred Marshall, *The Economics of Industry* (London: Macmillan, 1885), p. 231.

4. See Ezra Taft Benson, *Cross Fire* (Garden City, N.Y.: Doubleday, 1962), pp. 36, 194, 206, 511; also Emmet John Hughes, *The Ordeal of Power* (New York: Atheneum, 1963).

5. For example, see Henry Morgenthau, Jr., "The Struggle for a Program," in James N. Rosenau, *The Roosevelt Treasury* (Garden City, N.Y.: Doubleday, 1951), pp. 310–321.

6. Robert E. Sherwood, *Roosevelt and Hopkins* (New York: Harper, 1948), pp. 71, 756; also see John Gunther, *Roosevelt in Retrospect*, (New York: Harper, 1960), pp. 133–134; also see Rexford G. Tugwell, *The Democratic Roosevelt* (Garden City, N.Y.: Doubleday, 1957), p. 547.

7. Arthur M. Schlesinger, Jr., *A Thousand Days* (Boston: Houghton Mifflin, 1965), p. 807; also see Robert F. Kennedy, *Thirteen Days* (New York, Norton, 1969), p. 33.

two: ROOSEVELT'S FEUDING FRATERNITY

1. James MacGregor Burns, *Roosevelt: The Lion and the Fox* (New York: Harcourt, Brace, 1956), p. 165.

2. James D. Barber, *The Presidential Character* (Englewood Cliffs, N.J.: Prentice-Hall, 1972), p. vii.

3. Richard Hofstadter, *American Political Tradition* (New York: Knopf, 1948), p. 328.

4. Burns, op. cit., p. 219.

5. Lauren Henry, *Presidential Transitions* (Washington, D.C.: Brookings Institution, 1960), p. 385.

6. Burns, op. cit., p. 180.

7. Francis Biddle, "The Labor Board," Biddle Papers.

8. Burns, op. cit., p. 183.

9. Burns, op. cit., p. 51.

10. Ibid., pp. 86–87.

11. Joseph P. Lash, *Franklin and Eleanor* (New York: Norton, 1971), p. 432.

12. Burns, op. cit., pp. 93–94.

13. Arthur M. Schlesinger, Jr., *The Age of Roosevelt: The Coming of the New Deal* (Boston: Houghton Mifflin, 1958), p. 535.

14. Henry, op. cit., p. 33.

15. John Gunther, *Roosevelt in Retrospect* (New York: Harper, 1950), p. 133.

16. Rexford G. Tugwell, Tugwell Papers, February 16, 1935.
17. Gunther, op. cit., p. 49.
18. Schlesinger, op. cit., p. 547.
19. Robert E. Sherwood, *Roosevelt and Hopkins* (New York: Harper, 1948), p. 70.
20. Ibid., p. 71.
21. Ibid., p. 547.
22. Ibid., p. 547.
23. Ibid., p. 537.
24. Burns, op. cit., p. 265.
25. Francis Biddle, *In Brief Authority* (Garden City, N.Y.: Doubleday, 1962), p. 5.
26. Schlesinger, op. cit., p. 538.
27. Francis Perkins, *The Roosevelt I Knew* (New York: Viking Press, 1946), p. 137.
28. Schlesinger, op. cit., p. 539.
29. Louis Koenig, *The Invisible Presidency* (New York: Rinehart, 1960), p. 269.
30. Rexford G. Tugwell, *The Democratic Roosevelt* (Garden City, N.Y.: Doubleday, 1957), p. 547.
31. Lash, op. cit., p. 505.
32. Burns, op. cit., p. 332.
33. Ibid., pp. 457–458.
34. Koenig, op. cit., p. 319.
35. Ibid., p. 325.
36. Ibid., p. 324.
37. Ibid., pp. 324–325.
38. Henry L. Stimson, *On Active Service in Peace and War* (New York: Harper, 1947), p. 494.
39. Koenig, op. cit., p. 321.
40. James MacGregor Burns, *Roosevelt: The Soldier of Freedom* (New York: Harcourt, Brace, 1970), p. 190.
41. Harold L. Ickes, *The Secret Diary of Harold L. Ickes, Vol. III, The Lowering Clouds, 1939–1941* (New York: Simon and Schuster, 1954), p. 194.
42. A. J. Wann, *The President as Chief Administrator* (Washington, D.C.: Public Affairs Press, 1968), p. 136.
43. Ibid., p. 145.
44. Cabell Phillips, *The Truman Presidency* (New York: Macmillan, 1966), p. 37.
45. James F. Byrnes, *Speaking Frankly* (New York: Harper, 1947), p. 18.

46. Stimson, op. cit., p. 495.
47. Alfred Steinberg, *The Man From Missouri* (New York: Putnam, 1962), p. 201.
48. Burns, *Roosevelt: The Soldier of Freedom*, p. 230.
49. Ibid., p. 230.
50. Edgar E. Robinson, *The Roosevelt Leadership, 1933–45* (Philadelphia: Lippincott, 1955), p. 349.
51. Sherwood, op. cit., p. 789.
52. Burns, *Roosevelt: The Soldier of Freedom*, p. 409.
53. Sherwood, op. cit., p. 696.
54. Koenig, op. cit., p. 333.

THREE: TRUMAN'S MANAGEMENT BY TRANSGRESSION

1. Harry S. Truman, *Years of Trial and Hope, 1946–1952* (New York: New American Library, 1956), p. 13.
2. James D. Barber, *The Presidential Character* (Englewood Cliffs, N.J.: Prentice-Hall, 1972), p. 278.
3. Cabell Phillips, *The Truman Presidency* (New York: Macmillan, 1966), pp. 160–161.
4. Margaret Truman, *Harry S. Truman* (New York: Morrow, 1973), p. 322.
5. Barber, op. cit., p. 280.
6. Phillips, op. cit., p. 171.
7. Harry S. Truman, op. cit., p. 129.
8. Margaret Truman, op. cit., p. 74.
9. Alfred Steinberg, *The Man from Missouri* (New York: Putnam, 1962), p. 24.
10. Ibid., p. 24; also see Phillips, op. cit., pp. 10–14.
11. Barber, op. cit., p. 259.
12. Ibid., p. 260.
13. Ibid., p. 260.
14. Phillips, op. cit., p. 27.
15. Barber, op. cit., p. 262.
16. Arthur Krock, *New York Times*, June 14, 1938.
17. Margaret Truman, op. cit., p. 104.
18. Steinberg, op. cit., pp. 147–148.
19. Ibid., p. 134.
20. Ibid., p. 167.
21. Margaret Truman, op. cit., p. 95.
22. Ibid., p. 112.

23. Ibid., p. 3.
24. Ibid., p. 55.
25. Phillips, op. cit., p. 153.
26. Steinberg, op. cit., p. 188.
27. Margaret Truman, op. cit., p. 147.
28. Ibid., p. 140.
29. See Phillips, op. cit., p. 37; also Steinberg, op. cit., p. 197.
30. Margaret Truman, op. cit., p. 253.
31. Ibid., p. 449.
32. Steinberg, op. cit., p. 348.
33. Margaret Truman, op. cit., pp. 161–162.
34. Ibid., pp. 254–255.
35. Steinberg, op. cit., p. 352.
36. Barber, op. cit., p. 273.
37. Ibid., p. 273.
38. Margaret Truman, op. cit., p. 3.
39. Ibid., p. 26.
40. Ibid., pp. 35–36.
41. Ibid., p. 260.
42. Patrick Anderson, *The Presidents' Men* (Garden City, N.Y.: Doubleday, 1968), pp. 95–97.
43. Ibid., p. 116.
44. Glen Paige, *The Korean Decision* (New York: Free Press, 1968), p. 331.
45. *New York Times*, June 28, 1950, p. 4.
46. David S. McLellan, "Dean Acheson and the Korean War," *Political Science Quarterly* 83 (1968), p. 32.
47. Ibid., p. 37.
48. Irving L. Janis, *Victims of Groupthink* (Boston: Houghton Mifflin, 1972), p. 55.
49. H. A. deWeerd, "Strategic Surprise in the Korean War," *Orbis* 6 (1962), p. 451.
50. George F. Kennan, *Memoirs (1925–1950)* (New York: Bantam, 1969), p. 513.
51. Dean Acheson, *Present at the Creation* (New York: Norton, 1969), p. 468.
52. John Hersey, "Profiles: Mr. President II–Ten O'Clock Meeting," *The New Yorker*, April 14, 1951, p. 53.
53. Richard E. Neustadt, *Presidential Power* (New York: Wiley, 1960), p. 140.
54. Phillips, op. cit., p. 69.

55. Margaret Truman, op. cit., p. 450.
56. Steinberg, op. cit., pp. 277–278.
57. Ibid., p. 13.
58. Ibid., p. 254.
59. Ibid., p. 279.
60. Phillips, op. cit., p. 196.
61. Steinberg, op. cit., p. 253.
62. Ibid., p. 387.
63. Ibid., pp. 393–400.
64. Ibid., p. 145.
65. *New York Times,* July 16, 1948, p. 18.
66. Phillips, op. cit., p. 397.

FOUR: EISENHOWER'S ORGANIZED ABSENTEEISM

1. Herman Finer, *Dulles Over Suez* (Chicago: Quadrangle Books, 1964), p. 1.
2. Ibid., p. 11.
3. Ibid., p. 46.
4. Ibid., p. 47.
5. Ibid., p. 48.
6. Ibid., p. 48.
7. Robert Murphy, *Diplomat Among Warriors* (Garden City, N.Y.: Doubleday, 1964), p. 379.
8. Finer, op. cit., p. 64.
9. Ibid., p. 64.
10. Murphy, op. cit., p. 381.
11. Emmet John Hughes, *The Ordeal of Power* (New York: Atheneum, 1963), p. 216.
12. Finer, op. cit., p. 88.
13. Hughes, op. cit., p. 215.
14. Lloyd A. Free, ed., *French Motivations in the Suez Crisis* (Princeton, N.J.: Institute for International Social Research, November, 1956).
15. Finer, op. cit., p. 438.
16. Sherman Adams, *Firsthand Report* (New York: Harper, 1961), p. 260.
17. Hughes, op. cit., p. 178.
18. "Too Little Too Late," *New York Herald Tribune,* September 23, 1956.
19. Adams, op. cit., p. 87.

20. Ibid., p. 88.
21. Ibid., pp. 90–91.
22. Ibid., p. 91.
23. Finer, op. cit., p. 70.
24. Ibid., p. 72.
25. Adams, op. cit., p. 53.
26. Ibid., p. 62.
27. Ibid., p. 76.
28. Marquis Childs, *Eisenhower: Captive Hero* (New York: Harcourt, Brace, 1958), p. 167.
29. Patrick Anderson, *The Presidents' Men* (Garden City, N.Y.: Doubleday, 1968), p. 135.
30. Finer, op. cit., p. 50.
31. Richard E. Neustadt, *Presidential Power* (New York: Wiley, 1960), p. 71.
32. Ibid., p. 74.
33. Adams, op. cit., p. 208.
34. Ibid., p. 206.
35. Ibid., pp. 5, 6.
36. Ezra Taft Benson, *Cross Fire* (Garden City, N.Y.: Doubleday, 1962), p. 134.
37. Author interview with Jack Walsh, June 1972.
38. Adams, op. cit., p. 101.
39. Henry A. Kissinger, *The Necessity for Choice* (New York: Harper, 1960), pp. 356–357.
40. Robert J. Donovan, *Eisenhower: The Inside Story* (New York: Harper, 1961), pp. 333–334.
41. Ibid., p. 335.
42. Ibid., pp. 339–340.
43. Ibid., p. 339.
44. Richard Rovere, *The Eisenhower Years* (New York: Farrar, Straus, 1956), p. 356.
45. Ibid., p. 356.
46. Anderson, op. cit., p. 175.
47. Louis Koenig, *The Chief Executive* (New York: Harcourt, Brace, 1964), p. 170.
48. Ibid., p. 170.
49. Ibid., p. 171.
50. Adams, op. cit., p. 51.
51. Ibid., p. 75.
52. Anderson, op. cit., p. 152.

53. Interview with Jack Walsh, June 1972.
54. Anderson, op. cit., pp. 159–166.
55. Finer, op. cit., pp. 518–519.
56. Adams, op. cit., p. 76.
57. Ibid., p. 76.
58. Ibid., p. 76.
59. Ibid., p. 76.
60. Ibid., p. 75.
61. Neustadt, op. cit., p. 155.
62. Dwight D. Eisenhower, *At Ease* (New York: Avon, 1968), p. 58.
63. Kenneth Davis, *Soldier of Democracy* (Garden City, N.Y.: Doubleday, 1945), p. 192.
64. Chester Wilmot, *The Struggle for Europe* (New York, Harper, 1952), pp. 467–468.
65. Elmer E. Cornwell, *Presidential Leadership of Public Opinion* (Bloomington: Indiana University Press, 1965), p. 177.
66. Interview with Jack Walsh, June 1972.
67. Adams, op. cit., pp. 21–22.
68. Ibid., p. 22.
69. James D. Barber, *The Presidential Character* (Englewood Cliffs, N.J.: Prentice-Hall, 1972), p. 157.
70. Ibid., p. 158.
71. Hughes, op. cit., p. 125.
72. Ibid., p. 143.
73. Adams, op. cit., p. 106.
74. Hughes, op. cit., p. 144.
75. Donovan, op. cit., p. 76.
76. Barber, op. cit., p. 162.
77. *New York Times,* July 4, 1957.
78. *New York Times,* July 18, 1957.
79. Adams, op. cit., p. 349.
80. Virgil T. Blossom, *It Has Happened Here* (New York: Harper, 1959), p. 95.
81. Ibid., p. 95.
82. Adams, op. cit., p. 355.
83. *Time,* October 21, 1957.
84. *New York Times,* October 15, 1957.
85. Hughes, op. cit., p. 301.
86. Ibid., p. 103.
87. Ibid., p. 106.
88. Ibid., p. 107.

89. Adams, op. cit., p. 97.
90. Ibid., p. 98.
91. Ibid., p. 98.
92. Hughes, op. cit., p. 116.
93. Adams, op. cit., p. 91.
94. Ibid., pp. 177–178.
95. Anderson, op. cit., p. 142.
96. Adams, op. cit., p. 186.
97. Ibid., p. 187.
98. Ibid., p. 293.
99. Ibid., p. 74.
100. Ibid., p. 183.
101. Childs, op. cit., p. 215.
102. Adams, op. cit., p. 185.
103. Barber, op. cit., pp. 158–159.
104. Evelyn Lincoln, *Kennedy and Johnson* (New York: Holt, Rinehart & Winston, 1968), p. 190.
105. Neustadt, op. cit., p. 152.

FIVE: KENNEDY'S GAMBLES ON GROUPTHINK

1. Hugh Sidey, *John F. Kennedy, President* (New York: Atheneum, 1963), p. 204.
2. Leo Damore, *The Cape Cod Years of John Fitzgerald Kennedy* (Englewood Cliffs, N. J.: Prentice-Hall, 1967), p. 86.
3. Ibid., p. 91.
4. James MacGregor Burns, *John Kennedy* (New York: Harcourt, Brace, 1959), p. 20.
5. Theodore C. Sorensen, *Kennedy* (New York: Harper & Row, 1965), p. 41.
6. Burns, op. cit., p. 261.
7. Ibid., p. 262.
8. Ibid., p. 217.
9. Louis W. Koenig, *The Chief Executive* (New York: Harcourt, Brace, 1964), p. 174.
10. Arthur M. Schlesinger, Jr., *A Thousand Days* (Boston: Houghton Mifflin, 1965), p. 129.
11. Ibid., p. 135.
12. David Halberstam, *The Best and the Brightest* (New York: Random House, 1972), p. 458.

13. Jim Bishop, *A Day in the Life of President Kennedy* (New York: Random House, 1964), p. 217.

14. Schlesinger, op. cit., p. 912.

15. Ibid., p. 123.

16. Ibid., p. 155.

17. Sorensen, op. cit., p. 258.

18. Ibid., pp. 373–374.

19. Koenig, op. cit., p. 175.

20. Sorensen, op. cit., p. 374.

21. Schlesinger, op. cit., pp. 69, 687.

22. Sorensen, op. cit., p. 260.

23. Schlesinger, op. cit., p. 207.

24. Sorensen, op. cit., p. 262.

25. Ibid., p. 262.

26. Patrick Anderson, *The Presidents' Men* (Garden City, N.Y.: Doubleday, 1968), p. 197.

27. Ibid., p. 197.

28. Ibid., p. 197.

29. Sorensen, op. cit., p. 261.

30. Koenig, op. cit., p. 176.

31. Ibid., p. 176.

32. Ibid., p. 176.

33. Sorensen, op. cit., p. 372.

34. Ibid., p. 372.

35. Schlesinger, op. cit., p. 688.

36. Ibid., p. 241.

37. Stewart Alsop, "The Lesson in the Cuban Disaster," *Saturday Evening Post*, June 24, 1961, p. 68.

38. Irving L. Janis, *Victims of Groupthink* (Boston: Houghton Mifflin, 1972), p. 15.

39. Ibid., p. 36.

40. Schlesinger, op. cit., p. 250.

41. Roger Hilsman, *To Move a Nation* (Garden City, N. Y.: Doubleday, 1967), p. 58.

42. Janis, op. cit., p. 42.

43. Hilsman, op. cit., p. 31.

44. Sorensen, op. cit., p. 343.

45. Janis, op. cit., pp. 43–44.

46. Ibid., p. 148.

47. Ibid., p. 148–149.

48. Halberstam, op. cit., p. 76.

49. Thomas Halper, *Foreign Policy Crisis* (Columbus, Ohio: Merrill, 1971), p. 196.
50. Halberstam, op. cit., p. 77.
51. Richard Smoke, "The Berlin 'Aide-Mémoire' Crisis in 1961." Unpublished working paper, Stanford University, August 1972, pp. 26–27.
52. Ibid., pp. 29–30.
53. Ibid., p. 16.
54. Halberstam, op. cit., p. 90.
55. Ibid., p. 90.
56. Ibid., p. 92.
57. Sidey, op. cit., p. 329.
58. E. Abel, *The Missile Crisis* (New York: Bantam, 1966), p. 36.
59. Halper, op. cit., p. 192.
60. Schlesinger, op. cit., p. 803.
61. Janis, op. cit., p. 150.
62. Ibid., p. 145.
63. Sorensen, op. cit., pp. 692–693.
64. Janis, op. cit., p. 145.
65. Sorensen, op. cit., p. 692.
66. Janis, op. cit., p. 152.
67. Halper, op. cit., p. 194.
68. Halberstam, op. cit., p. 257.
69. Ibid., p. 271.
70. Ibid., p. 271.
71. Ibid., p. 263.
72. Ibid., p. 264.
73. Ibid., p. 263.
74. Ibid., p. 264.
75. Sorensen, op. cit., p. 281.
76. Koenig, op. cit., p. 175.
77. Ibid., p. 179.
78. Ibid., p. 179.
79. Interview with Jack Walsh, June 1972.
80. Schlesinger, op. cit., p. 685.
81. Ibid., p. 685.
82. Ibid., p. 314.
83. Ibid., p. 315.
84. Leonard Baker, *The Johnson Eclipse* (New York: Macmillan, 1966), p. 96.

85. Schlesinger, op. cit., p. 506.

86. Sidey, op. cit., p. 270.

87. Schlesinger, op. cit., p. 87.

88. Ibid., p. 98.

six: JOHNSON'S TYRANNY OF PERSUASION

1. Remarks by Doris Kearns, American Political Science Association Convention, September 1971; reported by Don Bacon, "New Look at What Drove LBJ," *San Francisco Chronicle*, September 19, 1971.

2. Alfred Steinberg, *Sam Johnson's Boy* (New York: Macmillan, 1968), p. 13.

3. Ibid., p. 12.

4. Ibid., p. 31.

5. Ibid., p. 36.

6. Ibid., p. 282.

7. Ibid., p. 28.

8. Ibid., p. 26.

9. Ibid., p. 27.

10. Ibid., p. 29.

11. Doris Kearns, "Johnson's Early Life." Draft manuscript prepared for Harper & Row, 1972.

12. Steinberg, op. cit., p. 68.

13. Ibid., p. 68.

14. Ibid., p. 68.

15. Ibid., pp. 78, 79.

16. Ibid., p. 79.

17. Ibid., p. 124.

18. Rowland Evans, Jr., and Robert D. Novak, *Lyndon B. Johnson: The Exercise of Power* (New York: New American Library, 1966), p. 108.

19. Steinberg, op. cit., p. 127.

20. Ibid., p. 131.

21. Ibid., p. 283.

22. Ibid., p. 278.

23. Ibid., p. 279.

24. Evans and Novak, op. cit., pp. 107–108.

25. Steinberg, op. cit., p. 280.

26. Hugh Sidey, *A Very Personal Presidency* (New York: Atheneum, 1968), p. 217.

27. Steinberg, op. cit., p. 381.
28. Interview with Barry Goldwater, "CBS Evening News," January 24, 1971.
29. Evans and Novak, op. cit., p. 104.
30. Steinberg, op. cit., p. 425.
31. Evans and Novak, op. cit., p. 10.
32. Patrick Anderson, *The Presidents' Men* (Garden City, N.Y.: Doubleday, 1968), p. 307.
33. Ibid., p. 382.
34. Lee C. White, "Symposium on the Office of the President: Formulation and Implementation of Domestic Policy," in Gordon Hoxie, ed., *The White House Organization and Operations* (New York: Center for the Study of the Presidency, 1971), p. 73.
35. Philip Geyelin, *Lyndon B. Johnson and the World* (New York: Praeger, 1966), p. 34.
36. Eric F. Goldman, *The Tragedy of Lyndon Johnson* (New York: Knopf, 1968), p. 22.
37. "The White House Staff Versus the Cabinet" (an interview with Bill Moyers), in Charles Peters and Timothy Adams, eds., *Inside the System* (New York: Praeger, 1970), p. 27.
38. Sidey, op. cit., p. 254.
39. David Halberstam, *The Best and the Brightest* (New York: Random House, 1972), p. 434.
40. Anderson, op. cit., p. 299.
41. Ibid., p. 330.
42. Ibid., p. 331.
43. Steinberg, op. cit., p. 632.
44. Ibid., p. 632.
45. Ibid., p. 633.
46. Ibid., p. 634.
47. Evans and Novak, op. cit., p. 344.
48. Anderson, op. cit., p. 300.
49. Geyelin, op. cit., p. 258.
50. Evans and Novak, op. cit., p. 430.
51. Sidey, op. cit., pp. 255–256.
52. Goldman, op. cit., pp. 59–60.
53. Sidey, op. cit., p. 86.
54. Geyelin, op. cit., p. 15.
55. Ibid., p. 101.
56. Ibid., p. 100.

57. Ibid., p. 237.
58. Sidey, op. cit., p. 178.
59. Halberstam, op. cit., p. 300.
60. Ibid., p. 300.
61. Ibid., p. 458.
62. Ibid., p. 361.
63. Ibid., p. 362.
64. Ibid., p. 437.
65. Townsend Hoopes, *The Limits of Intervention* (New York, McKay, 1969), p. 31.
66. Neil Sheehan, et al., *The Pentagon Papers* (New York: Benton, 1971), p. 332.
67. Irving Janis, *Victims of Groupthink* (Boston: Houghton Mifflin, 1972), p. 111.
68. Halberstam, op. cit., p. 414.
69. J. G. Thompson, "How Could Vietnam Happen?" *The Atlantic Monthly*, April 1968, p. 49.
70. Halberstam, op. cit., p. 618.
71. Lyndon B. Johnson, *The Vantage Point, 1963–1969* (New York: Holt, Rinehart & Winston, 1971), p. 37.
72. Halberstam, op. cit., p. 622.
73. Hoopes, op. cit., pp. 59–60.
74. Lee C. White, in Hoxie, ed., op. cit., p. 73.
75. Sidey, op. cit., p. 99.
76. Ibid., p. 85.
77. "The White House Staff Versus the Cabinet," op. cit., p. 25.
78. Evans and Novak, op. cit., p. 373.
79. Geyelin, op. cit., p. 133.

SELECTED BIBLIOGRAPHY FOR CHAPTER SIX

Anderson, Patrick, *The Presidents' Men*. New York: Doubleday, 1968.
Evans, Rowland, and Novak, Robert, *Lyndon Johnson: The Exercise of Power*. New York: New American Library, 1966.
Goldman, Eric F., *The Tragedy of Lyndon Johnson*. New York: Knopf, 1968.
Geyelin, Philip, *Lyndon B. Johnson and the World*. New York: Praeger, 1966.
Hoopes, Townsend, *The Limits of Intervention*. New York: McKay, 1969.
Reedy, George E., *The Twilight of the Presidency*. New York: World, 1970.

Roberts, Charles, *LBJ's Inner Circle*. New York: Delacorte Press, 1965.
Sherrill, Robert, *The Accidental President*. New York: Grossman, 1967.
Sidey, Hugh, *A Very Personal Presidency*. New York: Atheneum, 1968.
Steinberg, Alfred, *Sam Johnson's Boy*. New York: Macmillan, 1968.

SEVEN: NIXON'S COURTSHIP WITH CRISIS

1. *Time*, May 14, 1973, pp. 22–23.
2. "Text of Statement by the President on Allegations Surrounding Watergate Inquiry," *New York Times*, May 23, 1973, p. 28.
3. Gary Wills, *Nixon Agonistes* (Boston: Houghton Mifflin, 1972), p. 171.
4. James D. Barber, *The Presidential Character* (Englewood Cliffs, N.J.: Prentice-Hall, 1972), p. 399.
5. Interview with Harry Jefferies, Whittier, California, June 22, 1972.
6. Ibid.
7. Bela Kornitzer, *The Real Nixon: An Intimate Biography* (Chicago: Rand McNally, 1960), p. 57.
8. For an interesting discussion of the Nixon character see Barber, op. cit., Chapter 11.
9. Ibid., p. 401.
10. Richard Nixon, *Six Crises* (New York: Pyramid Books, 1968), p. 92.
11. Ibid., p. 101.
12. Ibid., p. 108.
13. Ibid., p. xxviii.
14. Ibid., p. 217.
15. Ibid., p. 219.
16. Ibid., p. 219.
17. *Time*, May 14, 1973, p. 17.
18. *New York Times*, April 21, 1970, p. 14.
19. Saul Pett, "Nixon, with a Brief Look Back," *Los Angeles Times*, January 14, 1973, p. 20.
20. Ibid., p. 22.
21. Ibid., p. 22.
22. *Time*, July 23, 1973, p. 15.
23. Pett, op. cit., p. 21.
24. Ibid., p. 20.
25. Ibid., p. 22.
26. Barber, op. cit., p. 359.
27. Pett, op. cit., p. 22.
28. Ibid., p. 21.

29. Barber, op. cit., p. 374.
30. Pett, op. cit., p. 21.
31. John Oberdorfer, "Ehrlichman Emerges on Top," *Washington Post*, November 6, 1969, p. 23.
32. Allen Drury, *Courage and Hesitation* (Garden City, N. Y.: Doubleday, 1971), p. 134.
33. "The President's Palace Guard," *Newsweek*, March 19, 1973, p. 25.
34. Ibid., p. 25.
35. Interview with an unnamed White House aide, March 29, 1973.
36. Ibid.
37. "The President's Palace Guard," op. cit., p. 25.
38. Rowland Evans, Jr. and Robert D. Novak, *Nixon in the White House* (New York: Random House, 1971), p. 220.
39. Richard Johnson, "Presidential Style and Staff Behavior in the White House." Unpublished doctoral dissertation, Harvard Graduate School of Business, 1971, pp. v–3.
40. James Reston, "A 'Small Staff' and 'Open' Administration," *New York Times*, June 17, 1970.
41. "Mr. Nixon's Honest Broker," *Newsweek*, January 19, 1970, p. 19.
42. Ibid., p. 19.
43. Drury, op. cit., p. 114.
44. John Osborne, *The First Two Years of the Nixon Watch* (New York: Liveright, 1971), p. 57.
45. Juan Cameron, "Richard Nixon's Very Personal White House," *Fortune*, July 1970, p. 59.
46. Ibid., p. 59.
47. "How Nixon's White House Works," *Time*, June 8, 1970, p. 17.
48. "The President's Palace Guard," op. cit., p. 24.
49. Ibid., p. 24.
50. Ibid., p. 26.
51. Interview with an unnamed White House aide, March 29, 1973.
52. Drury, op. cit., p. 162.
53. Interview with an unnamed White House aide, March 29, 1973.
54. Ibid.
55. *White House News Summary*, March 28, 1973, p. 12.
56. Ibid., p. 13.
57. Drury, op. cit., p. 128.
58. Cameron, op. cit., p. 104.
59. Evans and Novak, op. cit., pp. 356–357.
60. "The President's Palace Guard," *Newsweek*, March 19, 1973, p. 25.
61. Barber, op. cit., p. 426.

62. Evans and Novak, op. cit., p. 162.
63. Ibid., p. 163.
64. "Mr. Nixon's Secret Agent," *Newsweek*, February 7, 1972, p. 15.
65. Ibid., p. 15.
66. Ibid., p. 15.
67. Hugh Sidey, "Disarray in Government," *Time*, July 23, 1973, p. 27.
68. Arthur M. Schlesinger, Jr., *A Thousand Days* (Boston: Houghton Mifflin, 1965), p. 413.
69. *Time*, August 30, 1971, p. 5.
70. Ibid., p. 5.
71. Evans and Novak, op. cit., p. 247.
72. "Nixon's Continual Quest for Challenge," *Time*, January 22, 1973, p. 11.
73. Pett, op. cit., p. 21.

EIGHT: CONCLUSION

1. Richard Martin, "The Making of Theodore White," *Wall Street Journal*, October 31, 1971, p. 1.

INDEX

74 75 76 77 10 9 8 7 6 5 4 3 2